The Intensive-Image in Deleuze's
Film-Philosophy

Para mi abuela Eufemia (1922–2009)

The Intensive-Image in Deleuze's Film-Philosophy

Cristóbal Escobar

Edinburgh University Press is one of the leading university presses in the UK. We publish academic books and journals in our selected subject areas across the humanities and social sciences, combining cutting-edge scholarship with high editorial and production values to produce academic works of lasting importance. For more information visit our website: edinburghuniversitypress.com

© Cristóbal Escobar, 2023, 2025

Edinburgh University Press Ltd
13 Infirmary Street
Edinburgh EH1 1LT

First published in hardback by Edinburgh University Press 2023

Typeset in 11/13 Ehrhardt MT Pro
by Cheshire Typesetting Ltd, Cuddington

A CIP record for this book is available from the British Library

ISBN 978 1 3995 1753 9 (hardback)
ISBN 978 1 3995 1754 6 (paperback)
ISBN 978 1 3995 1755 3 (webready PDF)
ISBN 978 1 3995 1756 0 (epub)

The right of Cristóbal Escobar to be identified as the author of this work has been asserted in accordance with the Copyright, Designs and Patents Act 1988, and the Copyright and Related Rights Regulations 2003 (SI No. 2498).

Contents

Acknowledgements   viii

Introduction: Difference of Intensities (Difference is Intensity)   1
   Towards a Theory of the Intensive-Image   2
   On the Notion of (Cinematic) Intensity   9
   Deren, Pasolini, Ruiz and the Poetics of the Intensive-Image   14
   The Combinatorial Potential of the Intensive-Image   18
   The Shape of the Book   20

SECTION ONE: RE-THINKING DELEUZE'S FILM-PHILOSOPHY

1. Towards the Intensification of the Cinema   27
   The Movement-Image: A Solid Cinematic Form   31
   The Time-Image: A Liquid Cinematic Form   40
   The Frame Intensified: A Gaseous Passage in Pedro Costa's *Colossal Youth*   44

2. Luis Buñuel's Nomadic Vision: Departures from an Originary World   53
   Deleuze's Reading of Buñuel: An Idiosyncratic Surrealist   55
   The Intensive-Image: A Descendant from Aby Warburg's *Mnemosyne Atlas*   60
   Los olvidados, or *The Forgotten Ones* of Deleuze's Neorealist Act   62
   Buñuel's (Slit) Eye: The Mirror to Deleuze's 'Soul of the Cinema'   64

3. Human Infancy and the Language of Beginnings: *The Wild Child* and *The Enigma of Kaspar Hauser*   72
   Childhood: An Early Field of Intensities   75

Truffaut's *Enfants Terribles* 80
The Reversibility of Truffaut's Face: Looking at and through
the Window in *The Wild Child* 82
But What is to Become? 84
Herzog's Kaspar: A Man of Beginnings 87
A Classical/Modern Continuum: Origin qua Originality 89

4. In Between Modernities and the Contemporaneous 92
Modernity 1. The Age of Reason and the Emergence of the
Subject 96
Modernity 2. The Age of Art and the Fracture of the 'I', or the
Inhumanity of Deleuze's Cinema 98
El Sueño de la Razón Produce Monstruos 101
The Intensive-Image and the Idea of the Contemporaneous 105

SECTION TWO: THE POLITICS AND POETICS OF THE INTENSIVE-IMAGE IN CONTEMPORARY CINEMA

5. Resistance in *The Lobster*: Mapping an Intensive-Image in
Contemporary Popular Film 117
The Hotel: A Coercive-Administrative Ensemble 120
The Internal Resonance of Resistance: A Case for the
Intensive-Image 125
The External Resonance of Resistance: Tactics, Pass-Words,
Counter-Attacks . . . 128
What You Hear Above All is Loving: The Forest, the City and
the Two Maritime Lovers 131

6. *Zama* and the Method of Dramatisation: From Di Benedetto's
Novel to Martel's Film 139
First Drama: From Di Benedetto's Novel to Martel's Film 143
Second Drama, or the Drama of Deleuze's Cinema(s): From
One Level of Intensity to Another Level of Intensity 153
Third Drama: Intensification Passes Through the Body of
Zama 158

7. What do Animals Teach Us About Intensity? On *Sweetgrass* and
SEL's Bodily Praxis 163
In Search of the Body: Philosophical and Artistic Strategies in
Re-Thinking the Status of the Animal 165
Sweetgrass and the 'Becoming-Sheeple' 172

Conclusion: The Passion of Intensity	177
Postscript	184
Bibliography	185
Index	200

Acknowledgements

I wish to express my gratitude to many people who have contributed to the writing of *The Intensive-Image*. Primary, thanks to Barbara Creed and Joe Hughes for their intellectual generosity, support and encouragement to publish this book. Their expertise and advice made this monograph a much better one than it would otherwise have been. I would also like to thank my colleagues in the School of Culture and Communication at the University of Melbourne for the lengthy discussions and help in many different ways: Justin Clemens, Seán Cubitt, Janice Loreck, Mihai Bacaran, Sanja Mladenovic, Brendan Casey, Duncan Caillard, Nonie May, Corey Cribb, Alicia Byrnes, Wendy Haslem, Laura Henderson, Mark Nicholls and my friends from the Critical Research Association Melbourne (CRAM).

I am also grateful to the University of Melbourne for a number of funding opportunities, including the Melbourne Research Scholarship, which made this project financially possible; and the Faculty of Arts FARE, GRATS and RAGS grants, which allowed me to attend a number of conferences, seminars and film festivals that I benefited from in the writing of this monograph. Also, as an author, I cannot have hoped for a more sympathetic and efficient publisher and I am very grateful for all the support given to me by Edinburgh University Press, by Gillian Leslie, Grace Balfour-Harle, Christine Barton and Sam Johnson in particular.

I also wish to thank a number of people who invited me to write and speak in public events on cinematic intensity as these opportunities always provide inspiration. These include Antonia Girardi from the Festival Internacional de Documentales de Santiago (FIDOCS); Valeria de los Ríos and Pablo Corro from the Pontificia Universidad Católica de Chile; Josh Wilson from the Bulleke-Bek Brunswick Cinema in Melbourne; and Serdar Öztürk from the SineFilozofi journal. Special thanks are also due to my family and friends whose ideas have resonated deeply into this work: to my parents Carmen Dueñas and Miguel Escobar (1947–2007); to Robinson Trafilaf, Rafael Echeverría, Mary Sitarenos, Felipe Escobar,

Emilio Moreno, Marcela Santibáñez, Leandro Cappetto, Nicolas Molina, Vicente Matte; and to Rodrigo Arteaga for the wonderful book cover.

Finally, and most deeply, I would like to thank my *compañera* Josefina and my daughters Flora and Eloísa for sustaining me through this project with care, friendship and intensity.

INTRODUCTION:
Difference of Intensities
(Difference is Intensity)

In the preface to the North American edition of *Nietzsche and Philosophy* (2006), Deleuze introduces the thoughts of his predecessor by recalling the famous metaphor of the arrow. The thinker, says Nietzsche, is like an arrow propelled by the bow of Nature: no matter the distance it travels, or the strength of the shooting, the aim is to reach the ground of civilisation and, hopefully, stick it in its core. Hence Nietzsche's description of the philosopher as a physician of civilisation; it is an 'untimely' arrow that Deleuze will throw also to other regions. Here, to properly 'do philosophy' as Deleuze writes in *Difference and Repetition* (1968/2014, xii), it is necessary to take the arrows crafted by your ancestors and send them somewhere else – that is, to search for unknown spaces within a given region that have not yet been explored by your predecessors.

This book will seek to pick up Deleuze's film-arrow and send it to a new destination. It aims to analyse Deleuze's film-philosophical system under the notion of intensity, a category that I carry from Deleuze's earlier works into his theory of the cinematic image. I use this concept to reconceive his classification of the cinema as constituted by two separate periods, the classical movement-image and the modern time-image, by arguing that the intensive-image both transits across and differentiates these two periods from each other. Hence, the purpose is to show that the concept of intensity is central to all periods of the cinema and indeed provides a certain foundation to thinking about the cinematic image as such. The intensive-image, I argue, is one based on the primacy of difference and sensation, and it is present (though not exclusively so) in avant-garde, poetic, experimental, documentary and surreal films from the silent period to the present. In this capacity, however, intensity also has to be understood as the generic and morphological sign animating Deleuze's cinemas: it unites them under one escalating form of difference.

Other scholars, as I will demonstrate, have analysed specific films to question and to try to unify Deleuze's theories of the cinema (Totaro

1999; Rancière 2011/2014; Fotiade 2013; Nagib 2015; Fairfax 2016; Viegas 2016). It is my view, however, that the presence of an 'intensive-image' across these periods adds even stronger weight to this continuity argument, particularly because of the significance that Deleuze attaches to the concept of intensity: 'There will always be an image-intensity complex. For us, the key is non-representative intensities because intensities are deterritorializing, they break up territories' (Deleuze and Guattari 1973/2020, 225). My argument is that the intensive-image also breaks up Deleuze's divide between classical and modern films by recognising its activity and potency as central to all periods of the cinema.

The history of avant-garde and poetic film traditions supports this continuity thesis. In a sequence of studies, I follow the complications of the intensive-image in its affective mode of address and in the frequency of its appearance over time. This is particularly true of films that belong to new movements called slow cinema, cinema of boredom and post-human cinema. However, the intensive-image can also be found, I argue, in more recent popular films such as *First Cow* (Reichardt 2019), *High Life* (Denis 2018), *The Lobster* (Lanthimos 2015), or *Under the Skin* (Glazer 2013). The films that I study in this book, whether from recent world cinemas or high modernism, belong to a filmmaking style that privileges the gap, the sudden shifts of focus on-screen, or the indifference of a viewer's gaze that is lost viewing a landscape, as in those contemplative and irrelevant moments of a story contributing nothing to the central plot. These cinematic operations style broadly define the 'cinematic avant-garde' (Benjamin 1936/2003; Farber 1971/2009; Quaranta 2020). My aim is to show that these operations are also formal characteristics of the poetics and politics of the intensive-image. This is a displacing image that opens up the screen space in undetermined directions, whether by freeing the screen frame from its fixity or by filling it up with a felt visual richness that leads to an infinite connection between images and sounds, thus altering the organic formula of many suspense-filled blockbuster films where the viewer is absorbed by the cohesion of its linear narrative.

Towards a Theory of the Intensive-Image

Deleuze has famously proposed that the cinema can be best understood as consisting of two main image types: the classical movement-image and the modern time-image. The former is described as a system of actions and reactions that oscillate around a privileged centre, hence an image that is inseparable from the actions it exercises on, and the reactions it suffers from, all of the other images composing the film. This system, according to Deleuze, is predominantly present in the pre-war cinema of Hollywood, the Soviet school of montage and continental Europe, although movement-image films will continue to be made up to this day, and it is 'the greatest commercial successes [that] will always take that route' (Deleuze 1985/2013, 220). The modern time-image, on the contrary, will no longer be connected to a privileged centre but to an infinite set of images that never stop acting and reacting on each other, and with each other, *on all their faces and in all their parts*. This later system, which only appears with Italian neorealism and the New Wave films in Europe, will be characterised by Deleuze as an image that 'increases thought' (2013, 220) by emancipating time from the previous closed schema of actions and reactions on which the cinema had relied on up to that point.

Deleuze presented his thesis in two volumes: *Cinéma 1: L'image-movement* (1983) and *Cinéma 2: L'image-temps* (1985) which I will discuss in depth in the following chapter.[1] This book will explore the possibility that Deleuze's separation is ultimately not sustainable, and that there is potential overlap as a detailed study of what I term the 'intensive-image' hopes to demonstrate. My argument, however, is not disputing Deleuze's complex taxonomical construction of the cinema, comprising more than forty images with their respective signs of composition, some of which will be examined closely in this book. On the contrary, it accounts for the existence of a new image which has the potential to change the way in

---

[1] Deleuze's two books on film have been widely read and discussed within the international film studies community since their publication in the early 1980s. Rapidly translated into English by the end of the decade, his film-philosophical theory has been used by film scholars, art historians, aesthetic philosophers, artists and filmmakers in order to reflect upon the immanent status of the moving image and its connection to the world of perception, the body and thought. His project, which will be described in greater depth in the next chapter, can preliminarily be understood via two of his major theoretical influences; that of Henri Bergson's vitalist philosophy – from where Deleuze takes the primacy of the image as moving-matter – and that of Charles Sanders Peirce's semiotics – from where he produces an exhaustive taxonomy of images and signs. Drawing on these two thinkers, among many others, Deleuze's interest in films and filmmakers is understood in two complementary ways. First, it stands as a corrective endeavour of the cinematographic apparatus developed by his contemporaries who conceived of the image as a mirror reflection of a hidden structure – as proposed by Jean-Louis Baudry (1986), Jean-Louis Comolli (1980) and Christian Metz (1974). And secondly, Deleuze's theories are posed as a reaction against psychoanalytical film theories of the unconscious as well as the phenomenological split between consciousness and its content as explored by Edmund Husserl and Maurice Merleau-Ponty. For Deleuze, who tries to overcome both the transcendental plane of Platonic ideas and the Cartesian division between mind and matter (*res cogitans* and *res extensa*), the cinematographic image exists in itself as matter, and not as a sign to be found underneath the image. This explains why, unlike other approaches based on representational forms of camera-consciousness, the cinema appears for him on an immanent plane, that is to say, as a spatio-temporal dynamism that connects body, brain and screen into one *lived* reality rather than as the *duplication* – or re-presentation – of that reality.

which we think about Deleuze's philosophy in connection to his reading of film and filmmakers.

'Everything', say the authors of *Anti-Oedipus*, 'must be interpreted as intensity' (Deleuze and Guattari 1972/2009, 173), or as Deleuze explains in his 1968 masterwork *Difference and Repetition*: 'we only know intensity as already developed within extensity' (2014, 223); that is, a 'pure difference' (2014, 144) that cannot be perceived or captured in the actual image (extensity) to which this form of difference gives rise. This means that intensity, a pre-personal form of perception, denotes a multiplicity that cannot be apprehended instantly in the mind as an image-unit, but as Claire Colebrook remarks, it becomes a 'differing difference' that goes below and beyond the level of perceptual representation: 'a unique quality that is not yet grounded in a [thinking] subject or thing' (2020, 140). On the contrary, intensities are felt; they are deterritorialising images that interrupt our entire field of audio-vision, hence 'a quality' that cannot be thought of in an articulated or *mediated* way, but felt as *immediate* impressions. Like Kant's notion of intuition, which he defines as 'direct capture' (1790/2005, 301), the intensive-image is also and can only be apprehended directly – that is, an image whose plurality appears in an instant to *present* what is not yet *represented*. In an interview with Raymond Bellour, Deleuze and Guattari state that:

> Intensities drain images, they are fluxes of images (...) We are not saying that cinema is [bad] because it's images, on the contrary. Cinema is great because it can bring such a flux of images, for example in Godard, that it reconstitutes intensities in a pure state (...) There is no dualism at all. There is such an image/intensity relationship that at the same time, the image is the extension that an intensity takes when it dies; but a precipitation of images or a still image where things happen in all four corners; or a color goes through the image and restores the intensity completely through the image (...) What is important is to reach what is not representative. What interests us is to discover intensities. (1973/2020, 226)

Given Deleuze writes so much about intensities why doesn't he propose the concept of the 'intensive-image' in cinema? And why is it that intensity, according to Deleuze, only develops within the qualified image that this 'pure difference' gives rise to? How are we to connect these two apparently opposed realms of existence? What might the significance of an intensive-image be for Deleuze's classical and modern film periods? And how might the idea of an intensive-image prove significant in relation to contemporary cinema?

First and foremost, it should be noted that in Deleuze's philosophy there is a permanent underlying process through which his ideas are formed. Such is, for example, the primacy given to notions of becoming over being, molecular assemblages over molar formations, or the nomadic (smooth) space over the sedentary (striated) state. The concept of intensity is privileged in this regard, for it too undergoes constant change, but it is also pre-eminently the name for that underlying process of variation. It is a differing force of creation which, although imperceptible, is that which guarantees *actual* reality and its perception. However, to state that intensity goes unnoticed is not the same as saying that it is unreal, immaterial or imaginary, for as much as it is what animates images to move and change, intensity demands a full reality of its own. Put differently, it is Deleuze's intensive approach to philosophy which makes of his ontology not the result of pre-given, *a priori* structures, but quite the opposite, the result of an ongoing process of differentiation. 'Individuation', says Deleuze in a brief sentence, 'is the act by which intensity determines differential relations to become actualised [in extension]' (2014, 246).

Secondly, it is also important to mention that Deleuze's distinction between the intensive and the extensive categories is not a creation of his own. Rediscovered by modern Kantian metaphysics, such a distinction has been long debated by classical and modern thinkers,[2] and in his commentaries on these thinkers, especially in his early works on philosophers,[3] Deleuze re-examines both properties to outline his own differential approach to *physis*, the natural world. With Kant, he refers to intensity mainly as a problem of measurement. It stands for the *degree* of energy by which all magnitudes are said to vary in potency although never to settle in homogenous or immobile forms. (Hence, to say that 'we only know intensity as already developed within extensity' is to claim that its power of affection is only noticeable in the divisible, in the actual image or quality that intensity yields.) In Kant's critique, in the second part of his chapter on intensive quantities entitled 'The Anticipations of Perception' (1781/2008), the category of quantity generates extensive difference which always leads to the creation of new forms, whereas the category of quality generates intensity of sensation, defined as an invisible or imperceptible force by which the actually given is given as 'diverse' in the world.

---

[2] Deleuze argues that in medieval physics and classical philosophy even, intensive qualities were always shadowed or 'obscured' by the primacy given to extensive properties. With Kant, and later on, with Pierre Klossowski, intensity assumes a new 'philosophical and theological depth' (Deleuze 1980/2007, 179). For further discussion, see Deleuze, 'Eight Years Later: 1980 Interview' (2007, 119–66).

[3] In his early works, Deleuze develops his concept of intensity in dialogue with a number of key thinkers: Kant, Hume, Bergson and Nietzsche, among others. In what follows, I will briefly make some remarks about Deleuze's engagement with these thinkers.

With Hume, the problem is quite similarly posed as an issue of gradation, that is, in an increase or decrease of sensation. This time, however, intensity stands as the passage from the early impressions of the human subject (what Hume calls 'vividness', or the principle of *minima sensibilia*) to its later cognitive formation in the rational mind of the adult. Consequently, the main question informing *Empiricism and Subjectivity* (1953/1991), Deleuze's first published book on Hume, can also be read *in intensio*, that is to say, as that threshold separating the early state of a mind defined by its perceptual vividness or 'the imagination', to its later synthesis in the mind of adults which transforms sensible imprints into rational categories. To paraphrase Hume (and this is a point that will be further discussed in Chapter 3 through the figure of the cinematic child), we can state that whereas impressions (intensities) are those 'perceptions which enter with most force and violence [into the mind of the subject]', conceptual ideas (extensities) are 'the faint images of those impressions in thinking and reasoning' (quoted in Deleuze 1991, 10).

In line with Hume's perceptions which are more vivid than the tiniest of rational ideas,[4] Nietzsche's philosophy is also fruitful for Deleuze's thinking about thermodynamic intensity. His reading of intensity, as described in Chapter 5 of *Difference and Repetition*, is articulated in terms of Nietzsche's will to power: the generic force by which not only what appears on the surface becomes explicable but also, and more importantly for Deleuze's Nietzsche, the principle by which every process of differentiation can be thought in its own terms as the inexplicable – hence, Nietzsche's disparity and heterogeneous movement of becoming. Self-implicated as the differential, the intensive-image will preliminarily be defined as that which according to Deleuze 'never ceases to be in itself even while it is constantly explicated outside itself' (2014, 301). This 'will' of intensity, according to Nietzsche, represents an orientation, the indivisible direction of a force. It is what expresses the inner potential of every intensive-image, its *sense-abilities* and their degrees of affection relative to both cinematic periods. As invoked by Nietzsche in the final pages of *The Will to Power* (1901/1968), this is an image of ever-intensifying and ever-transforming force relations, capable of alliances with other images, free to connect with or disconnect from any other elements, epochs or forms:

---

[4] This 'minimum' under which we no longer have an impression of an object is defined by Deleuze's Hume as atomism. As he notes while preparing his course on Hume (1957–8): 'There are always objects smaller than the object identified as the smallest idea I have (. . .) Atomism is the theory of impressions or ideas as indivisible and external to each other' (1957/2007, 178).

> This world [of intensity]: a monster of energy, without beginning, without end; a firm, iron magnitude of force that does not grow bigger or smaller, that does not expand itself but only transforms itself; (. . .) a sea of forces, flowing and rushing together, eternally changing, eternally flooding back, with tremendous years of recurrence, with an ebb and a flood of its forms. (1968, #1067)

These definitions inform the concept of the intensive-image and my belief that such a category is crucial to an understanding of the way in which the imagination and the senses find expression in films that operate directly with the flow of time and its process of 'differentiation' – that is, as sheer audiovisual impressions that are not yet schematised in firm rational categories. And such a decision is marked, among other reasons, by the dynamic organisation of Deleuze's theory of intensity which shifts from his works on philosophers (emerging with *Empiricism and Subjectivity* all the way up to *Difference and Repetition*) towards a theory of multiplicity and haecceity in his later works, especially those written with Félix Guattari and where the figure of the (Nietzschean) artist escapes from the depths to become superficial, or out of profundity:

> The theory of intensity which I was drafting [up to *Difference and Repetition*] was marked by depth, false or true; intensity was presented as stemming from the depths. In *Logic of Sense*, the novelty for me lay in the act of learning something about surfaces. The concepts remained the same: 'multiplicities', 'singularities', 'intensities', 'events', 'infinities', 'problems', 'paradoxes' and 'propositions' – but reorganized according to this [new] dimension. (Deleuze 1976/2007, 65)

I have adopted Deleuze's own definition of intensity, which I am drawing on as a theoretical basis for my concept of the intensive-image. This is an image of sensation, before it is an image of cognition and reasoning. I will expand on this definition as I progress through the book and the film analyses. Structures, properties and formal qualities central to the intensive-image will include: the off-screen space; processes of subtraction and de-visualisation; the scanning of the cinematic frame at a slow pace; or crowded, baroque surfaces where one cannot isolate an object for distant viewing; free-indirect-discourse [*quasi-direct discourse*]; embodied perspectivism; among others. I will propose that the intensive-image, by means of these signs and operations, represents an essential category with which to read Deleuze's cinema(s) as one escalating form of difference, defined by its continuous process of variation, in a range of avant-garde works from the classical to the modern and the contemporary periods.

Hence, what all of these cases will suggest is that the notion of intensity not only manifests a general displacing energy leading to my critique of

Deleuze's division of the two periods (as an image-in-becoming that is prolonging the cinema's past into its present moment and towards its yet-to-be-actualised future) but also, as my film analyses will aim to more specifically demonstrate, an image of affection [*une image-affection*] that is completely independent from the perception that actualises it, conditioned by its differential and heterogeneous parts that are responsible for the intensive shock felt in the viewer. The intensive-image, be it classical or modern, will thus arise as a unit-complex that does not consist of actions-perceptual-and-affective parts that are consecutively connected to one another (say, through the schema of resemblance and the understanding), but as one sensuous image (of difference and of the different) that results from its impact on the body by fluid impressions that cannot (yet) be schematised in reasoning. This is, in other words, a rebellious image-matter that is not formed from a firm, *a priori* ground but from a principle of indetermination that intensifies the viewer's experience of sensations depicted onscreen.

Like Deleuze's affection-image in *Cinema 1*, intensity will be read as another image that 'surges in the centre of indetermination' (2005, 67), but unlike this form of affection which only occupies a momentary interval between action and perception, the intensive-image will constitute the organising principle of both classical and modern films, mainly described under the cinema's poetic tradition that is no longer or not only understood as an 'affective instance' set in isolation from the film as a whole but as a 'negative space' or in between images that, in Manny Farber's words, remain faithful to the transitory, multi-suggestive complication of the movie image:

> Negative space, the command of experience which an artist can set resonating within a film, is a sense of terrain created partly by the audience's imagination and partly by camera-actors-director (. . .) It has to do with flux, movement and air: a movie filled with negative space is always a textural work throbbing with acuity. (1971/2009, 696)

So, how can we read Deleuze's cinema books through the lens of intensity? If intensity is understood as ongoing difference – 'pure difference in itself' – and therefore linked to *sensibilia* and variability, then I argue that this concept is quite crucial in highlighting the (dis)continuities, as well as the poetic excesses at play, in Deleuze's early images, such as the affection-image or the impulse-image, and cannot be separated according to his two ages of film, the classical movement-image and the modern time-image.[5]

[5] In an interview, Laura U. Marks was asked a similar question: 'Isn't your reading of the senses and the body [an aesthetic of sensation that she puts forward by reading diasporic films] somehow

Intensity – an image like a crystal that changes without ceasing – is that which associates, rather than separates, both of these film periods under its production of sensations that are independent from the actions and reactions they actualise. A 'bloc of sensation', after all, is the very definition Deleuze and Guattari give in *What is Philosophy?* (1991/1996) to the work of art – a being of the sensible which is both able to observe and be in the world:

> The aim of art is to wrest the percept from perceptions of objects and the states of a perceiving subject, to wrest the affect from affection [i.e. feeling] as the transition from one state to another: *to extract a bloc of sensations, a pure being of sensation.* (1996, 167; my emphasis)

On the Notion of (Cinematic) Intensity

My concept of the intensive-image is also situated in relation to the rich secondary literature on Deleuze's film-philosophy. Lately, on the side of film criticism, there has been a growing interest in this notion. However, to my mind, no one has conceptualised it with due attention, or with enough proximity to the work of Deleuze and thermodynamics. Adrian Martin, for example, in his thought-provoking essays on Raúl Ruiz, reads intensity as that 'general energy' which gives movement to the cinema: 'as a time-based art, [cinema] depends on precisely that kind of intensity: a film moves, or it dies'. In Ruiz's films, he continues, such intensity 'is everywhere (. . .) [it is] what animates the telling of stories (. . .) the erotic attraction and repulsion of bodies' (2004, 45). The text is titled, and for good reason, 'Displacements'. It is a striking formulation that Martin re-elaborates later on in *Mise en Scène and Film Style* (2014), when suggesting that the 'potentially transformative [nature of] intensity' is produced by those enigmatic moments of a film that are 'too strange, dream-like, and multidirectional' (2014, 19). Intensity becomes for him a loosely defined category (probably because it cannot be defined firmly) that is central to his reading of films and filmmakers. This is a mode of cinematic viewing based on displacements and intuition, more than on images based on denotative meanings and cause-and-effect logic. 'The magic of a film, its intensity' says Ruiz in his *Diario* (2017), 'depends on

---

shattering Deleuze's movement-image system?' (Escobar 2020). Her answer demonstrated that the concept of the intensive-image may well enhance this critique based on the powers of affection and the body: 'Yes, completely; in fact, the concept of the affection-image is proposed there, in *Cinema 1*. It's an element of classical cinema that, if suspended for long enough, breaks down the movement-image by way of the body' (2020).

the enigmas of an image originating in the interstices of the plot' (2017, 538).

Moreover, and in closer proximity to the work of Deleuze, Paolo Bertetto also analyses intensity in terms of a cinematic style that moves (itself and the viewer) through the non-linear wires of sensation. In his book *Il cinema e l'estetica dell'intensità* (2016) and later article on 'Deleuze's Theory of Art and Cinema' (2017), the Italian scholar rightly identifies intensity as that displacing movement which never settles in homogeneous forms. 'Concepts and sensations are forms of intensity, and they are flows, rather than firm configurations' (2017, 792). For Bertetto, what is so central about Deleuze's film-philosophy is not so much the focus on the rupture he sets among classical and modern periods but on what the cinema produces philosophically: 'What I find most relevant in Deleuze is not his reconstruction of an anomalous history of cinema, but his ability to trigger forms of conceptual creation originating from cinema' (2017, 792). Bertetto's work is indeed pivotal in locating the intensive category at the crossroads of film and philosophy – a proximity that Deleuze himself remarks at the end of *The Time-Image*, when stating that: 'cinema's concepts are not given in cinema [but in philosophy] (. . .) Cinema itself is a new practice of images and signs, whose theory philosophy must produce as conceptual practice' (2013, 280).

Hence, Bertetto's reading of intensity can be defined not only by its dual Deleuzian imprint as philosophical concept and cinematographic image, but also, and most importantly for my hypothesis, it represents an invisible yet transformative movement associated with the notions of 'flow, difference, and variability' (2017, 795). This allows me to read the two cinematic periods in terms of differences of intensity, or more generally, *of intensive degrees*, but not in terms of differences *in kind*, as it is in both image regimes where an intensive continuity can be found. As Deleuze himself remarks in his film seminars at the University of Vincennes: 'an intensive movement has degrees [it's a multiplicity], while an extensive movement has parts [it's a unity] (. . .) In its essence, the intensive movement is not the product of an addition of parts, but a function of zero' (1983/2011, 469).

In this direction, one could even talk about the 'intensive-image', following Deleuze's lexicon, as a 'quasi-concept' or an 'embryonic-image', in that its meanings and operations are so unstable, subjected to such variability and flow, that intensity qua image can never be secured in actual form or extensity – that is, in a system of capture that any conceptual category necessarily implicates. However, unlike Bertetto who is uninterested in examining the 'anomalous history of [Deleuze's] cinema[s]', I put forward a critique of such a rupture between classical and modern images by proposing an intensifying continuity among them based on an ongoing process of differentiation that has carried the cinema towards higher, or more complex, destinies. Hence, what the intensive category represents, if anything, is an image-in-becoming which recognises and brings back the fundamental difference of the 'classical-old', such that the 'modern-new' originates in it, as well as departs from it. It is, in essence, an evolving image that not only looks back at Deleuze's cinematic past, but also one that pushes his cinematic modernity forward in time, towards new genesis and sensations to come.[6]

With these considerations in mind, however, it is also crucial to distinguish, or give a more accurate definition of what intensity means and what intensity is doing exactly in the work of art. This demands to address the specificity of such notion: Why focus on *intensities* rather than the *virtual* when conceptualising Deleuze's cinemas? It is true, for instance, that Deleuze's thought, as expressed in *What is Philosophy?* is mostly concerned with the relationship between the intensive and the virtual, although the demarcation between the two categories remains constantly subjected to interchange: the former being defined as the 'plane of composition' of artistic sensation whereas the latter is defined as 'the plane of immanence' of conceptual thought. So, if we talk about a system that is double, as in Deleuze's film-philosophical taxonomy, then isn't such a merging between the intensive-virtual what generates his reading of *images that think*?

For Brian Massumi's *Parables for the Virtual: Movement, Affect, Sensation* (2002), as well as Constantin V. Boundas's *Gilles Deleuze: The Intensive Reduction* (2009) that seems exactly to be the case. For both of these authors, intensity is read, almost cinematographically, as that 'narratively delocalized event [which is] most directly felt in the skin' (2002, 25). In Massumi's words:

> Intensity is outside [of] expectation and adaptation (. . .) as disconnected from meaningful sequencing, from narration, as it is from vital function. It is narratively

---

[6] In his article 'Gilles et Jacques se disputen Béla', Daniel Fairfax also takes on these problems and further contends Deleuze's separation of the two periods by aligning with Rancière's inclusive historicity of film. One of the examples Fairfax suggests for this 'continued vitality of the cinema and [its] capacity for rebirth' (2016, 4) is brought by the contemplative films of Béla Tarr, a Hungarian director associated with the slow cinematic movement and whose 'collapsing of the distinction between cinematic epochs' testifies for Rancière's more dialectical relation to film history. In his study, Fairfax claims that the image 'explode[s] the chronological demarcations of the movement-image/time-image duality' (2016, 5) and adds, quoting Rancière, that Tarr's films 'typify a cyclical relationship between cinematic classicism and modernism (. . .): "[His] is the time after *histoires*, the time when one is interested directly in sensuous matter"' (2016, 9–10).

delocalized, spreading over the generalized body surface like a lateral backwash from the function-meaning interloops that travel the vertical path between head and heart. (2002, 25)

This means that for Massumi, as well as for Boundas, it is the transformative power of intensity which allows for the constant 'differentiation' of Deleuze's virtual. As Boundas suggests, intensity represents a 'necessary ontological reduction [safeguarding] the reality of the actual (the actually given) through the continuous interaction between the *extended* actual/real and the *intensive* virtual/real' (2009, 3; my emphasis). Again, what is learnt from their description is that the intensive-image (common to the arts) is inseparable from those forces populating the virtual-idea (common to philosophy): '*Virtual intensities* raise problems and questions; the actual constitutes solutions and responses; and solutions do not resemble or copy the parent problems' (2009, 3).

In the light of this coupling between sensual intensities and virtual ideas, what needs to be stressed, I suggest, are the singularities delimiting their domains of existence. So, whereas 'intensities' are associated with the percepts and affects of the work of art (or what Deleuze calls 'the being of sensation'), the 'virtual', on the other hand, is associated with the figure of the philosopher – that is, by a 'conceptual personae (...) who lives intensely within the thinker that forces him [her] to think' (Deleuze and Guattari 1996, 70). This means that if Massumi is looking for *parables for the virtual* to better visualise the philosophical ideas developed by Deleuze, my book is in search of an intensive-image that engages directly with the beat of cinematic sensation. Thus, in a very literal sense, as Deleuze and Guattari state, 'art is concerned with making *perceptible* the usually hidden realm of the intensive. Similarly, philosophy must make the virtual *intelligible*' (1996, 126).

In this train of thought, Elisabeth Grosz's various works on Deleuze and the arts are essential contributions to my analysis of Deleuze's conceptual reading of the cinema – that is, a form of virtual thinking that engages directly with the intensities of the moving image. Here, Grosz's oeuvre is key in connecting the thermodynamic nature of Deleuze's philosophy and the arts through their common, yet well demarcated ways of framing chaos:

Art, according to Deleuze, does not produce concepts, though it does address problems and provocations. [On the contrary] the arts produce and generate *intensity*, that which impacts the nervous system and *intensifies sensation*. Art is the art of affect more than representation, a system of dynamized and impacting forces rather than a system of unique images that function under the regime of signs. (2008, 3; my emphasis)

Next to Grosz's approach to the arts as intensive machines of sensation, it is also from Manuel DeLanda's reading of intensity that I take the flowing movement of this cinematic category. DeLanda's *Intensive Science and Virtual Philosophy* (2013) becomes here an important work which allows for the conceptualisation of an intensive-image under its ongoing thermodynamic differentiation. Drawing on a branch of physics that deals with the relationship between various forms of energy, DeLanda proposes an introductory definition of the intensive and the extensive categories in order to grasp their ontological (and I would also add cinematographic) importance. In his words:

> Thermodynamic properties can be divided into two general classes, namely intensive and extensive properties. If a quantity of matter in a given state is divided into two equal parts, each part will have the same value of intensive properties as the original, and half the value of the extensive properties. Pressure, temperature, and density are examples of intensive properties. Mass and total volume are examples of extensive properties. (2013, 116)

This means, for DeLanda as well as for Deleuze, that while extensive properties are intrinsically divisible in space (e.g. when dividing an area into two equal parts you get two areas with half the initial extension) the intensive properties cannot be so divided (e.g. when dividing a volume of water into two half volumes you don't get two equal parts having the same degrees of temperature). As Deleuze explains in an interview with Bellour:

> What you take simultaneously, in an instant, by definition is a unit. The length of this table is an extensive quantity: whatever division I make of its length, I apprehend in an instant. As soon as I apprehend it in an instant, I constitute it as a unit. Intensive quantity is the opposite. It is a multiplicity that you take in an instant as multiplicity. When you say: it is 20 degrees warm, you do not mean 10 degrees plus 10 degrees. It means: it makes the multiplicity of 20 degrees that I apprehend in an instant. A multiplicity apprehended instantly as multiplicity is an intensive quantity. (1973/2020, 230)

Intensity, in simpler words, is not so much a property that is 'indivisible' in space but one that is always in flux and shifting, thus one that 'cannot be so divided without involving a change in kind' (DeLanda 2013, 18). This amounts to say, as my film analyses will try to demonstrate, that the intensive-image can indeed be organised under different states of itself, but these states are nothing other than the accumulation of its singular energy – like a snowball on the snow rolling upon itself in an amassing movement. This intensification of the image represents, then, the connection of its phases under a movement that expresses itself without the fixity of a unified schema, but open to its becoming as an ongoing multiplicity.

Therefore, if thermodynamic intensity can help us establish a more elastic continuity in Deleuze's taxonomy of images, then one could also describe his passage from the classical to the modern era as one incremental flow of intensities – that is to say, as a preservation of the cinematic past into the present moment which develops as it advances. Because if intensity is defined as 'flow' (and this is a term that I derive from thermodynamics as much as from its Greek etymology as *rheûma*, which is the sign of composition for Deleuze's liquid state of perception), then what I suggest is that Deleuze's movement from one cinematic order to the next should not be made visible by the opposition between two epistemological realms, but by the continuation of one and the same image divided into its divergent lines of evolution. Following Henri Bergson's understanding of becoming as the coexistence of present and past, that is, as an old-new sequence which entails the continual elaboration of the new, I argue that the intensive-image, too, involves 'a careful consideration of the ways in which the past, present and future are entwined' (Grosz 2000, 230–1) – hence, a theory which recognises that intensity itself is constituted by the indeterminate, differential potential of time. This is the intensive-image complex characterised by the sensuous and poetic language of film, bounded to a cinematic tradition where images remain flowing and non-representative, combined in a multiple manner that excludes any simple reduction to signification.

Deren, Pasolini, Ruiz and the Poetics of the Intensive-Image

In Nietzsche, as we briefly saw before, this notion of intensity was introduced by the differential continuity of his 'will-to-power', namely the principle of becoming under which the never-ending transformations of the natural world can be explained in extension or actuality. Now, the same dynamic reading of the cinema – literally, a *moving image* – can be heard from Deleuze's notion of thermodynamic intensity, when he asserts that:

> Difference is the sufficient reason of change only to the extent that the change tends to negate difference [in actual forms or extension]. Since intensity is already difference, it refers to a series of other differences that it affirms by affirming itself. (2014, 223–4)

In cinema, similarly, such a differing force of intensity is explained in terms of those indirect and sensuous moments departing from the expected outcomes of the blockbuster film. It is an image that can be described under those 'stylistic fragmentations and narrative incoherencies' that, according to David Bordwell, Hollywood films are not (2002, 16). In this capacity, and for the lack of a better terminology, the type of 'intensity' that I'm looking at is not echoed by the cohesiveness of the action-sequence model as in Bordwell's 'Intensified Continuity: Visual Style in Contemporary American Film' (2002)[7] but by the type of 'vertical intensification' that Maya Deren attempted to link to a tradition of film poetry in a symposium devoted to the subject in 1953, 'Poetry and the Film'.

Deren, an avant-garde filmmaker herself, as well as a dancer, ethnographer, artist and aesthetic theorist, lends support here to the notion of an early intensive-image that expands upon and even enlarges Deleuze's classical affection-image from its broader sensory-motor-scheme. As seen in her 16 mm cine-poems *Meshes of the Afternoon* (1943), *At Land* (1944), *A Study in Choreography for Camera* (1945), *A Ritual in Transfigured Time* (1946) and *Meditation on Violence* (1948), the filmmaker conveys a sense of affection and 'becomingness' that frees the image from its rigid time-form in order to give birth to a different mode of temporality that she refers to as 'the time-quality of a woman's body' (1951/2016, 9). In Deren's films, this represents a metamorphic sense of temporality in which 'one image is always becoming another' (2016, 9), thus displacing the visual immediacy of 'what is of any moment' (2016, 9) for the invisible and affective content of a feeling. This imperceptibility of intensity is what she refers to as film-poetry:

> A poem, to my mind, creates visible or auditory forms for something that is invisible, which is the feeling, or the emotion, or the metaphysical content of a moment. Now it may also include action, but its attack is what I call the 'vertical' attack, and this may be a little bit clearer if you will contrast it to what I would call the 'horizontal' attack of a drama, which is concerned with the development from situation to

---

[7] In his article 'Intensified Continuity: Visual Style in Contemporary American Film' (2002), David Bordwell sets out to describe some tactics in recent US studio filmmaking practice that are amplifying traditional methods of storytelling and editing by what he calls 'an intensification of [narrative] established techniques' (2002, 16) This is, I believe, the right track to assess any form of 'intensification' and its continuity, let it be 'narrative' or 'counter-narrative', mainstream or avant-garde, and so, like this book does, the way in which Bordwell takes such a notion of intensity is also by linking, and not by separating, the new (contemporary Hollywood) film with its old (classically coherent) studio formula, although 'amp[ed] up to a higher pitch of emphasis' (2002, 16). This means that for Bordwell, unlike many critics suggest, the so-called 'cinema of narrative incoherence and stylistic fragmentation' (2002, 16) of the North American blockbuster film today, represents a speeding-up of the previous organic formula of the Hollywood action-sequence. As Bordwell states, from the mid- and late 60s onwards 'Hollywood filmmakers have progressively edited their films more rapidly than ever (. . .) Certainly, some action sequences are cut so fast (and staged so gracelessly) today as to be incomprehensible. Nonetheless, many fast-cut sequences [in contemporary North American cinema] do remain spatially coherent' (2002, 17).

situation, whereas a poem is concerned with the development, let's say, within a very small situation from feeling to feeling. (Quoted in Maas 1953, 57)

Deren's theory of vertical intensification of the emotions and the poetic image, composed exclusively of intense moments apprehended by the viewer's body, is also echoed by Pasolini's 'cinema of poetry'. Plotting a distinction between 'the language of poetry' and 'the language of prose', the filmmaker and writer describes the former as a free stream of utterances, or what he calls 'free-indirect-discourse' [*discorso indiretto libero*], in allusion to the naturalist tradition of literature, and which translates, later in cinema, as the purely expressive quality of an image. Prose narrative or content, as in Deren's 'horizontal attack of a drama', is also perceived by Pasolini as a small pretext towards the affective development of the poetic film, which he sees as the essence or 'purity' of art cinema. He cites Salvador Dali and Luis Buñuel's *Un chien andalou* (1929) as one of the forerunners of such a tradition in filmmaking. It is an early form of the intensive-image which I will examine closely in Chapter 2 under what Ramona Fotiade calls 'Buñuel's Surrealist Time-Image' (2013), and which Pasolini describes in terms of an image that intensifies, and runs through the different periods of poetic cinema – and through Buñuel's filmography more particularly:

> A common technical/stylistic tradition is taking form; a language, that is, of the cinema of poetry. This language by now tends to be placed diachronically in relation to the language of the film narrative, a diachronism that would appear destined to be always more pronounced, as it happens in literary systems (. . .) There are of course extreme cases, where the poetic character of cinema is altogether evident. *The Andalusian Dog*, for example, is flagrantly obedient to a will to pure expression; but to get there, Buñuel had to have recourse to the descriptive panoply of surrealism and one must say that, as a surrealist product, it is of the first order. (1965/2001, 44)

In Ruiz, too, we find reference to this involuntary and expressive quality of the poetic image. In his rejection of the central conflict theory of narrative, characteristic of the Hollywood scriptwriting manual, the Chilean filmmaker and playwright adopted a different mode of storytelling under what many scholars have associated with 'the baroque' (Buci-Glucksmann 1987/2010; Goddard 2004, 2013; Bégin 2009/2010; de los Ríos 2019) that is, a system of concealments and illusions that destabilises reality by opening up 'the poetic spaces of language' (Foucault 1966/1968, 58). The baroque is here understood as an episodic and loose style of filmmaking which welcomes spectatorial states of wonder over the multiplicity of images (characters, situations, landscapes . . .)

that create tension and suspense in the viewer, thus inverting the logic of the Hollywood film cautiously crafted by the conflicts of its central protagonist. For Ruiz, this central conflict economy dominating great part of mainstream cinema today, is more epistemologically described as a 'predatory practice': 'a system of ideas that devours and enslaves any other idea that may limit its activity [by] forcing to eliminate all stories that do not include confrontation in a film' (Ruiz quoted in de los Ríos 2019, 43). On the contrary, what makes cinema 'intense and mysterious', as noted by the filmmaker in his *Poéticas del cine* (2013), are those 'magical accidents, the alteration of ideas [and characters] in the story, and the inexplicable wonders (. . .) left in the spectator's mind by the end of the movie' (2013, 96). According to this logic, what constitutes the baroque are those images that do not allow us to reply easily to the question 'what is the film about?', precisely because its images are intense, miscellaneous or indeterminate, composed 'of multiple situations loosely interwind with each other and connected episodically by a random selection of life-events' (2013, 97).[8] In Michael Goddard's words, this is a cinema that replaces the assumption 'everything is fundamentally simple' with its opposite 'everything is fundamentally complex':

> It is clear that this idea of infinite relations between images and signs, that images are always resonating with other images, forms a kind of perverse general economy in relation to the restricted one of Central Conflict Theory. The logic of this general

---

[8] Let me clarify this method of the baroque by recounting a brief anecdote from the country where I was born and the indirect, shifting dialect that we speak at home. In Chile, it's often said, the Spanish spoken is not only presented in an ornamental, rhetorical manner, as characteristic of many Latin American languages, but also in a highly babbling way, as a hypothetical mode of discourse that rarely gives you the full picture of the reality depicted, often allowing the listeners to come up with their own subjective interpretations, to the point where the actual, real meaning of the sentence becomes quite confusing and blurred. Once a Chilean friend who was in need of cash asked a foreign friend and myself if he could borrow some 'plata viva' [living money] from us. The person from overseas thought he was asking for money to pay his 'living' expenses, such as groceries or bills (after all, it is reasonable to interpret 'living money' that way, I thought), but in reality, what our friend meant by this term was simply 'cash' (material money; money that is 'alive', physically present), as opposed to 'plata muerta' [dead money], which, in his odd lexicon, stood for 'credit card' (virtual money; money that is invisible, physically absent). In other words, what I want to suggest with this anecdote is that in Chilean language, as well as in Ruizian cinema, there is often an out-of-field or a fracture in the image of speech that must be accounted for by the receiver in order to grasp the intended meaning of the utterance, so just as in the previous example 'to borrow some living money', it is the indirect, ornamental element 'living money' that defines, and to a certain degree controls, the central request 'to get cash'. It is a *figuring figure* that forces the listener and viewer to engage in an endless game of interpretation, crystalline instead of organic composition, shamanic instead of scientific montage: 'Filmmaking', notes Ruiz in his chapter 'Towards a Shamanic Cinema' is an '*ars combinatoria* that mixes discontinuous images constantly' (2013, 96).

economy is clearly an interstitial one in that images are combined in a multiple manner that excludes any simple reduction to representation or signification; in the final analysis every image and every sequence of images, even the most classically constructed cannot be assigned a fixed meaning because it will always be in a relation to a multiplicity of other images, whether present or virtual, real or imagined (. . .) And it is precisely this Baroque multiplication of images and their combinations that appears in Ruiz's own cinema. (*Senses of Cinema*, 2004)

Here, what is most interesting about Ruiz's films in connection with Pasolini's free-indirect-discourse, or with Deren's building of affection from one image to the next, is that poetry and the intensive-image are felt in the same 'crossing of images originating in the interstices of the plot' (2013, 167). Drawing on Pierre Klossowski's reading of Nietzsche, Ruiz characterises intensity as an endless reservoir of relations which combines and interchanges images through their common 'sequence of durations':

In our field, the practice of cinema, the notion of intensity – an intuition that is so pertinent, luminous, and evident – (. . .) allows us to associate ideas, sequences, and situations which, placed in different sections of a film, no matter how distant from each other they may be (the more distant the better I'd say) can indeed re-intensify themselves in their multiple connections. And this is not only because they share a similar emotional intensity but also because they participate in a similar 'sequence of durations'. (2013, 191)

It is the nature of this connection between similar intensities and durations that I want to explore in what follows under the combinatorial potential of the intensive-image.

The Combinatorial Potential of the Intensive-Image

Deleuze's conception of the moving image proposes an innovative taxonomical construction that can be put into question by Ruiz's notion of intensity *qua ars combinatoria*. By dealing 'exclusively with cinematic masterpieces' (1995/2007b, 275), as Deleuze writes in his preface to *Cinema 1*, intensity represents, it seems to me, that flowing energy of a tradition of film poetry which arises from the conjunction of his two eras, classical and modern. The intensive-image, as I will argue, is one which abolishes historical distinctions between indirect and direct representations of time by adjoining the two periods into one intensifying image of *durée*, or 'similar durations', as Ruiz states. (Let's remember here that for Deleuze, post-war filmmakers will continue to make movement-image films, mostly linked to the 'commercially successful' cinema of Hollywood (Deleuze 2013, 220), but what we do not have, according to him, are direct time-images of thought in his classical pre-war era. In this way, the new image-category that I am proposing does not aim for or is not marked by 'the advent of a third-age of the image' (Fairfax 2016, 7), but rather inscribes intensity as a trans-historical category that has always made manifest those deterritorialising tendencies of Deleuze's time-image.) This will require me to engage critically with Deleuze's classical conception of film, largely composed of closed sets, or cause-and-effect chain of events, and suggest that from the earliest days of film the audience has participated in an encounter with pure intensive difference – that is to say, in Deleuze's lexicon, an encounter with the intervallic and the inexplicable, as a direct image of time that brings into play the world beyond the plot. Deleuze's reflection-image (Mizoguchi), affection-image (Dreyer), perception-image (Vertov) relation-image (Hitchcock), and impulse-image (Buñuel), as discussed mostly in *Cinema 1*, are all notions related to the non-actualised tendencies of the intensive-image.

Take, for instance, Carl Theodor Dreyer's *La passion de Jeanne d'Arc* (1928). This is a pivotal work on the use of the extreme close-up that relates not only to those expressive powers of affection which Deleuze discusses alongside Béla Balázs's theories of the close-up, but an equally autonomous image-face that disconnects from the film as a whole by taking the viewer into a completely new physical and emotional realm. Evidently, *La passion de Jeanne d'Arc* cannot be said to follow the unified schema of classical movement. There is a certain preponderance of sensation over the film's narrative logic which creates spaces of tactile value, that is 'any-space-whatever' that are disconnected from the film as a whole (Deleuze 1982/2011, 193). For instance, if Dreyer's close-up creates an early case for the study of the intensive-image it is because his fragmented, de-framed face(s) of Maria Falconetti may well be said to depart from, or break with, the general economy of the movement-image film. It is an intense facial space which, as mentioned by Adrian Martin, 'goes beyond the dramaturgical demands of characterization [in order to] fragment the totality of a scene' (2018/2020, 146).

Similar intensive effects are discussed by Gilberto Perez next to the use of the close-up and the off-space in Dovzhenko's films, most notably in *Earth* (1930). This is another early poetic work which interrogates Deleuze's classical reading of the cinema by enacting what Deren calls 'the vertical attack' of intensity. *Earth* can indeed be read as an enlarged form of Deleuze's affection-image which, by continually offering 'moments of pure intensity' (Perez 1998, 165) transforms the visibility of action into the invisibility of a feeling, thus breaking down the system of the movement-image by way of the body.⁹ Deleuze, however, never deterritorialises completely the classical poetic film by giving enough duration [*durée*], or enough autonomy to such an enlarged modality of the affective instance. It is only with Michelangelo Antonioni that Deleuze's 'power of affection' pairs with his modern 'any-space-whatever, [a sign] which Antonioni in turn pushes as far as the void' (1983/2005, 119–20). Neither his notion of intensity, which I claim is essential to comprehend the differential nature of both of his cinematic periods, is stressed with enough autonomy in *Cinema 1* – not at least with the sufficient energy required to shatter his closed sensory-motor schema by way of affection. It is true, for instance, that the 'sublime-intense' is found next to the early expressionist works of F. W. Murnau and Fritz Lang, but the type of image Deleuze accounts for in these cases does not escape 'the closed dynamic interplay of light and darkness' proper to the German pre-war school of montage (Deleuze 2011, 58). So, just as Perez observes this unmediated power of intensity in Dovzhenko's *Earth*, or in regard to those scenes left empty, often unfinished in the films by Murnau, 'as in the gaps that appear in the trolley in *Sunrise* [1927], or the space around the lovers' hut in *Tabu* [1931]' (1998, 143), I similarly account for an intensive-image that confronts the set demarcations of Deleuze's classical era by creating situations that are at the edge of the visible and which create doubts about what we see and hear on-screen.

The Shape of the Book

Drawing on this groundless notion of intensity, my book will engage not only with Deleuze's writings on philosophers and the arts, or with the work of other cultural theorists who have thought – and are still thinking – intensively, but it will also engage with the way Deleuze's large philosophical project can account for his smaller, yet immense work on the cinema, *The Movement-Image* and *The Time-Image*. The former, which the author draws as material signs immobilised by their own sensory-motor cohesion,

---

⁹ In the overture of Dovzhenko's film, at the moment when the viewer glimpses a shot of wheat fields cutting to a close-up of a woman standing still, Perez describes how the immobility of the young girl represents an act of passivity from which a plethora of meanings radiate: 'It is a resistance to being swayed, an assertion of her intrinsic energy, her own intensity, before the surrounding energies and intensities of nature. In the next shot the swaying sunflower fills the whole screen: it too has its own intensity (. . .) Not only the close-up but every shot [in Dovzhenko's film] is a detail, a section of a larger field extending out of frame, continuing without bounds in the space off-screen: a painting is a whole, a theatre stage is a whole, but what we see on screen is always a part of a whole. More than any other filmmaker, Dovzhenko makes us forget the space off-screen as we apprehend the thing we have before our eyes' (1998, 165; 168–9).

represents an image of *adaequatio* or 'a plane of consistency' (2011, 17–58) where intensities rest and are stopped, whereas the latter, which Deleuze sketches *in intensio*, stands for his artistic image of thought dynamised by its own creative force – that is, as non-representative flux of images that become, to employ Jean-François Lyotard's terminology, 'figural'. If that is the case, and the intensive quality of early film is somehow cancelled by the primacy given to extensive movement, then what this book aims to achieve is to apply Deleuze's theory on intensities into the cinema in order to create a continuity between his two periods. This theory of intensities, as I have mentioned it above, is one that moves from Deleuze's early works on 'difference' and its depths into one of the 'multiple' and the surface. However, and despite his later reorganisation of intensities as a theory of haecceity, multiplicities and interstices, what remains constant, in my view, is the transformative potential of his notion of becoming. In fact, one could also take this dynamic push that carries the intensive-image towards more and more complex forms, and more differentiated destinies, from Bergson (the author that most influenced Deleuze's cinema books),[10] when stating in *Creative Evolution* (1907/1998) that the evolution of life must be read as a singular indivisible force: 'a creation that goes on forever expanding in virtue of an initial movement [which] constitutes the unity of the organized world' (1998, 105). Such initial movement, according to Bergson, must carry with it the irreducible difference that prevents any system (in this case, the cinema) from ever attaining any form of completion or closure. Hence, and with regard to my critique of Deleuze's classical/modern division, Bergson's becoming will mean that there is no essential difference between passing from one image-period or one image-state to another and persisting in the same state, because the state of intensity itself is nothing but change.

In examining closely Deleuze's film-philosophy, this book reads the intensive-image in two complementary ways. The first one, which thinks of intensities as a continuous dynamism or flow [*rheûma*], rather than as completed or unified forms, suggests that the image, foreseeable only in extension, is constantly being transformed within itself, because as much as intensity is that which animates bodies to obtain an actual form and to change in themselves, the same energy is said to mobilise the cinema, and my reading of Deleuze's cinemas more particularly, into different – heterogeneous – states of itself. (It is important to remember here that for Deleuze, as well as for Ruiz, the cinema is a living organism that is

---

[10] In fact, it is probably *Matter and Memory* (1896/1990) the book that most influenced Deleuze's views on the two cinemas: the movement-image (matter) and the time-image (memory).

changing constantly, so that the image, in every point of its trajectory, is as 'intense' and expressive as it can be.) In other words, I do not propose to separate Deleuze's classical and modern regimes as completely *different in nature*, but as evolving or *differing in degrees of intensity* – that is, as one open bloc of sensation that changes without ceasing. This is what I call, in the next chapter, 'towards the intensification of the cinema'. It is a morphogenetic process, or an image of becoming that gathers force in time, in films from the silent to the contemporary era, ranging from Buster Keaton's 'comedy of mind' (Perez 1998, 92–122) or Mario Peixoto's 'early slow cinema' (Cousins 2021) to the current 'poetry of exchanges and displacements' of Pedro Costa's aesthetics (Rancière 2014, 127–42). Here, unlike Deleuze who describes classical films as mainly driven by their sensory-motor closure (except for Yasujiro Ozu perhaps)[11] – thus, as images devoid of 'difference' in their being flawlessly coherent in a firm system of sensory-actions, motor-affections and perceptual-schemes – I seek to free the sensuous power of early intensive-images by pointing out, along with Jacques Rancière, those 'aftereffects [of] classical art' (2001/2016, 75–94). The purpose, once again, will be to outline an intensified continuity of the cinema by suggesting that Deleuze's *new* conception of the time-image should not be opposed or detached from his *old* schema of the movement-image, but accompanying each other in the combinatorial potential of what I call the intensive-image.

The second dimension of the intensive-image, already at play in this movement of intensification and becoming, has to do with embryology rather than morphology. This means that every intensive-image, be it classical or modern, is defined as more than the representation of itself, always open to becoming more, or to further orders of self-complexity. Hence, if intensity is said to be difference, and difference is that which goes underneath the given ('difference is not diversity', says Deleuze, just as intensity is not the purely visible in the image), then this book argues that there are singular disparities, in each of the cinema's periods, that match the prenatal strength of intensity with a certain notion of the incommensurable. It is an imperceptible form of audiovisuality that, echoing Gregory Flaxman,

---

[11] Ozu was already developing in the early 1930s a cinema of weak sensory-motor-connections based on Deleuze's notion of any-space-whatever and the pure optical and sound situations of his modern time-image, in films such as *The Woman of Tokyo* (1933); *A Story of Floating Weeds* (1934); and *What Did the Lady Forget?* (1937). As Felicity Colman argues in her 'Deleuze's Kiss: The Sensory Pause of Screen Affect': 'Deleuze names Japanese director Yasujiro Ozu as "the inventor of opsigns and sonsigns" for the use of specific filmic moments that enable the spectator and those onscreen to perceive the change that has occurred within the whole' (2005, 104). These moments, as Deleuze remarks in his seminars at the University of Paris, are called 'affective-intensive' (2011, 194).

some forms of cinema, in the very sense of breathing, are 'inspiring' (2000, 1–57). So, when taken in itself as the inexplicable, intensity follows the pure differential nature of the image rather than the varying degrees of intensity through which the cinema moves and intensifies across its history. Singular cases of the intensive-image will be examined under films by Luis Buñuel (*Un chien andalou*, 1929; *Los olvidados*, 1950); Anthony Mann (*Winchester 73*, 1950); Merian C. Cooper and Ernest B. Schoedsack (*Grass: A Nation's Battle for Life*, 1925); François Truffaut (*The Wild Child*, 1970); Werner Herzog (*The Enigma of Kaspar Hauser*, 1974); Lucrecia Martel (*Zama*, 2017); Pedro Costa (*Colossal Youth*, 2006); the Sensory Ethnography Lab (*Sweetgrass*, 2009); among others. According to this logic, as in Deren's film-poems, the intensity of an image can neither be divisible nor extended to the narrative progression of action; it can only be arranged on a 'vertical scale of sensation' which allows the viewer to speak about intensities and their displacing degrees of affection. Chapter 5 on 'Resistance in *The Lobster*' will offer a pedagogical study of this imperceptible form of sensation passing through the body of both characters and viewers.

The following chapters seek to define the meanings and conventions of the intensive-image through a close analysis of avant-garde, poetic and realist films encompassing the classical, modern and contemporary periods. Accordingly, each of the following chapters will discuss relevant aspects of the intensive-image to demonstrate its originality, formal characteristics and relationship with the history of image-forms.

Section One

Re-Thinking Deleuze's Film-Philosophy

CHAPTER 1

Towards the Intensification of the Cinema

In *What is Philosophy?*, the last collaboration between Gilles Deleuze and Félix Guattari, the authors reflect upon the privileged position that the arts have occupied in their lives and discuss how is it that the aesthetic field connects with what they do. The main premise of the book is that what they call 'thinking' (traditionally monopolised by philosophy) and what they call 'creativity' (traditionally associated with the arts) are coextensive in life and offer nothing to distinguish the domains of one from the other: philosophers as much as artists are said to experiment with the unknown and to create the new, what Deleuze and Guattari define as two similar modes of 'confronting chaos' (1996, 197). What changes, though, is how philosophers and artists experiment over this plane, and the reason to pose the question is to set the limits that makes one activity irreducible to the other. In their view, while philosophers are concerned with the creation of concepts, so that philosophy makes sense of reality out of its own capacity to think about the world, artists are concerned with the creation of affects or intensity, so that art gives ideas a sensuous form (1996, 24). This amounts to saying that while philosophy creates *conceptual images* by constructing blocs of utterances (in Wittgenstein's sense of 'making pictures of facts') art, in its turn, extracts sensation from its materials in order to create an *affective discourse* (in Hegel's sense of art as 'the sensual presentation of ideas'). As a result, even though their planes revolve around different objectives and compose autonomous fields, their activities, nevertheless, produce an overlapping frame – that of the philosophical concept becoming visible to the mind of the reader and that of the artistic sensation producing an intensive shock in the viewer.

By referring to Deleuze's film-philosophy, this chapter reflects upon the cinematic categories of movement and time as a medium akin to philosophical thinking. Movement, which Deleuze links predominantly to the form of realism portrayed by the classical Hollywood montage, is understood as an action-whole whose parts – perceptual and affective – fit together exactly in the trajectory of the moving image. Here, there are three main units making up Deleuze's classical system of the movement-image: perception-images (generally linked with the long shot); affection-images (akin to the face or the close-up); and the motor force of action-images (associated with the mid-shot), all of which form an organic or *solid* structure, organised by rational cuts determining the cohesiveness of shots, and these shots subsequently determining the action-movement of the film as a whole. Here, by interlocking the primacy of action in a firm system of events, what I call the 'solidity' of Deleuze's classical era is advancing a philosophical tradition that he calls, after Plato, 'the dogmatic image of thought' (2014, 137) – that is, a type of rational consciousness that is sure of itself and the world it inhabits. In contrast, Deleuze's notion of time qua duration or alteration, which he links exclusively with the emergence of the modern time-image, is one that rejects the previous teleological mandates of classical cinema in order to connect screen events by disjunction or fragmentation – that is to say, as a more *liquid* flow of audiovisual relations. Deleuze's time-image, which appears for the first time at the end of the Second World War, with Italian neorealism, is thus characterised by a movement of intensity, differentiation and becoming. It is an open system of relations that the philosopher describes under five cinematic operations: 'the dispersive situation, the deliberatively weak link, the voyage form, the consciousness of clichés, [and] the condemnation of the plot' (2013, 210). This means that if the solidity of the classical tale portrays a place that is somehow complete and univocal for the mind of the viewer, the routes of the time-image will project a milieu that is more uncertain and vaguer; hence a 'liquid' territory in which the relationship between philosophy and film will be said to follow the intensive line of the problematic.

What is central for my analysis, however, is not so much to focus on the rupture between classical movement-images and modern time-images as if they were two unrelated categories belonging to different ages or philosophies, but to treat the two periods as one continuous image that experiences the art of crossing a verge – that is to say, as a passage of intensity bridging Deleuze's classical-modern binary.[1] Hence, 'Towards the intensification of the cinema', the title for this chapter, denotes a first departure from Deleuze's classification of images. Here, instead of speaking about two separate regimes of art, I examine intensive-images that

[1] As Bergson states at the beginning of *Creative Evolution* when referring to the indivisible flow of the different states of an organism: 'This amounts to saying that there is no essential difference between passing from one state to another and persisting in the same state (. . .) [These different states] stand out against the continuity of a background on which they are designed, and to which indeed they owe the intervals that separate them' (1998, 2–3).

are present in, and differentiate across, the classical and modern periods. This is a movement that deals more directly with films that increase our capacity for thought, that is to say 'time-image' according to Deleuze, but which I nonetheless describe under a new form of the image, the intensive-image, which questions his classical system of relations by affirming difference, or by expressing an image of *durée* that is continually creating the new: 'Continuity of change, preservation of the past in the present, [that is] real duration' (Bergson 1998, 23). Thus, the notion of intensity that I am investigating is one that entails a coexistence between present and past under a principle of indeterminacy that helps to elaborate the new. And such indivisible continuity of the intensive-image which gathers force through its material evolution, is also what Bergson calls 'a function of time' – that is, 'a living being [that] essentially has duration' (quoted in Grosz 2000, 230).

* * *

Using the analogy of different states of water (that is solid, liquid and gas) I will describe the movement of intensity as the transition from Deleuze's 'icy' form of classical realism to the more 'liquefied' fluctuations of his modern age. Subsequently, and to complete the hydrological cycle, I will account for the 'gaseous' phase of Deleuze's cinema(s) under a contemporary form of realism that is radicalising the fragmented links of his film modernity. Here, unlike other scholars who exemplify Deleuze's solid, liquid and gaseous states of perception under a range of contemporary popular films, as David Deamer so convincingly does in his *Deleuze's Cinema Books* (2016, 177–88),[2] my intention is rather to expand and unify the spatio-temporal breaks of Deleuze's two eras by accounting for an image-continuity that differentiates across films from the solid-classical to the liquid-modern and the gaseous-present. In this sense, the current cinematic state that I am proposing accounts for a more vaporous image that shifts away from the centre of action towards the margin, and simultaneously pushes the margin towards the off-screen space. It is an image that confronts thought in virtue of all the indeterminacy that thinking is: it is thus an intensity that creates doubts about the reality we perceive on-screen; an uncertain viewing experience that blurs the boundaries between the inside and the outside, interiority and exteriority, on- and off-screen. Echoing Paola Marrati, the purpose of this cinematic streamflow will be

---

[2] For further discussion see David Deamer's 'Le scaphandre et la papillon/The Diving Bell and the Butterfly. Solid perception; Timecode. Liquid perception'; and 'Naqoyqatsi. Gaseous perception' (2016, 177–88).

to examine in-depth 'forms of action and agency and their *transformation*' (2008, x; my emphasis) in Deleuze's two film periods as well as in contemporary cinema. It is a form of becoming that, I argue, creates the grounds for an intensive-image which carefully considers the ways in which the past, present and future are entangled, thus typifying a more cyclical relationship between cinematic classicism and modernism.

It is important to clarify again that the notion of the intensive-image, which is based on Deleuze's primacy of difference and sensation, is one that looks back at his classical art of the homogenous to reintroduce such displacing energy of intensities. By claiming certain fissures in Deleuze's movement-image schema, intensity is read, as the philosopher does next to his modern cinematic phase, in terms of a rebellious image that displaces vision and identification by making its familiar objects strange. In Flaxman's words:

> Sensation always initially betokens a kind of violence insofar as the dogmatic image of thought solidifies itself in its own inertia (habits, rituals, conventions), sensation is like the setting off of a trip wire, the communication of a kind of synaptic frenzy through the faculties. (2000, 13)

As I will show shortly, this is also the case for classical intensive-images that free the movement-image system from its solidity by offering 'parametric narratives' that are intrinsically poetic in style (Bordwell 1985, 274). It is, to echo Bergson once again, an image of ever-intensifying relations that orients itself towards the unknown and which 'never stop[s] changing' in its divergent evolution (1998, 11).

Hence, it is not surprising to notice that the concept of intensity, as developed by DeLanda from a branch of physics called thermodynamics (2013, 1–35), is central to a reading of the cinema that continuously transforms – insofar as its duration becomes here the pure intensive change. Natural philosophy, the early term for physics, is what drives Deleuze's two main images as the genetic element of a film tradition that literally *moves* in *time*. It is an intensive trajectory that, as Bertetto demonstrates in his reading of Deleuze's philosophy, represents the qualitative motion of his uninterrupted, non-pulsated image of time:

> Cinema is movement, of course. But its movement is continuous flow, effected through recomposed and remodeled discontinuities. It is flow because it is a more or less effective orchestration of intensities. It is flow because it is an art of becoming (. . .) *Cinema is flow, that is, it is intensity*. (2017, 796; my emphasis)

Before I begin to describe in greater depth my trajectory in films from solid to liquid and gaseous states of perception, let me offer first a pedagogical example of this tripartite hydrological cycle. I am talking about Victor Kossakovsky's *Aquarela* (2018), a film that clearly evaporates narrative structures to welcome more of an ebb-and-flow of cinematic viewing. This is a documentary film shot at ninety-six frames per second and which is based on the threatening powers of water in what seems to be a speedily disappearing human environment. *Aquarela*'s opening sequence begins in the frozen Lake Baikal, at the time when the icy waters start to melt, hence it is not safe to walk or drive through, despite some people still crossing the lake. In a wide shot of the Siberian Lake, we see vehicles crashing through the ice with some of the survivors screaming for a missing person. Once the rescuers arrive at the scene human dialogue is minimal, or at least indistinguishable, but the cracking soundscape of the ice is enough of a messenger to set the tone and the atmosphere for the film to come, one in which the uncontrollable forces of nature are placed against desperate tiny humans trying to escape from an unavoidable catastrophe.

In this direction, *Aquarela* helps to illustrate not only what global warming is doing to the planet in the age of the Anthropocene but also, and more specifically for my hypothesis, to show the liquefied narrative links that Deleuze's time-image advances in dissolving the previous solid structures of the classical movement-image. Here, Kossakovsky's film portrays a melting environment and an image-intensification that exemplifies exactly the sort of meteorological transformations I will investigate in this chapter. After the ice cliffs and glaciers start to collapse at the beginning of the film, Kossakovsky's camera takes the viewer to a vast oceanic landscape where a sailing boat confronts dangerous waves. In terms of the film's narrative arc, this episode marks the passage from the previous, more solid sequence in the frozen Lake Baikal, conveyed in a fixed long shot with some humans acting and reacting in it, to an increasingly de-humanised, abstract and liquid environment where the camera is lashed by the immense oceanic waves the filmmaker is trying to capture. Subsequently, the film ends at Angel Falls in Venezuela, in a passage from liquidity to steam that offers a metacommentary on both the film's vanishing storyline as well as the becoming-gaseous of Deleuze's cinemas through the intensities of the image.

The Movement-Image: A Solid Cinematic Form

First act: *Cinema 1*. Deleuze argues that what predominates in the movement-image is a rational trajectory between action-images, perception-images and affection-images, all of which are interlocked in a sequence of narrative events: the perception of an image drives a certain logic of action which in turn entails an affective situation that consecutively leads to a new perception and action. For Deleuze, such a (foreseeable) structure of events is what prevails in classical narrative montage. Following Bergson, who defines this system as the 'sensory-motor schema', Deleuze argues that:

> The cinema of action depicts sensory-motor situations: there are characters, in a certain situation, who act (...) according to how they perceive the situation. Actions are linked to perceptions and perceptions develop into actions. (2005, 51)

Broadly speaking, this schematism refers to the dominant action-image portrayed by Hollywood's productions running from the early decades of the twentieth century up to the late 1950s. It is a classical form of realism that Deleuze describes according to the plot-line trajectory of the melodrama (*Casablanca*, Curtiz 1942); the musical (*The Love Parade*, Lubitsch 1929); the western (*Stagecoach*, Ford 1939), the gangster film (*Scarface: The Shame of the Nation*, Hawks 1932) and the sociopolitical film (*Birth of a Nation*, Griffith 1915), the latter being a remarkable example for Deleuze to show how in classical political films the notion of the common people (e.g. the unified nation) prevails for the audience to identify with. This formula, as I will demonstrate later on with the advent of the time-image, stands in stark contrast to the 'missing people' and social fragmentations of Deleuze's modern age; an image without a 'hero' tightening the classical sense of political unity, or the narrative unity of the movement-image apparatus. For now, however, what I want to highlight is that although Deleuze's sensory-motor formula fails to account for the sociopolitical complexities of the North American film tradition (Bordwell 1986, 17–34; Perez 1998, 233–59; Isaacs 2005, 126–38) his action-montage is well suited to inform a dominant principle in the organisation of films which functions according to a 'central conflict theory' (Ruiz 2013, 15–33) that secures the coherence of the classical tale. And the fact that most of these films have a central conflict commanding the action (usually with a hero wanting something and a villain trying to stop him from obtaining it), as well as an Aristotelian three-act structure as its backbone, is one of the reasons why I refer to Deleuze's movement-image system as a frozen type of architecture. Because as much as there might be agreement that this sensory-motor arrangement creates no detours in the organisation of events, then classical cinema becomes, according to Deleuze, a static homogeneity stabilised by its own 'immobile sections of duration' (2005, 8).

In fact, Deleuze makes at times some derogatory remarks about the linearity of the movement-image, especially in regard to Hollywood's commercial films. On some occasions, he refers to this closed functioning totality as an uncreative image ridden by 'the dark organisation of clichés', which marks the 'cretinization' and the 'mental deficiency' of the viewer (2005, 210). Clearly, in line with his *temps modernes*, and by equating the meaning of an image to its level of zero variational degree, Deleuze turns a blind eye to those thought-operations at play in various pre-war films, as noted by contemporary philosophers and film scholars such as Totaro (1999), Perez (1998, 2019), Badiou (2010/2013), Rancière (2014), Nagib (2015) and Viegas (2016). This is to say that by excluding the perceptual gaps in the development of the chronicle, what Deleuze's modernity aims for is to undo the links of classical cinema whose trajectories are somehow complete; this suggests films without fissure or lacunae that makes it impossible for the viewer to separate the image from what it comes to represent. Yet, if ambiguity and incompletion are indeed lacking in the Hollywood golden age, as Deleuze argues, how are we to read a number of pioneering films from this period by directors such as Nicholas Ray, Buster Keaton or Anthony Mann?

The powers of subtraction and the strange relationships presented by the epics of Ray offer a case in point. When Mildred summarises the novel she has read to Dixon in *In a Lonely Place* (1950) and says to him: 'You know, there are lots of little plots and things I didn't even tell you about!', isn't she suggesting that the viewer may well be left in state of uncertainty and wonder, too? Or when asked by Dixon what an epic film is: A 'dreamy picture' she says, inferring the multiplicity of meanings populating the classical take: 'You know, [the epic is] a picture that is real long and has lots of things going on.' *In a Lonely Place*, as Adrian Martin and Cristina Álvarez observe, represents one of the cinema's most deeply felt, atypical and intense love stories ever made:

> The electricity of immediate attraction between two people, the period of ecstatic romance, the sadness of eventual parting: Nicolas Ray indeed depicts these immortal peaks and valleys of love with a remarkably concise intensity, and at a telling distance from Hollywood convention. (Martin and Álvarez 2021)

Or consider, along the same lines, Keaton's strange finale in *Collage* (1927): 'What is this abrupt slap in the face doing at the end of an otherwise unquestioning love story?' (1975, 242) writes Walter Kerr in *The Silent Clowns*. As commented on by Gilberto Perez in his chapter 'The Bewildered Equilibrist', dedicated to Keaton's comedies of the mind, the burlesque filmmaker also seems to be questioning this classical closure by providing a screen-world that is rather fractured and incomplete. Keaton's cinema, we may say, introduces an image of the gap: another early filmmaker 'whose propensity is to leave the space of action unresolved' (Perez 1998, 122), with a preference for the use of the long take and the unsettled conflict that may be compared to those later films made by Michelangelo Antonioni, Jean-Marie Straub and Danièle Huillet, or Jean Renoir – all time-image filmmakers according to Deleuze. This means, in short, that by revealing the displacements of classical cinema, as Ray and Keaton demonstrate, there is a case for an early intensive-image freed from solid measures. This is an image of sensation that undoes, or at least problematises, Deleuze's argument about the 'mindlessness' of classical narrative. In Perez's words:

> Keaton's work indeed resembles, and more than in the use of this or that similar technique, the work of such later directors as Renoir and Antonioni, who also employ the camera to conduct an inquiry into the world rather than to parcel out the answers. His films differ from theirs, however, in being as much the actor's as the director's (. . .) The director performs as deftly in his shots as the actor does in his acrobatics, but they both seem precariously poised in their dealings with an uncertain situation. (1998, 114)

Similar arguments are drawn by Rancière in relation to Ray's 'missing shots' and Anthony Mann's 'poetics' (2016, 95–104). In his view, both directors taken together represent what he calls the 'aftereffects [of] classical art' – that is, as described by Perez, too, the perceptual gaps left by an image of intensity which breaks with the prevailing logic of the action film. Referring to Mann's open-ended stories, Rancière suggests that:

> The only good end is the one that contains the action within its proper limits, the one that leaves open the possibility that the action may be continued, restarted. This is what's called the risk of art, and Anthony Mann has always assumed that risk. (2016, 94)

Here, Rancière's 'aftereffects' of the classical era are also thought in terms of intensive-images that challenge Deleuze's inflexible account of the early movement-image which fails to see the subversive and fluid nature of many of these films. By welcoming the viewer to decipher apparently unrelated signs in works that are not finished but suspended, classical filmmakers such as Keaton, Ray or Mann are thus able to thwart Deleuze's sensory-motor schema by generating situations that are not readily at hand.

Winchester 73 (Mann 1950) and its hero Lin McAdam (James Stewart) is another film that reveals such a disconnection between action, perception and affection by problematising our identification with the hero's elusive way of being. James Stewart, says Mann in regard to his role as Lin McAdam, 'is not the "broad-shouldered type" [of man], so that you must take a lot of "precautions" if you want to show him "taking on the whole world" [onscreen]' (Mann quoted in Rancière 2016, 78). The protagonist, who is a stranger to the community of Dodge City and a solitary wanderer of the West, introduces 'ambiguous signs' (2016, 84) that certainly interrupt the unity of the sensory-motor chronicle. Such an aporia is seen, among other moments of the film, towards the end when the hero confronts his villainous brother Dutch Henry (Stephen McNally) for a duel. In this episode that goes for about six uninterrupted minutes, McAdam makes Dutch Henry spend, very methodically and patiently, all his ammunition on top of a cliff in the deserted landscape of the southwest. In addition to the long duration of the shooting, and the empty space where the action happens, Mann's calmness in recording the battle portrays a flux of intensive moments that place the viewer quite away from the general logics of the narrative, thus taking the viewer towards a more haptic and gestural space.

Accordingly, if unresolved perceptual gaps are said to exist in the classical chronicle, then I would argue that by no means should Deleuze's movement-image and time-image regimes be placed in historical separation. The concept of the intensive-image proposes, in fact, a radically different approach to Deleuze's film-philosophy and its relation with the cinematic past, founded on a more cyclical structure, as well as on an incessant intensification, between the classical and the modern. As I have noted previously, intensity stands for an image-in-becoming that suggests a continuity between the two periods, old and new, by questioning Deleuze's closure of early cinematic practice. This is to say that while transiting from the more or less stable unity of Deleuze's classical age, to the weaker links of his film modernity, what the viewer experiences is not so much the separation between two different images, but the intensification of one image, the intensive-image, that phases into a more differentiated state of itself. This is why, among other reasons, I propose the analogy of water states to illustrate such a continuous transformation. It is intensity that not only gathers force from Deleuze's 'icy' movement-image unity to his 'liquid' time-image period but also one that further differentiates into a 'gaseous' form of audiovisuality that dissipates narrative interaction in favour of more contemplative and sensory experiences. I will illustrate this thesis with the work of two contemporary realist filmmakers: Pedro Costa in the final section of this chapter, and Lucrecia Martel in Chapter 6. For now, however, let me show how the transition from *Cinema 1* to *Cinema 2* is actually made.

The key component for Deleuze in the movement-image is the relationship between his schema of action-perception-affection and time: how is it that such a system arises in time? In keeping proximity with Bergson, he argues that early filmmakers represent time in an indirect way, meaning that the motion of classical action predetermines time in a measurable or closed unity that is incapable of altering its sensory-motor course of events (2005, 58–63). The idea can be shown briefly by what Bergson calls the 'image-puzzle' in the last chapter of *Creative Evolution*. Like Deleuze's movement-image, Bergson's image-puzzle uses time not to create a figure, but to reconstruct a picture that is already conceived before the assemblage of the puzzle. Needless to say, the process of completing a puzzle requires time for its picture reconstruction, but as far as the image is *a priori* given, the category of time, as Bergson exclaims, becomes only 'an accessory (. . .) that may be lengthened or shortened without the content [of the work] being altered' (1998, 340). In terms of its form of content, such is also the case for Deleuze's action cinema: at the centre of the story there is someone who attempts to solve a mystery, uses a prescribed set of clues, undertakes possible actions and completes the puzzle, so that the viewer may already glimpse how the story is going to end. In this way, as long as the connections between images circulate in a closed functioning totality, Deleuze argues that the filmic trajectory only involves quantitative or *extensive* motion in space, but never qualitative or *intensive* change in time. As he declares while referring to the movement-image system: 'there is never anything else or anything more than there is in the thing [because] the thing and the perception of the thing are one and the same thing' (2005, 65).

This is, of course, what I have put into question when considering the narrative gaps developed by Ray, Keaton and Mann, or by Buñuel's early intensities as it will be discussed in the next chapter. Deleuze, however, remains vague in unblocking the deterritorialising forces of time in his description of classical film, essentially read as a mimetic image of thought that imposes a metric cadence cancelling the inventiveness of time. While reflecting on Mann's westerns as symptoms of the sensory-motor formula, whose 'heterogeneous elements are interconnected directly' (2005, 173), Deleuze nonetheless leaves open the possibility of reading some of his films as almost pure optical and audible signs. Referring to *Winchester 73* and its construction of a 'skeleton-space with missing intermediaries' (2005, 172) the philosopher declares that '[the film] is a drama of the visible and of the invisible as much as an epic of action' (2005, 72). This suggests, as Deleuze further states in relation to *Man of the West* (Mann 1958) that the action can no longer be determined by the 'straight lines' of classical narrative but by the 'elliptical lines [of a new] vector-space, with temporal distances' (2005, 173). So, if Mann introduces here a more ambiguous signs for Deleuze, it is only because his late (1950s and 1960s) westerns represent a transitive old/new image summoning the limits of the previous epoch. However, it is only with Alfred Hitchcock that Deleuze makes his way out of this sensory-motor closure.

Deleuze positions Hitchcock at the juncture between the two cinemas and describes him as a liminal director (next to Orson Welles and Roberto Rossellini) who brings into completion the movement in the image to make room for a direct presentation of time in cinema. Hitchcock creates a system of relations, and of mental operations, that Deleuze describes as being qualitative in time: 'By paralysing his characters Hitchcock opens them, and thus the audience, to a chain of relations which constitute the mental image, in opposition to the thread of actions, perceptions and affections' (2005, 118). So, if the filmmaker entails this threshold standing in the middle of Deleuze's two cinemas it is because he presents a disjunction between actual and virtual events which generates the new mental relation for the viewer.[3]

Now, before I analyse Deleuze's time-image system and its virtual, more relational structure, it is important to note first that his interest in film and filmmakers is philosophical rather than cinematographic. That is why, for instance, the various analytical aspects of his cinema books, and of his books on the arts more generally,[4] are always subordinated to the construction of a concept designed to discuss philosophical ideas – such as those of 'movement' and 'time' in relation to the cinema. Hence, by looking at his film taxonomy it is reasonable to argue that in expressing what the movement-image *shows*, Deleuze is also mimicking what his classical image of philosophy *says*. Most particularly, by describing the schematism

---

[3] This is a topic that I have elaborated on in an article devoted to 'Hitchcock's Simulacra' (2017c, 76–91). Here, I analyse a scene of mental relations from *Rear Window* (1954) that illustrates this process of intensification in Deleuze's image-periods. In a crucial moment of the film, the protagonist L. B. Jeffries, who is a photographer struck with motor (leg) paralysis, comes to interpret a series of events as an indication that a crime has been committed in the neighbourhood. The fact that his neighbour, Lars Thorwald, has made a few late-night trips with a knife wrapped in newspaper, three rings and an alligator purse in his suitcase, is a clear indication for Jeffries that Thorwald has murdered his wife. However, whether a real crime has happened is quite uncertain throughout the movie, and it is the viewer who must decide whether Jeffries's position is right or wrong. By this technique, as Deleuze suggests, Hitchcock's mental-image indicates not only how the hero comes to attribute meaning to what he sees but more importantly, how he erroneously interprets a sign that will eventually involve the viewer in the (mis)creation of meaning (2005, 204–9): 'Tell me everything you saw', says Lisa to Jeffries at one moment of the film, '*and what you think it means.*' Hence, by making the viewer aware of the act of perceiving images, the director introduces a mental relation, which is an external element, that liberates the movement of time from its internal, cohesive blockage.

[4] His books on art and philosophy include *Proust and Signs* (1964), *Francis Bacon* (1981/2005), *Cinema 1* (1983), *Cinema 2* (1985), *The Fold* (1988). In collaboration with Guattari, he also co-authored a book on Kafka (1975), among other minor works.

of classical film, what the philosopher is accounting for is a type of mediation that he refers to as 'the dogmatic image of thought' (2014, 137). Like the logic of the movement-image system, Deleuze argues in *Difference and Repetition* that philosophy has long constituted a restricted form of thinking that works according to fixed norms and which aspires to totalise any encounter into one of resemblance and recognition:

> Thought is thereby filled with no more than an image of itself, one in which it recognises itself more than it recognises things: this is a finger, this is a table, Good morning Theaetetus. (2014, 138)

Explicitly announced, the critique is pointed towards Platonism and the old triad of the model, the copy and the simulacrum. The story is well known: for Plato, the sensible environment and the things we see in it are *modelled* on the realm of eternal ideas, so that our experiences of the world are derived as *copies* of a deeper reality – what Plato calls the model or the intelligible. As discussed in *The Republic* (c. 375 BC/2006), such hierarchy separating immanent copies from transcendent ideas further marks a decline in his mimetic conception of the arts, because as much as Plato's material world stands as a copy of an ideal system, then the visual arts, and their value in representing the 'superficial' can only produce a simulation that is irrelevant for his deeper, eternal realm. This is the reason why art becomes for Plato a *copy of a copy* for which there is neither usefulness nor truth. On the contrary, by following the Kantian (Copernican) revolution in philosophy, and the subsequent Nietzschean reversal of Platonism, Deleuze wants to applaud art for its ability to magnify a world of pure appearances and simulations.

According to Deleuze, the philosopher who clearly abolishes this distinction between the real and the copy is Friedrich Nietzsche – the artist-philosopher par excellence. He refers to Nietzsche as the writer who gave him the taste for speaking through the forces of 'affects, intensities, [and] experiments' (1962/2006, 6), all expressions of an image which demands thought to operate without the transcendental form of Platonic consciousness (whether this may be called God, the model, or the subject). As this sort of philosopher of aesthetic experience, Nietzsche shows, similar to Kant, that knowledge can never be formed outside of sensible encounters, but unlike Kant, whose conditions for experience are always universal and transcendental, Nietzsche wants to demonstrate that the encounter is always singular and superficial – that is, happening on the surface, instead of the depths. As a result of this reversal, life for Nietzsche becomes dynamic and elastic, no longer related to univocal causes or pre-existing events. And also, like Deleuze's time-image, Nietzsche's reality is one that happens through the unexpected encounter, by the multiple configurations of a character's vital forces:

> One should have more respect for the bashfulness with which nature has hidden behind riddles and iridescent uncertainties (...) What is required is to stop courageously at the surface, the fold, the skin, to adore appearance, to believe in forms, tones, words, to be superficial – *out of profundity* (...) Are we not, in this respect, artists? (Nietzsche 1882/1974, 38)

So, if the relation between film and philosophy has found an organisational structure bringing together Deleuze's *Cinema 1* and his dogmatic image of thought in Plato, then how is it that Deleuze's theory transits from the predetermination of movement (in classical cinema) to the liberation of thought (in the time-image)? We already know that this passage is separated by two extensive vectors; one concerned with quantitative movement in space, the other concerned with qualitative change in time. But how does this shift really occur? In order to answer the question, let me introduce again Bergson's image-puzzle and confront it with another figure he distinguishes from it – that of the image-painting.

It is important to note that for Bergson the comparison between the puzzle being assembled and the painting being created is one fundamentally linked to the effects of time in the outcome of the work. So, while the puzzle suggests that time is only an accessory to the reconstruction of the image (because the final figure is already there for us to look at), the painting, on the contrary, suggests that time is integral to the final result of the work. According to Bergson, it is only by altering the process of the artist's creation that time enacts all its inventive force:

> To the artist who creates a picture (...) the duration of the work is part and parcel of the picture. To contract or dilate it would be to modify both the physical evolution that fills it and the invention which is its goal. (1998, 340)

Here, Bergson's distinction between quantitative *time-length* (the puzzle) and qualitative *time-invention* (the painting) should also be read as a Kantian category. In *The Critique of Pure Reason* (1781/2008), Kant presented time as a generative feature by which the succession of movement necessarily becomes the effect of time rather than its cause. For him, time is no longer subordinated to a series of movements in space (e.g. as the actions required to assemble the figure of the puzzle) but it is movement which, on the contrary, presupposes time in order to act. This is the reason why for someone like Bergson and Deleuze, who clearly follow the Kantian formulation, everything moves and changes in time, because: 'Time is not in us, for we are in time, it is our limit and our condition for action' (Bergson quoted in Grosz 2012, 148).

Put differently, it is only by distinguishing the Bergsonian notion of quantitative time-length (indirect representation of time; a movement determining time; the image-puzzle) from qualitative time-invention (direct representation of time; a movement presupposing time; the image-painting) that the shift in Deleuze's cinemas can actually occur. As Deleuze sums it up:

> When the cinema goes through its 'Kantian' revolution, that's to say when it stops subordinating time to motion, when it makes motion depend on time (. . .) the cinematic image becomes a time-image, an auto-temporalization of the image. (1995a, 122–3)

The Time-Image: A Liquid Cinematic Form

The Bergsonian idea of time being inventive is what Deleuze's modern cinema precisely creates. His time-image, unlike classical montage, is no longer equivalent to the succession of movements marking a character's transition from one action-perception-affection unit to another. On the contrary, once delinked from the laws of schematism and its progression of events, modern cinema performs a non-commensurable relation between audiovisuals in which each shot assumes the form of a non-link. As Flaxman writes: 'By developing new images, modern cinema develops a new kind of montage (. . .) A gap opens between one image and another, an "interstice" in which thought experiences its own duration' (2000, 6). Time as such introduces the randomness of life onto the screen; a cinema that experiences a delay, a crack in perception and in the viewer's mind. Accordingly, if the failure of action and the collapse of its solidness is what gives rise to the liquefied solution of the modern era, then Deleuze's direct representation of time becomes the fissure, the lacunae and the 'out of joint' (*Hamlet*, Act 1, scene 5). This is how, according to the philosopher, modern cinema gives rise to 'a little bit of time in its pure state' (Proust quoted in Deleuze 2020a, 241). It is time, this non-pulsated movement freed of all measure, which is now in action.

Deleuze situates this sense of disjunction around the European crisis of the Second World War. For him, drawing heavily on André Bazin to locate the new image, post-war European filmmakers, and most particularly Italian neorealists, were the first to develop a cinema of pure optical and sound situations. This new style stands, according to Bazin, 'in opposition to the traditional dramatic system [of action] and rejects analysis, whether political, moral, psychological, logical, or social, of the characters and their situations' (1967/2005, 20–1). In this post-war Europe devoid of human agency and moral guidelines, Deleuze's 'new race of characters' (2013, x) represent erratic heroes of inaction and scepticism: lost wanderers (*Germany, Year Zero*, Rossellini 1948) who no longer know how to orient and make sense of the world they live in (*8 ½*, Fellini 1963); how to speak about it (*Persona*, Bergman 1966) or how to come to terms with what they perceive in it (*Blow-Up*, Antonioni 1966). Similar circumstances affected the North American New Wave filmmakers, who, years later, begin to witness the traumas of the Vietnam War (*Full Metal Jacket*, Kubrick 1987) and the necessity 'to get tough on drugs' to cope with the reality lived there (*Apocalypse Now*, Coppola 1979). The unsteadiness of the 'American Dream' and the general sense of despair with the situations in which these characters were immersed was also felt in terms of youth disaffection (*Bonnie and Clyde*, Penn 1967), personality disorders (*Taxi Driver*, Scorsese 1975) and emotional struggles (*Shadows*, Cassavetes 1959), all expressions of a life that confronts the individual with unresolved dilemmas rather than ready-made solutions. As such, and even though the North American film trajectory arguably followed a more question-answer logic and a more character-centred story than its European counterpart, both cinematic waves shared a fall of some type – a form of Greek katabasis which offered the new mental *durée* and perceptual delay for the emergence of Deleuze's time-image period.

Katabasis, an old expression designating the gradual descending of a force – such as a movement downhill, or a trip to the underworld – is also helpful to describe the shift that I am suggesting from image solidity to liquidity. Directors of time, from the 1950s onward, enact a new audiovisual route that is defined by the deregulated links of Deleuze's modernity. As suggested by the philosopher, the previous centre of gravity locked in logical plots and motivated actions transits into a more fluid system of audible and optical events:

> [Liquid perception] is one in which, all the images vary not to a central and privileged image but in relation to one another, on all their facets and in all their parts (. . .) For the more the privileged centre is itself put into movement, the more it will tend towards an acentred system where the images vary in relation to one another and tend to become like the reciprocal actions and vibrations of a pure matter. (2005, 79)

The time-image, like flowing water, appears to be a more elusive form of material existence. Time becomes the *a priori* ground for which, according to Kant and Bergson, the material and incorporeal bodies of the earth move and change in all directions. And that is also why the actions of Deleuze's modern characters are paused by the caesuras of their own perception: in Fellini's *8 ½*, Guido Anselmi (Marcello Mastroianni) is a famous Italian filmmaker who is unable to complete his film; in Bergman's *Persona*, Elizabeth Vogler (Liv Ullman) is an actress who goes mute on stage; and in Antonioni's *Blow-Up*, Thomas (David Hemmings) is a photographer who no longer knows whether he has witnessed a scene of a murder. Their visions have all failed to respond to the 'celestial' realm of the Hollywood 'star' (or the Italian 'divo', also denoting the transcendental figure of 'the divine'). On the contrary, reality becomes for them anomie and exhaustion, physical and spiritual dislocation: the time of Chronos is deregulated as much as Euclidean space is fragmented. Rossellini's *Germany, Year Zero* and its boy protagonist who aimlessly wanders around a city laid in ruins, is probably the best example to illustrate this sense of disjunction and moral devastation in European cinema after the war. It tells the story of a drifter, a boy called Edmund, who walks towards the void of his own death.

In his article 'The Imagination of Immanence; An Ethics of Cinema' (2000), Peter Canning offers a notable interpretation on why the actions of Edmund, like the actions of Deleuze's modern characters, have failed to find motivation to live in post-1945 Berlin. For Canning, the lack of bonding with the world after the Holocaust, the general shock and disillusionment following the war, and the loss of faith in humanity's place on earth are all strong reasons to link the collapse of the classical sensory-motor system with the ethical impossibility of recognising and finding an explanation for the atrocities experienced there (2000, 330). The refrain of the time-image 'Eros is sick' is the clearest sign to announce such a predicament. Canning relates this malaise to the rupture of the representational structures, as much as the moral foundations, of the previous movement-image schema:

> Morality and representation go hand in hand (...) Whenever the human schema is about to break down before the inevitable fact of illness, suffering [or] death, the moral vision comes like a sudden revelation of Truth to save the sensory-motor apparatus [of the movement-image] from anxiety and despair. (2000, 328)

In the next chapter, I will call into question this ethical reversal of Deleuze's modernity by looking at a classical filmmaker, Luis Buñuel, who is also performing (like Rossellini after him) such a rupture and moral disillusionment with the world. Here, I will suggest that the 'intolerable situation' proper to Deleuze's time-image is not something that arises exclusively after the Second World War in Europe, but something that has already been happening elsewhere, and which has previously interrupted the solidity of his movement-image thesis. This is the case of an early intensive-image that I analyse next to Buñuel's characters of *Un chien andalou* and *Los olvidados*, or as Vivian Sobchack also does in relation to his documentary subjects of *Land Without Bread* (1933). I will argue that Buñuel's films from his early naturalist period are also questioning Deleuze's representational structures and moral meanings by introducing an image of violence and affection that is producing the intensive shock in the viewer. So, similar to how Canning rejects the moral sensory-motor schema as a way of judging life from above, Buñuel's cinematic ethics will be placed alongside Deleuze's rejection of Platonism and its clairvoyant subjects, despite the filmmaker being located under the fixity of Deleuze's movement-image system.

Now, the point that I want to stress in this section is that by following the Nietzschean affirmation of a world-in-flux, Deleuze's time-image becomes a more disperse form of audiovisual perception. It is a liquid-image that, devoid of any point of origin or destination, is taken to rest in a perpetual dynamic of change. As he writes in *Cinema 2*:

> It is not a matter of judging life in the name of a higher authority which would be the good, the true; it is a matter, on the contrary, of evaluating every being, every action and passion, even every value, in relation to the life which they involve. Affect as immanent evaluation, instead of judgment as transcendent value: 'I love' or 'I hate' instead of 'I judge'. (2013, 146)

The task of turning a morality tied to mediation into an ethical process of interconnection with all that lives consists, as Deleuze suggests, in cultivating as many 'joyful encounters' as possible – that is, in maximising those relations that will expand our capacity 'to act freely and creatively' (Deleuze quoted in Pisters 2003, 86). Affect as in Spinoza's *affectus* then: the capacity of a body to affect and to be affected. However, as Rossellini shows in those last moments of *Germany, Year Zero*, when Edmund had no other choice but to kill his father, we learn that it is not always possible to rework our negative passions (what makes us sad and sick) into positive affection (what fulfils our capacity to live). For Edmund, who has constantly played around the streets of a war-torn Berlin (e.g. by kicking the ball and shooting with an imaginary gun) life is sadly turning away from him (e.g. children no longer play with him in the streets; his teacher calls him 'a monster' and tells him that it is 'only the strong who survive'). As a result, Edmund's final gesture of rubbing his hand over his face and jumping into the void represents a radical contestation of his infernal milieu: by not accepting any connection with this reality, by rejecting life in a place that negates his freedom to play, Edmund decides to put an end to his life and becomes another falling body from Berlin.

In Canning's view, who similarly draws on Primo Levi's failure to connect with a world hindering his powers to live, Edmund's suicide may well express the Spinozist denial of a world refuting his *potential* – namely, the capacity of a body to enact its own freedom to act. Although, what is central, is not so much the affection of positive or negative interactions with a given environment as is the revelation of an ethics without morality; one in which the cinema is devoid of any moral-God-character and its happy, conciliatory ending. *Germany, Year Zero* then, with all its uncertainty and cruel imagery, not only portrays the intolerable situations of Deleuze's post-war age, but more importantly for the author, it refuses to supply a moral tale for this reality that has been 'shattered from within' (2013, 41). This is why, in Canning's view, time-image filmmakers must overcome the signifying gaze of the visual medium in order to discover new intensive fields of relations: 'an absolute ethics that begins where symbolic-moral mediation leaves off and an aesthetic experience of nonrelations appear' (2000, 351).

This form of cinematic experimentation, which I will be tracing back to classical cinematic poetry, generates precisely the type of intensity that this book argues for: an aesthetic of affective relations which experiments with structures of meaning in both pre- and post-war periods by connecting us directly with the beat of sensation. Intensity represents here an image of difference and of the different that incessantly invents 'new relations and new [affective] powers' (Canning 2000, 351). So, by connecting moments of a film through invisible feelings or the sensuous, rather than through the rational and moral understanding of a situation, the intensive-image is in close proximity to those non-mediated powers of Deleuzian art. In Deleuze and Guattari's words:

> The visual material must now capture non-visible forces. Render *visible*, Klee said; not render or reproduce the visible (. . .) The forces to be captured are no longer those of the earth, but those of an immaterial, nonformal, energetic Cosmos (. . .) The essential thing is no longer forms and matters, or themes, but forces, densities, intensities. (2005, 28)

The Frame Intensified: A Gaseous Passage in Pedro Costa's *Colossal Youth*

Intensity, like sensation, is a force that must be thought in terms of unframing – the cracking of the ice. Similar to the revolution in art which took painting from representation to abstraction (say, from Malevich to Kandinsky), abstract expressionism (Pollock) and figural painting (Cézanne, Bacon . . .), the revolution in cinema that Deleuze has in mind is also pushing against the frame to confront its fixed demarcations. Following Pascal Bonitzer's notion of 'deframing' [*décadrage*], Pascal Auger's 'any-space-whatever' [*l'espace quelconque*],[5] and Pier Paolo Pasolini's 'free-indirect-discourse' [*quasi-direct discourse*], Deleuze attempts to decompose the solid trajectory of the movement-image by unfolding an abstract aesthetic of non-relations – that is, a cinema that gives birth to what I identify as a gaseous intensive-image freed of all measures or shapes. Irrational cuts, missing shots, superimpositions, displacements, de-framings, spatio-temporal leaps, or an editing connected haptically through feeling-images are all features Deleuze sketches to account for a more vaporous state where images act on each other, and with each other, without definitive purposes. Referring to the genetic sign of his perception-image, the philosopher defines the gaseous as a gramme [*engramme*] that perceives 'things in themselves': 'a universal variation [where] any point connects with any point (. . .) a gaseous state defined by the free movement of each molecule' (2005, 83–4). A scene from Pedro Costa's *Colossal Youth* works well to illustrate such an emancipation from the frame and the becoming-molecular of his experimental filmmaking practice.

As in later works by Costa (*Centro Histórico*, 2012; *Horse Money*, 2014), *Colossal Youth* follows the fate of Ventura, an elderly Cape Verde immigrant who has come to work in Lisbon's construction sites. The film is set when the Portuguese government demolishes his slum and the protagonist is relocated in a marginal housing complex on the outskirts of Lisbon. Ventura, who spends his days visiting neighbours and who reconnects with people from his past, constantly wanders between spaces (between his old and new enclosures) and different times (between his present and past lives). An example of this spectral exchange can be seen during a passage of high intensity in the film. Here, we start to hear Ventura reciting a love letter about immigrants to his friend Lento in a dark and small room. Suddenly, there is a cut and the camera moves to the kitchen of the apartment while we hear his vocalisation of the letter dying away. Right after, we move to another dark room where an illuminated painting hangs at the centre of the frame. Wandering in this seemingly expressionist space,

---

[5] Pascal Auger attended Deleuze's seminars, first at the University of Vincennes, and then at Saint-Denis, from 1975 to 1987. He worked with Deleuze on the concept of *l'espace quelconque* [any-space-whatever], which Deleuze was developing in the seminars for *The Movement-Image*.

our ears become accustomed to the footsteps of a character (later on we will know is Ventura) who appears in the next shot. Ventura's presence, however, assumes all its physicality only when we see him leaning against the wall in the Gulbenkian Foundation. He is placed between two portraits, one by Peter Paul Rubens and the other by Anthony van Dyck (Rancière 2014, 131). After he contemplates these paintings, the sequence ends with a guard of the museum asking Ventura to leave. He first whispers a few words in Ventura's ear and then cleans the surface where our protagonist, an immigrant in the country and a trespasser in the museum, is standing.

The knotty ambivalence between these series of events – between the visual and the audible, between the intervals of time and the shifting of space – remains largely unexplained. The sound-image, placed here in juxtaposition, has formed an ensemble of constant splits, so that the passing from one place to another can be linked, or not linked at all, by a multiple number of ways (e.g. by a dream, by a temporal loop, by a love letter, by the viewer's mental *durée* . . .). Hence, if my reading of the film proposes a sequence of gaseous relations, and even one of indeterminacy, it is because its meanings are flowing in the air – an intensive-image without fixity or constraints; that is, an image 'suspended in nothingness', as Martin Heidegger may suggest (quoted in Sloterdijk 2011, 89). *Colossal Youth*, in this sense, is full of feeling rather than meaning. And feeling must be understood in the abstract, as affect or intensity, before it is connected to an emotional form of content, which only comes later, through reasoning and the understanding.[6] The same can be said about the intensive-image more generally: it creates 'visible and auditory forms for something that is invisible' (Deren 1953, 57), which is the immediacy of a feeling – a poetic consciousness – characteristic of Costa's cinema: haptic editing, sequences connected rhythmically, various speeds and textures, expressionist colours . . . As Deleuze and Guattari put it in an interview with Bellour: 'It is intensities that pass, and these intensities are not representative (. . .) *When intensities pass, there is no image*. You no longer know where you are' (Deleuze 1973/2020, 222–3; my emphasis).

At first glance, this quote seems to point at the impossibility of having an 'intensive-image' in cinema: on the one hand you have 'images', and on the other hand you have 'intensities' that pass underneath. However, as soon as one describes the intensive-image in terms of a vibrant moving matter, then a generation of intensities is perfectly possible in films: there

---

[6] *Feeling and Form*, written by Susanne K. Langer in 1953, is a book that may help us to navigate through Costa's film *in a key note*, that is to say, as a musical composition that makes sonorous the forces that are not sonorous in themselves

you have an image that is non-representative, deterritorialised; a body of sensation that withdraws from the film's representational structures, and which plunges the viewer into an affective meltdown. Hence, what the authors call an 'image', *strictu sensu*, would only appear later, through the understanding, once you stop watching the film and start thinking about what had just happened on-screen. Intensity, in short, remains in the realm of the body – an unmediated affect or invisible feeling.

And this is, too, the experience of inhabiting Ventura's puzzling subjectivity in *Colossal Youth*. Here, in order to 'visualise' its intensity, I propose three different ways to read the protagonist's displacements, as well as our own spectatorial leaps. The first one has to do with Sigmund Freud's 'free association method', an important technique employed in his investigations of the psyche based on the assumption that ultimate meaning is a slippery business when it comes to the interpretation of dreams. His displacement, as defined in *The Interpretation of Dreams* (1965), transmutes the allegorical work of dream-analysis into a paradoxical process of 'looplines or short-circuits' that renders uncanny the origins or destinations of dreams: 'Even if the solution seems satisfactory and without any gaps', Freud writes, 'the possibility always remains that the dream may have yet another meaning' (1965, 313).

Freud's insight into the free association method opens up a film analysis where the intensive-image affirms its own differential energy to connect events through a gaseous interplay of relations and sensations. It is a poetic image that shifts away from the logics of action in order to advance a more episodic form of cinematic storytelling, like the surreal sequences created while dreaming. Freud's method, largely disregarded by Deleuze's philosophy of multiplicities, is taken to animate here the centripetal force of an avant-garde tradition that Pasolini has associated with the 'free indirect discourse' in cinema, and which Costa's Ventura, in my view, is pushing towards higher levels of 'indirectedness' and cinematic abstraction. Referring to Pasolini's 'cinema of poetry', Deleuze notes that free indirect discourse arises as 'a system which is always heterogeneous, far from equilibrium (. . .) [It] consists of an enunciation taken within an utterance, which itself depends on another enunciation' (2005, 75).

As seen in *Colossal Youth*, Ventura's cascade of symmetry-breaking relations is indeed helpful to describe the most heterogeneous pole of Deleuze's cinematic states – namely, the 'gaseous state', defined as the 'genetic element of all possible perception, that is, the point which changes, and which makes perception change, the differential of perception itself' (2005, 85). In this sense, I read Costa's intensive-image as a vaporous experience where perception similarly lingers in a limbo.[7] It is a form of audiovisuality, and a free association method, that undermines rational connections between events in order to generate states of spectatorial wonder – that is, contemplative and heterogeneous images constructing the filmic time for reflection. In the case of *Colossal Youth*, such an inactive mode of viewing is thought in terms of unframing – an image that shifts attention away from the centre to the margin, and from the margin towards the edge and the off-screen space. This is the case for a gaseous intensity that evaporates the fixity of the visual medium in order to turn its images into unknown realities, commanded by the thinking-feeling of what is happening, or not happening, onscreen.

Moreover, these types of temporal and spatial nicks characteristic of Ventura's journey are discussed, in a similar fashion, by Rancière. He also draws on Costa's 'politics of the sensible' to announce, in reference to *Colossal Youth*, a 'poetry of exchanges and displacements' (2014, 130). As informed by *Les écarts du cinéma* (2011), the original title for his *Intervals of Cinema* (2014), Costa's displacement, similar to Freud and Pasolini's free association method, can be summarised next to the double definition of the word *écart*: (1) displacement as the rupture of a movement in terms of an action's origin and destination; and (2) displacement as the temporal shift of one time taken for another. Referring to the film sequence described above, Rancière suggests that:

> Obviously [the Gulbenkian Foundation] is not in Ventura's neighbourhood. Nothing in the previous shot announced this visit, nothing in the film suggests Ventura has a particular taste for painting. This time the director seems to have departed from the paths of his characters. He has transported Ventura into the museum (. . .) The relationship between the paintings and the preceding still-life, between the dilapidated shack and the art gallery, but also perhaps between the love letter and the hanging of the paintings in the gallery thus compose a highly specific form of poetic displacement. (2014, 131)

This means that for Rancière, the film is similarly framed through moments of perceptual chaos, which is the type of intensive energy, a leap into the abyss, that I've been describing next to the idea of deframing.[8] As in modern abstract painting, where lines and colours tear the

---

[7] One could also think of Kurosawa's *Throne of Blood* here, where viewers also confront a world without clear objects at first, with images preceded by a kind of vapour, or fog, blurring the screen-world: 'It is the beginning of the world in the middle of a story, like dawn and dusk enclosed in [Kurosawa's] story' (Schefer 2016, 206).

[8] In his film review for *The Guardian*, '*Colossal Youth* is a colossal confusion', Samuel Wigley also describes the film as one 'not to be entered into lightly' and declares that 'I left [the cinema] certainly a little perplexed, not sure what to make of the film's peculiar energies, but with a head full

frame off to travel into thin air, *Colossal Youth* also introduces a form of disappearance that fades the frame out into the dark room of both the *cinémathèque* (where I watched the film) and the Gulbenkian Foundation (where Ventura was standing). Obviously, painting as much as cinema is an art form essentially bounded by the frame, but what its modern rearrangements achieve, echoing Deleuze, is that our visual navigation becomes spatially unlimited. This is what Grosz indicates when referring to contemporary painting as a mode of de-framing. For her, the history of art, and particularly that of painting, represents a project that 'distends and transforms frames', a movement that, also for Rancière, focuses on the *écart* in order to intensify it:

> In this sense the history of painting, and of art after painting, can be seen as the action of leaving the frame, of moving beyond and pressing against the frame, the frame exploding through the movement it can no longer contain. Art thus captures an element, a fragment, of chaos in the frame and creates or extracts from it not an image or representation, but a sensation or rather a compound or a multiplicity of sensations. (Grosz 2008, 18)

Lastly, it is also important to mention that Costa's gaseous intensity not only manifests here the discontinuities of a movement in space and time, but also the pure expressivity of an image which connects perception to things themselves. As read in *Cinema 1*, this is the sheer power of affection which Deleuze associates with Charles Sanders Peirce's qualisign, and which later on the philosopher transforms into the 'sign of composition' of his classical affection-image [*trait-icon*]. This image, which I have already discussed in my introduction, could well be read as an early case of the intensive-image, except for the fact that the deterritorialising powers of affection are cancelled under Deleuze's broader system of sensory-actions: 'Affection is what occupies the interval (. . .) without filling it in or filling it up. It surges in the centre of indetermination (. . .) in the subject, between perception and action' (2005, 67). For Peirce, however, this 'pure quality' of the sign – a qualisign – does not necessarily have an 'anticipatory role' transforming sensual impressions (affection) into perception-images and action-images, as Deleuze does (2005, 105). On the contrary, it stands for the pure expressive power of what Peirce calls 'Firstness', an image of *not-yet-identifiable forces* advancing intensity in itself.[9] It is a sign that, like the gaseous, is associated with the idea of 'freshness, life, and freedom' (Peirce

---

of indelible imagery, a lingering sense of sadness, though – mercifully – no rodents' (Wigley 2008).

[9] Secondness is where the sign-object emerges as an actual event in space; the image as a sinsign (1950, 79). And Thirdness is where the virtual operation of the observer takes place; the mental relation through which the viewer translates signs and interprets events – a legisign.

1950, 79) and which I link directly to my notion of a classical intensive-image as an enlarged, liberated form of Deleuze's affective instance.

For Laura U. Marks, who remains close to the unmediated powers of affection, qualisigns occupy a special place in her haptic reading of intercultural films:

> In our present Thirdness/symbol-saturated era, it seems urgent to look back for that source of renewal that is Firstness, to try to get past discourse to 'things themselves' [because] there are always elements of knowledge that cannot be mediated by Thirdness, that cannot be symbolized. (2000a, 200)

Such a philosophy of non-actualised tendencies,[10] which begins when the image does not yet have a clear meaning but a full openness towards its combinatorial potential, creates an interesting challenge for the study of the intensive-image in cinema. At the beginning of this chapter, I described intensity as a differential tendency explicating the sudden changes of Deleuze's two film periods, the classical movement-image and the modern time-image. I suggested that the passage from one solid unity (*Cinema 1*) to another more fluid trajectory (*Cinema 2*) was not marked by the separation between two different images, but by the same image, the intensive-image, which gathered force in films from the classical to the modern. Continuing with this hydrological cycle, the gaseous phase of Costa's cinema is now understood in terms of an 'intensification' of sensation that is radicalising the fragmented links of Deleuze's modernity. This is an image of Firstness, full of feeling rather than meaning, where images vary freely with one another without a privileged centre. Hence, the history of the intensive-image, and that of experimental and art-films more generally, can be read as this amplification of a fracture, or as the evolving de-visualisation of an image that becomes less and less dependent on solid ground. Here, in a very literal sense, art and the intensive-image

---

[10] This idea of a semiotic informing the unmediated powers of the image can also be read next to the old Aristotelian category of potentiality (*dynamis*) and its relation to actuality (*energeia*) through the workings of the Italian philosopher Giorgio Agamben. In his book *The Coming Community* (1993), Agamben articulates two different modes of potentials to think about philosophy and the *poietic* act. The first of the two kinds he discusses, which is the least significant side of the Greek *dynamis* (but equally the most important to think about Peirce's passage of signs) is what he sees as the Aristotelian *potential to be*, namely the possibility of a thing to pass into existence which further transforms qualities or forces (firstness) into legible signs (thirdness). To such desire for actualisation, on the other hand, Agamben opposes a second mode of enunciation in which the trajectory of the possible never really enters into the actual but remains suspended in the pure indeterminacy of the act, what he terms after Aristotle 'Impotence' (*adynamia*); 'the potentiality to not-be' (*dynamis me einai*) (1993, 35), defined as the most authentic and 'supreme theme of [Aristotelian] metaphysics' (1993, 36).

collide in the same ontological plane – that of 'the being of the sensible' in Deleuze and Guattari's sense.

Costa's filmmaking practice is one out of many contemporary examples performing such an audiovisual mode of sensation. Chantal Akerman (*No Home Movie*, 2015); Béla Tarr (*The Turin Horse*, 2011); Lucrecia Martel (*Zama*, 2017); Raúl Ruiz (*Mysteries of Lisbon*, 2010); Lisandro Alonso (*Jauja*, 2014); James Benning (*L. Cohen*, 2018); or Paz Encina (*Eami*, 2022) are some of the names that come to mind to suggest an 'ex-centric' (J. Harbord 2016) or a-centric form of cinema, one which confronts the frame as well as constructs the filmic time for reflection (whether by featuring an overabundant stimulation for the eye, or by producing 'inactive' images composed of very long duration). They all express, in different poetic ways, an 'aesthetic of sensation' (Marks 2000b) that privileges the tactile over the visual, and because of this, an intensity-image complex that suspends narrative action to favour eventlessness, a 'boring' form of cinema where the audience is 'suspended in nothingness'. This is, in similar terms, what Michel Ciment has called the 'cinema of slowness' in a conference paper delivered at the forty-sixth San Francisco International Film Festival, a film trend that has more recently been systematised as 'the most potent signifier of the Modern in post-war cinema (. . .) assuming [today] a diverse and changeable form' (Flanagan 2012, 4).

An aesthetics of slowness is here understood as audiovisual works composed of very long shots, and of very long duration, where the viewer is 'left empty' [*Leergelassenheit*] and 'held in a limbo' [*Hingehaltenheit*] by situations that are felt in the body rather than made accessible to understanding. Recent films such as *The Turin Horse* (Béla Tarr 2011), or *A Lullaby to the Sorrowful Mystery* (Lav Diaz 2016) lasting a little over eight hours, suffice to illustrate what an experience of dilated time or slowness may mean for the viewer. According to Chiara Quaranta, this is a sensuous style of filmmaking which, next to the broader category of art cinema, constitutes the most paradigmatic example of Heidegger's profound boredom:

> Because of its challenging of stylistically and narratively conventional cinematic worlds, art films at once subvert the immersive spectacle of [much] mainstream cinema and foster awareness of our often-distracted viewing. Boredom has the potential to stimulate a questioning of our attitude about images in two, seemingly paradoxical, manners thanks to its relationship with time: by killing time (. . .) and by making time conspicuous. (2020, 9–10)

In this capacity, contemporary slow films do constitute a paradigmatic example of what I call the gaseous intensive-image. By killing narrative time, and by favouring the sensuous over the discursive, slow cinema activates a process of de-visualisation that allows intensities to pass on- and off-screen. It is a mode of qualitative *durée*, or a relaxed form of temporality, which permits the contemporary intensive-image to be freed of all form, or to become-molecular. *Colossal Youth* was the case study I examined in this chapter, although there will be other recent films investigated throughout this book that dissipate narrative interaction in favour of more contemplative and sensory experiences. First, however, I will turn my attention to Buñuel's nomadic vision and his capacity to create a purely affective experience so as to indicate one of my last examples of an early intensive-image in cinema.

CHAPTER 2

Luis Buñuel's Nomadic Vision: Departures from an Originary World

Luis Buñuel, born in 1900 in Zaragoza, started his relationship with the cinema almost vis-à-vis the beginnings of the medium itself, at the time when the still and slow-motion representation of photography was being perfected, and perverted, by the animated flow of the celluloid strip. His close friend and collaborator, Jean-Claude Carrière, tells the anecdote that when Buñuel went to the movies for the first time in 1908, there was a man with a long stick translating the motion pictures on screen to him. The audience, not yet familiar with the automatic flow of the emergent technology, solicited an *explicador* [interpreter] to make sense of the strange operations of the visual language of film (Eco and Carrière 2009, 41). Today, more than 100 years after Buñuel's inaugural encounter with the cinema, one could only imagine the powerful effects such a mysterious assemblage of signs might have had for a kid like him. It is as if this primal encounter with the screen would drive, twenty years later with *Un chien andalou*, his first surrealist attempt to keep alive that original frenzy of film. Such a 'cinema of attractions', described by Tom Gunning as those early visual spectacles aiming to stimulate the curiosity of audiences, will arguably constitute the grounds for the filmmaker's uncanny associations of his later 'aesthetic of astonishment' (Gunning 1990, 56–62).

Buñuel's cinematic vision, which began in the dying moments of Gunning's 'spectacular period', at the time when he was still a boy in Zaragoza, traverses many of the technical and narrative developments of the medium in the decades to follow. From his directorial debut in 1929 (*Un chien andalou*) until his last production in 1977 (*That Obscure Object of Desire*), Buñuel went from the silent to the sound era, from black-and-white photography to the colour screen, and from the shoestring productions of his early period in France (his short film with Salvador Dalí was financed by his mother) to the more expensive budgets of his latest films. In the process, Buñuel experimented with the expressive possibilities of the medium, from its theatrical arrangements in the form of *mise en scène* (*The Phantom of Liberty*, 1974) to its more realist conventions in the documentary format (*Land Without Bread*, 1933), the ethno-fiction (*Los olvidados*, 1950), and the fiction film (*The Exterminating Angel*, 1962). He also experimented with various film lengths, from the short film (*Un chien andalou*, 1929) to the medium-length film (*Simon of the Desert*, 1965) and the long feature film (*Robinson Crusoe*, 1954); or innovated with hybrid genres, such as the surrealist comedy (*Illusion Travels by Streetcar*, 1954), the perverse family melodrama (*Viridiana*, 1961) and the psychological thriller (*This Strange Passion*, 1953). He also employed a wide selection of topics, ranging from anarchism (*L'âge d'or*, 1930) to Catholicism (*The Milky Way*, 1969) and probably his favourite, eroticism (*Belle de jour*, 1967). For as the Mexican poet Carlos Fuentes has put it, Buñuel should be read above all as 'the filmmaker of the multiple' (1973). I would further add, considering all these intellectual and aesthetic threads, that if Buñuel belongs to the plural, it is because his visions have never been encompassed by one singular artistic trajectory, or by one sole cultural tradition, but on the contrary by a nomadic and transcultural movement that, in Rosi Braidotti's words, shows 'the intense desire [of the nomadic subject] to go on trespassing and transgressing borders' (1994, 36). Buñuel's cultural legacy is clearly one embedded in the multiple: his cinema becomes an animated flow of images gathered from Francisco de Goya's paintings to the baroque literary systems of Octavio Paz; or from the Mexican and Spanish picaresque novella to the French *nouvelle vague*.

Arguably, for all his ability to create this migratory form of realism, that is, a psychological, sociopolitical, artistic, religious and philosophical realism – namely, a 'nomadism' – Buñuel has also been considered a director of significant theoretical importance. 'Great directors of the cinema', writes Deleuze in his preface to the English edition of *The Movement-Image*, should not only be compared with other artists (say, with writers, architects or musicians) but also, in producing images qua concepts, with great philosophical 'thinkers' (2005, xii). In the case of Buñuel, who allows the philosopher's aim to create an original taxonomy of film categories, there are two main images Deleuze extracts from his work; one 'impulsive', predominant in Buñuel's early naturalist period, and another 'oneiric', proper to the direct time-image of his final decade in France.

This chapter looks more closely at Deleuze's transition from Buñuel's naturalist coordinates of the classical movement-image to his modern time-image and interrogates the separation the philosopher makes between the two periods. I claim that if the interval – that negative space in-between images – is what inaugurates the non-representative intensities of Deleuze's modernity, then it is also through the 'insuppressible naturalistic possibilities' (Perez 1998, 262) of Buñuel's early films where such an interstice can be found. Echoing Perez, this is one of the reasons why naturalism (in nineteenth-century literature, for example) leads to the modernism of the new filmic medium as it was realised in the pioneering works by Buñuel:

> Where naturalism appears, modernism is not far behind. Ever since the Lumière brothers took their movie camera out into the streets, naturalism has kept coming back into the art of film (. . .) In France in the thirties, the surrealism of Buñuel and Vigo, the searching realism of Renoir, likewise brought together a vigorous naturalistic impulse and an equally vigorous impulse towards formal innovation and the challenge to convention. (1998, 262)

These modernist innovations are also what I investigate under the concept of the intensive-image, and its de/structuring techniques, by looking at the 'aftereffects' of Buñuel's naturalism. In the following chapters I will come back to this idea of 'the cinematic modern' not as a break with 'the pre-war classical' but as an ongoing succession of breaks that bridges the two periods and which leads, as in the case of Buñuel's films, towards an ever-intensifying displacing image. For now, as regards to Buñuel's 'movement-image schema', it is proposed that such an affective fissure in between action and perception is precisely what flows through a naturalist poetic tradition that, in thinking cinematically, Pasolini calls 'free-indirect-discourse' (2001, 43). According to the Italian filmmaker and writer, this is a heterogeneous system of relations, characterised by its expressive functions, which Buñuel inaugurates in cinema in *Un chien andalou*. In rethinking Deleuze's approach, I propose that the naturalist Buñuel, whom Deleuze sees as a classical movement-image filmmaker, becomes instead a nomadic artist of the heterogeneous – that is, a 'surrealist director of time' (Fotiade 2013, 156–71). First, however, it is necessary to understand what Deleuze means by this 'naturalism' embedded in the 'originary world' and 'impulse-images' of the early Buñuel.

Deleuze's Reading of Buñuel: An Idiosyncratic Surrealist

Deleuze's Buñuel makes his entrance in Chapter 8 of *Cinema 1*, 'From Affect to Action: The Impulse-Image' (2005, 127–37). This image, although described at length under the movement-image system, could well be the subject for Deleuze's later volume on *The Time-Image* (say, as a subcategory of the crystal-image, or as another liminal case of his Hitchcockian mental-image), except for the fact that in Deleuze's view, Buñuel's impulse-image is caught up in the four coordinates of his naturalism which cancels the opening of time and the differential effects of what I call the intensive-image. This naturalist impulse, described by Deleuze as an 'idiosyncratic surrealism' (2005, 128), is organised under four axes of two pairs: (1) the overflowing location that exhausts and yet explains the actual milieus of Buñuel's films (i.e. originary worlds/derived milieus pair) and; (2) the instinctual degradation of action that is extracted from Buñuel's *sur-real* whole and which explains his characters' *real* way of life (i.e. impulses/modes of behaviour pair). In Deleuze's view, this is what creates the closed tightening cycle of Buñuel's early films:

> The originary world only exists and operates in the depths of a real milieu, and is only valid through its immanence in this milieu, whose violence and cruelty it reveals (. . .) Actions or modes of behaviour, people and objects, have to occupy the derived milieu, and are developed there, while impulses and fragments people the originary world which carries the whole along it. (2005, 129)

This means that in the relics and symptoms of Buñuel's impulse-image, Deleuze finds an indirect time-image whose intensities and immanence, nonetheless, are still subordinated to the originary world where 'the whole of the film happens'. As Deleuze refers to Buñuel's classical cinema:

> [In the impulse-image], time finds its source in the originary world, which confers upon it the role of a destiny which cannot be expiated. Curled up in the originary world which is like the beginning and end of time, time unravels in derived milieux. This is almost a Neo-Platonism of time. And it is undoubtedly one of the naturalist cinema's greatest achievements to have come so close to a [direct] time-image. (2005, 131)

Put differently, this means that the reason why Deleuze's Buñuel reaches a 'direct time-image' only towards the end of his career is that he is able to emancipate his style from the elementary impulses and closed coordinates of his previous surrealism. So, to embrace time directly means for Deleuze's Buñuel an image existing outside, or being independent of, this higher – sur-realist – source. But isn't Buñuel's originary world, 'which is like the beginning and the end of time', the same immanent ground described elsewhere by Deleuze as the pure transcendental given of existence – also distinguished from real milieus to the extent that this 'given' is the pure 'pre-reflective impersonal consciousness [of experience]' (Deleuze 2007a, 338)? If that is the case, how then can Buñuel's immanence be delinked from his larger surrealist source? Isn't Buñuel's overflowing (originary) location a similar kind of 'transcendental given' that not only carries the whole and the impulses of his characters along it but also the very foundation of Deleuze's subjective experience qua empirical representation? If that is the case, then Buñuel's originary world runs vis-à-vis Deleuze's empirico-transcendental given, very much like the 'virtual wound' the surrealist poet Joe Bousquet describes as 'embodying before his birth', or Kafka's 'beautiful wound' that the writer refers to as 'being furnished with before coming into this world'[1] – two literary references that Deleuze engages with to explicate his empirico-transcendental principle:

> A wound is actualized in a state of things and in lived experience. A wound itself, however, is a pure virtual on the plane of immanence which leads us to a life. My wound existed before me . . . (Deleuze 2007a, 393)

Perhaps, the problem for Deleuze's Buñuel is that up to the early 1960s, the filmmaker's pre-existing (originary) wound is conceived of as a constant by-product of his universal/ascendant spirit, hence determined by higher, sur-real actualities rather than by actual behaviours in real milieus. Therefore, the cinema Buñuel develops from *Belle de jour* onwards is, according to the philosopher, one that effectively transforms this immanent ground qua virtuality into a transcendental field which functions as life itself. Referring to the direct time-image of Buñuel's latest period, Deleuze states that the filmmaker has now been able to depart from his naturalist and cyclical point of view:

> In *Belle de jour*, the husband's final paralysis does and does not take place (. . .); *The Discreet Charm of the Bourgeoisie* shows less a cycle of interrupted meals than different versions of the same meal in irreducible modes and worlds. In *The Phantom of Liberty*, the postcards are truly pornographic, even though they represent only monuments stripped of all ambiguity (. . .) And in *That Obscure Object of Desire* there blossoms one of Buñuel's finest inventions: instead of having one character play different roles, casting two characters, and two actresses, as one person (. . .) *Buñuel achieves here a direct time-image which was previously impossible for him because of his naturalist and cyclical point of view*. (2013, 108; my emphasis)

Thus, the grand cosmos existing 'outside of reality' is now – in Deleuze's modernity – part and parcel of Buñuel's immanent ground. This means that for the philosopher there is no longer a coexistence, or well-determined relation, between large cause and the impulsive behaviour pair. Since Buñuel's originary world does not prevail any longer over his characters who occupy it, the correlation becomes inherent to the film's empirical source.

---

[1] 'I came into this world with a beautiful wound; that is all I was furnished with' (Kafka quoted in Sloterdijk 2011, 218).

Deleuze's description, which reads Buñuel's cinema as an image that opens itself up by differentiating in historical time, thus resembles the process of image-intensification that I have accounted for in the previous chapters. However, this 'image-tendency' (Deleuze 1956/2004a, 22–31) which moves from Buñuel's early 'solidity' in the impulse-image to the more 'liquid' trajectories of his later dream-image, interrogates, precisely, the periodical separation Deleuze makes between the classical and the modern artist. The concept of the intensive-image, which the philosopher does not discuss in this section on affect and naturalism, and which I claim is of significant importance in reading Buñuel's evolving poetic vision, does bridge Deleuze's divide between the movement-image and the time-image periods. Intensity confronts here the fixity of rational subjects who refuse to seek the unstable or the unresolved in thinking by conveying images in which mad lovers and stray characters, as in Buñuel's early films, will feel most at home. Buñuel's intensive-image, which is understood as one of the earliest exponents of a cinema of immanence, and whose characters are understood not as beyond or above this world but existing within it, represents here a nomadism that transforms Deleuze's narrative fixity of the early period into looser – foamier – structures. In Grosz's view: 'The intensities that constitute the plane of immanence are ever changing, capable of alliance with other terms, undergoing endless mutations; [they] populate this plane "nomadically", that is, without a given location' (2017, 138).

Although clearly formulated, Deleuze's division between classicism and modernism, or between transcendental and immanent planes, becomes problematic, or at best ambiguous, as soon as one looks more deeply into the kind of natural taxonomy he had in mind for the cinema: 'My own view is that cinema is a composition of images and signs, an intelligible preverbal material' (2007b, 274). How then should we read Buñuel's two periods? Is such a rupture internal to his artistic process of creation? Or is it rather history, as an external event, which separates not only Buñuel but all of Deleuze's images into pre-and post-war systems? If considered historically, then the break entails a larger separation – that of the classical-old being opposed to the modern-new, hence an art that 'only reveals its essence after a detour in its evolution' (Deleuze 2013, 43). I suggest, however, that Deleuze's rupture is deeply problematic, for it creates a division between the classical qua expression of a non-art form[2] (e.g. in the mimetic functioning of his dogmatic image of thought) and the modern qua the 'soul of [his time-image] cinema' (e.g. in the artist-filmmaker who

---

[2] As long as we understand art, in words of Deleuze, as an immanent plane that confronts the new and the unknown.

searches for the unknown and thus confronts the unresolved in thinking by creating the new). However noticeable this separation might be when reading Deleuze's two cinema volumes, I don't believe such is the scope of his film-philosophical system. Mainly because his taxonomy of films is fully dedicated to those 'great *auteurs* of the cinema' (2005, xix), thus the modern-new should not be opposed to the classical-old, but 'to the new of the preceding sequence' (Badiou 2013, 84), which is the type of intensive violence that, as I will discuss shortly, Buñuel inaugurates with his early avant-garde films. (Avant-garde means, precisely, to put something upfront, a new image in the fore.) Deleuze warns us from the beginning about this commonly made error – an error that he himself initiates in many regards – which separates the art of the cinema from its history. In the preface to *The Movement-Image*, he writes:

> It would be pointless to claim that the modern cinema of the time-image is 'better' than the classical cinema of the movement-image. Here I deal exclusively with cinematic masterpieces which do not allow any such [artistic] hierarchy of evaluation. (2007b, 275)[3]

Following this premise, I propose the notion of the intensive-image to read Deleuze's cinema(s) as one indivisible art of the heterogeneous – an *ars combinatoria* that mixes discontinuous images together by way of poetic displacements and its sensation. While looking at Buñuel's nomadism, this means that the classification of films proposed by Deleuze will no longer reject the commonality of images to think together in their different epochs but, as Buñuel's case will demonstrate, to expresses their mutual capacity to do so. However, in order to make this claim clear – one certainly left in ambiguity and incompletion by the philosopher – I need to trace the interruptions of an early intensive-image, or what Deleuze's calls 'a pure time-image of thought', working within the naturalism of Buñuel's sensory-motor-apparatus. In Deleuze's words:

> ...we must look in pre-war cinema, and even in silent cinema, for the workings of a very pure time-image which has always been breaking through, holding back or encompassing the movement-image. (2013, xii)[4]

---

[3] Similar remarks are made at the end of *Cinema 2*, in the concluding chapter for *The Time-Image*, when Deleuze declares that there are many possible ways to combine the movement-image with the time-image: 'It cannot be said that one is more important to the other, whether more beautiful or more profound. All that can be said is that the movement-image does not give us a time-image. Nevertheless, it does give us many things in connection with it' (2013, 278).

[4] In 'Cinema-I, Premiere', Deleuze similarly states that: 'In cinema, people are not yet in the habit of disconnecting the classical (what has been done and is the object of overly confident university

The Intensive-Image: A Descendant from Aby Warburg's *Mnemosyne Atlas*

Those filmmakers called 'classical' were people to whom everything was new. From the perspective of this book's analysis on the intensive-image and its deterritorialising tendency, the naturalism embedded in Deleuze's Buñuel must necessarily escape its fixed cyclicality in order to enter into more genealogical dialogues with his later modern system – this is the reason why I juxtapose Deleuze's two regimes of art into one intensive sequence of the heterogeneous. This coexistence, in my view, bears direct resemblance to Aby Warburg's *Mnemosyne Atlas*, an immense repertoire of archaeological items and avant-garde objects left unfinished by the art historian in 1929, described in terms of a singular tableau of visual gestures taken from both classical-antique and modern-renaissance periods, and which arises not from the opposition between these two epochs, but from their common 'rifts, denotations, and deflagrations' (Michaud 2007, 253). It is, in the words of Philippe-Alain Michaud, a technique of 'cinematic arrangement' (2007, 240) that Warburg constructed 'not to find constants in the order of [the] heterogeneous but to introduce difference within the identical' (2007, 253). In this capacity, and in closer proximity to my reading of Buñuel's nomad vision, the 'iconology of the interval' that Warburg proposes with his atlas is similarly derived from an image of difference, or a singular sequence of interconnected images, proper to my notion of intensity. In the words of Georges Didi-Huberman, the German art historian employs:

> The same relations [of] 'nomad science' [than those employed by Deleuze and Guattari] in *Mille plateaux*. It is a knowledge that is 'problematic' and not 'axiomatic', founded on a model of 'becoming and heterogeneity, as opposed to the stable, the eternal, the identical, [and] the constant'. Where Panofsky again proposed a science of the *compars* in search of the 'invariable form of variables', Warburg had already proposed that science of the dispars which Deleuze and Guattari envisaged dynamically: 'it is not exactly a question of extracting constants from variables, but of placing the variables themselves in a state of continuous variation'. (2011/2018, 56–7)

Here, one could easily visualise Deleuze's film history, and Buñuel's cinematic career more particularly, as one shifting repertoire of intensive-images interconnected through their common intervallic gestures.

critics) from the modern (what is being done now and is judged haughtily). This disassociation between an art and its history is always ruinous. If it happens to cinema, it will be ruined as well' (2007, 3).

It is an atlas expressing a large series of visuals becoming confused with their own past, rearranged in the present moment and thus intensified, as in the case of Buñuel, by their continuous metamorphosis – a nomadism.

As a way of example, and in the wake of Warburg's method, one could suggest that the sadistic man with the razor at the beginning of *Un chien andalou* (played by Buñuel himself) bears direct resemblance to David (Colin Farrell) in *The Lobster*, the male protagonist who in the dying moments of the film is about to cut his eyes with a knife. There is also a deadly self-propelled coffin in Buñuel's *Simon of the Desert* (1965), originally appearing in *Nosferatu* (Murnau 1922), and which then reappears in Lucrecia Martel's *Zama* (2017) in the form of an uncanny moving box with a kid, or a ghost, in it. Or take, as one last (out of many other possible) example(s), that intriguing pictorial appearance of Vermeer's *The Lacemaker* which Buñuel references at various intervals of his career, most noticeably, as Fotiade remarks, 'in his first and last film' (2013, 156). (Interestingly enough, this first appearance of Vermeer's *The Lacemaker* in *Un chien andalou*, which is internal to the temporal progression of the story, when the female protagonist looks at this picture in a magazine after the black screen announces a gap of eight years, turns into an interval of approximately forty-eight years when taking Buñuel's career as a whole, from beginning to end, because it is in his last film, *That Obscure Object of Desire*,[5] that we also see Vermeer's *The Lacemaker* reappearing in the flesh behind the shop window somewhere in Spain.)

Such a speculative atlas consisting entirely of fragments of films could well be reorganised in a different manner every time we bring heterogeneous elements together under a common order of themes. This is what Warburg did not only with his *Mnemosyne Atlas* – by juxtaposing art figures from antiquity (the Apollonian) with those of renaissance art (the Dionysian) – but also with the books of his library that he repeatedly rearranged in a system he called 'the law of the good neighbour' (de la Durantaye 2009, xviii) – namely, a principle by which each book answers, or poses a specific question, to the book next to it. Similarly, I'm also posing questions about Buñuel's classical and modern cinemas as coming together under a common intensive-image and which intensifies throughout his filmmaking career. According to Fuentes, this bridging image that offers new ways of thinking about the past (instead of breaking with it) has to do with vision itself:

---

[5] *That Obscure Object of Desire* was realised in France at the same year of Claude Goretta's *The Lacemaker* (1977), the latter being awarded the Prize of the Jury at Cannes Film Festival.

> A really important director makes only one film; his [or her] work is a sum, a totality of perfectly related parts that illuminate each other. In Buñuel's films, from *Un chien andalou* (1929) to [*That Obscure Object of Desire*],[6] the essential unifying factor is sight. (1973)

Fuentes's Buñuel, a filmmaker who approaches cinema from the perspective of a surreal site of loss – that is, as an experience of time threatened by formlessness—thus helps me to identify Deleuze's two periods under one intensive tendency which provokes, in each of its ages, visual inclinations towards the unknown and the problematic: 'I could write a thousand essays on Buñuel and yet', Fuentes says, 'there is still room for a thousand more' (1973). This is, more clearly, an atlas of interconnected gestures that synthesises Buñuel's naturalism and modernism into one displacing image that cannot be classified according to strict rules. Hence, and next to what Deleuze sees as 'a pure time-image of thought that has always been breaking through [in cinema]', I aim to integrate Warburg's displacing method into the supposedly cyclical, naturalist films of Buñuel. In what follows, I will discuss Buñuel's creation of a modern time-image in *Los olvidados* to then analyse the formation of early intensities in Buñuel and Dali's debut film *Un chien andalou*.

Los olvidados, or *The Forgotten Ones* of Deleuze's Neorealist Act

Let's begin with Buñuel's *Los olvidados* (also known as *The Forgotten Ones*). This is a film subordinated to the general sensory-motor cohesiveness of Deleuze's *Cinema 1*, perhaps with the only exception of the dream sequence of the virgin mother and the chunk of meat that the philosopher describes in *The Time-Image* as 'the limit of the largest circuit' (2013, 60–1). In Deleuze's view, this is almost a time-image sequence except that it only brings about a limited virtual mobility:

> Characters do not move, but, as in an animated film, the camera causes the movement of the path on which they change places, 'motionless at a great pace'. This is a virtual movement, but it becomes actual at the price of an expansion of the totality of space and of a stretching of time. It is therefore the limit of the largest circuit. Of course, these phenomena already appear in Buñuel's *Los olvidados*; in the dream of the Virgin with the chunk of meat, the child is slowly sucked towards the meat rather than thrusting himself forward. (2013, 60–1)

---

[6] *The Discreet Charm of the Bourgeoisie* appears in the original. The text was written in 1973, prior to Buñuel's last film, *That Obscure Object of Desire*.

Los olvidados, which is a film without 'stars', devoid of a celestial protagonist, a film about a delinquent pack of teens wandering around the unbearable spaces of their Mexican slum, is read more generally by the philosopher as a cinematic attempt to expand the actuality of its spaces into a virtual movement that, nonetheless, it never fully reaches. Not at least in the way Rossellini's *Germany, Year Zero* does, which is one of Deleuze's paradigmatic examples of the new cinema as discussed in the previous chapter. (This is a neorealist work that calls upon the 'inaction' of its protagonist, the boy Edmund, who effectively witnesses the intolerable situations of a post-war Berlin destroyed by the war.) In the case of *Los olvidados*, however, the unbearable and marginal reality of Buñuel's slum-children are not taken by Deleuze as symptomatic of the modern time-image but rather subordinated to the general sensory-motor-cohesion of the classical movement-image film.

In an attempt to deconstruct Deleuze's formula by calling into question the 'eurocentrism' of his modern politics of the image, as David Martin-Jones (2011, 1–22) and Susana Viegas (2016, 239) effectively do, I suggest that Buñuel's characters in *Los olvidados* – most of them non-professional actors, as in Deleuze's 'new race of characters' – do not 'react' to the fissures of the European post-war period. Instead, they already belong to a territory that manifests the 'originary' conditions of marginality upon which these children have always had 'to act' (e.g. stealing and lying) and 'react' (e.g. they must hide or they die). This amounts to saying that since the Second World War's crisis never happened in Mexico, Deleuze's 'intolerable [European] situations' are nonetheless part and parcel of an ongoing reality that is integral to Latin America's (and Buñuel's) street-kids. Put differently: if Deleuze's broken link between '[the European] man and the world' (2013, 178) is what reveals the exhaustion of time and the emergence of a new image of thought, then a film like *Los olvidados*, with all its uncertainty and peripheral reality, is equally exposing the 'seers' and 'mutant characters' of Deleuze's modernity.

As a hybrid work of ethno-fiction, and with almost no use of background music, *Los olvidados* portrays a rich Bazinian aesthetic that rejects those representational guidelines and moral foundations of Deleuze's classical cinema in order to reveal a different space-time that has similarly 'shattered from within'. Here, it is next to the general sense of disjointedness produced by Buñuel's *Los olvidados* that I take his characters as forgotten representatives of Deleuze's time-image 'drifters': Don Carmelo (Miguel Inclán) for example, like Deleuze's modern 'seers', is a street-singer and a blind beggar who can nonetheless see things all the more clearly (in fact, he sees rather than acts); El Jaibo (Roberto Cobo) and his orphaned pack of followers hide in abandoned warehouses just as in Deleuze's children of the post-war age; or little Pedro (Alfonso Mejía), that wandering boy without a father and whose mother has put him in reform school due to criminal behaviour, can equally be placed next to Antoine (Jean-Pierre Léaud) in *The 400 Blows* (Truffaut, 1959), another homeless boy sent to reform school and who, like Pedro, has been treated with cruelty and indifference throughout the film (I will briefly discuss Truffaut's film in my next chapter, when examining the case of Victor of Aveyron as another of his *enfants terribles*).

All of these stray characters represent an image of difference and of the different that produces an intense viewing experience. *Los olvidados* depicts a confronting, immanent reality that dislocates the true, the beauty and the good not from a *sur-real*, other-worldly-realm, but from an empirical situation which, according to the philosopher in describing his direct time-image, is beyond characters and viewers: 'too awful, or too beautiful, or insoluble' (1995b, 59). However, unlike Deleuze who announces this fracture in the wake of Italian neorealism, Buñuel confronts the viewer in virtue of an indeterminate and violent image that not only operates outside of the European New Wave tradition, but also one which encompasses the previous sequence of the movement-image with sheer intensities. However, to properly introduce this correspondence between Deleuze's modern (neorealist) act and his classical (dogmatic) image of thought, or between Buñuel's dream-image and his impulse-image, it is necessary to look into an earlier film made by the filmmaker and to trace the presence of a displacing intensive-image operating within Deleuze's classical system. This bridging image – an 'iconology of the interval' in Warburg's sense – will be described in what follows under Buñuel and Dalí's short-film *Un chien andalou*.

Buñuel's (Slit) Eye: The Mirror to Deleuze's 'Soul of the Cinema'

Un chien andalou begins with a cinematic gesture embedded in a long literary tradition: the text on-screen reads 'once upon a time', and this overture is followed by an image of a young man holding a razor in his hand. The next – and most famous – film sequence, that in which a moon sliced by the clouds is intertwined with the extreme close-up of a woman's eye cut in half, interrupts the previous textual cohesion by placing an image of violence that not only anticipates the sadistic love story to come, but also one that attacks our own spectatorial eye by inflicting a destructuring cut in/sight. Like Georges Bataille's *Histoire de l'oeil* (1928), published a year before *Un chien andalou*, Buñuel and Dalí's eye story functions on at least two similar levels, both interconnected by the same seductive yet horrific transgression. On the one hand, it stands as the metaphor accounting for the bloody sexual play of lovers, visually schematised in several vignette-shots just as in Bataille's novel. (In addition, this violence introduced by the slit eye in *Un chien andalou* can equally be said to reverse the stereotypical story of the 'romantic Hollywood couple', which is this sort of image-cliché that the film begins with, where a young man in the balcony dreams about his lover while contemplating a full moon with a cigar in his mouth.) On the other hand, Buñuel's slit eye can similarly be said to be 'that obscure object of desire' organising visuality not just in this film, but as Fuentes states, on a more structural ocular level, too, one connecting the whole of Buñuel's filmography, sight as the 'essential unifying factor' of his entire filmmaking career. So, in the same way Roland Barthes describes *Histoire de l'oeil* not as the story of its characters, but as the story of an eye shifting from one subject to another (1972, 239–47) we could also infer that in Buñuel's film(s) 'sight determines content' as much as 'content is sight at all possible levels' (Fuentes 1973). This implies, next to the intensive-image continuum that I am investigating in relation to Buñuel's cinema, that the sliced eye in *Un chien andalou* not only anticipates the misogynistic[7] and disturbing love story to unfold later in the film but more allusively stands for the de/structuring technique of a 'nomadic' filmmaker who constantly performs 'an acute awareness of the nonfixity of boundaries' (Braidotti 1994, 36).

These aggressive associations at the beginning of *Un chien andalou* portray a systemic critique of Deleuze's rigidity of the movement-image system. It interrupts the closed fixity of his naturalist schema by introducing an event that disarticulates the gaze of characters as much as the look of viewers. As one of the forerunners of the cinematic avant-garde, *Un chien andalou* has been praised – and for good reason – as a key example of 'classical cinematic poetry' (Williams 1981, 54; Creed 2007, 115–33; Perez 1998, 159; Farber 2009, 662–7). Even for Bataille, who locates the sheer expressiveness of the film in its opening sequence that exceeds those 'logical connections of visuality', describes Buñuel's slit eye as a horrific object 'that we [viewers] will never bite' (1985, 17). Patrick ffrench, who also comments on such a transgressive gesture shared by Bataille

---

[7] Buñuel's misogynistic and violent act at the beginning of *Un chien andalou* (1929) has been widely debated by feminist film scholars. See, for example, the work by Dominique Russell, 'Blinding Women: Buñuel, Feminism and the Representation of Rape' (2003), in *Buñuel: El Imaginario Transcultural* and Linda Williams, *Figures of Desire: A Theory and Analysis of Surrealist Film* (1981).

and Buñuel's eye-stories, equally suggests that in both cases the play of ocular associations is arranged under the de/forming poetry of horror: 'Transgression ruins the dialectic of desire and recognition with the eye at its centre, as its pole, and inaugurates a different kind of structural movement, one of displacement and dislocation' (1999, 2). These poetic transgressions are, in other words, parables for the intensive-image in cinema: they all point to a site of destruction and loss where the physicality of space and the measurability of time are irremediable threatened by an experience of formlessness. Buñuel's dream-images come to us abruptly, one after the other, without them being rationally connected or cyclically determined in originary milieus. It is an oneiric, preverbal site where reason is loss and poetry elevated.

There is a similar idea in the work of Jean Louis Schefer, whose influence on Deleuze is crucial for his conceptualisation of the time-image, especially in the latter's chapter on 'Thought and Cinema' (2013, 161–93) where the poetic quality of early film manifests the same affective space that erases all of our rational dispositions towards meaning. Schefer describes the intensity of early film as a 'lived cinematographic space' where the 'psychic structure' of the viewer is never quite complete: 'he [or she] is porous to something fundamentally linked to time, which is to say anxiety' (2016, 56). Here, the images Schefer discusses in *The Ordinary Man of Cinema* are read, next to the burlesque and horror film traditions, in terms of 'disproportionate [and] mutant gestures' which, as in Buñuel's naturalism,[8] are 'lived affectively' by the viewer. In Schefer's words, this is a virtual movement 'whose centre of gravity I have ceased to be' (2016, 116).

Schefer's affective reading of classical cinema – a reading which ironically moves beyond that traditional system of representation outlined by Deleuze and Bazin – is further commented on by Deleuze to reflect upon his modern mode of film-thinking. Schefer, however, defines the modernity of this time-image as one that has already ceased to be sensory-motor in the pre-war period, where audiences were already accustomed to the intensities and disturbances of meaning. In Deleuze's words:

> According to Schefer, it is the suspension of the world, rather than movement, which gives the visible to thought, not as its object, but as an act which is constantly arising and being revealed in thought: 'not that it is here a matter of thought become visible, the visible is affected and irremediably affected by the initial incoherence of thought, this inchoate quality'. This is the description of *the ordinary man in cinema*:

---

[8] Buñuel's naturalism can be observed in films such as *Un chien andalou* (1929), *L'âge d'or* (1930), *Las Hurdes* (1933), and *Los olvidados* (1950).

the spiritual automaton, 'mechanical man', 'experimental dummy', Cartesian diver in us, unknown body which we have at the back of our heads [and] whose age is neither ours nor that of our childhood, *but a little time in the pure state*. (2013, 174; my emphasis)

And this is exactly the sort of intensity that Schefer shows to be erratic, governed by the unconscious, composed by multiple heterogeneous signs already at play in classical films. This is a poetic, avant-garde tradition whose origin many scholars have located in the expressive capabilities of Buñuel's inaugural film. Hence, whether we look at *Un chien andalou* via Bataille's 'cannibal delicacy' (1985, 17), ffrench's 'non-closed (. . .) play of deformation' (1999, 8), or Schefer's early film viewer who thinks affectively where he or she is not, the poetic character of Buñuel's eye-story is what transgresses, in all its free-associative spirit, the logics of storytelling itself.

In reference to Buñuel's 'poetic consciousness', as his peer Andrei Tarkovsky puts it (1989, 51), I argue that the intensive-image generated by *Un chien andalou* is more precisely the type of enlarged affective instance Deleuze thinks the film does not fully possess. By suggesting that *Un chien andalou* is caught up in the four coordinates of Buñuel's naturalist schema, the movement of the image is described as cyclical, thus the dream remaining closed in its perpetual originary loop:

[Buñuel's naturalist dream-image] is subject to the condition of attributing the dream to a dreamer, and the awareness of the dream (the real) to the viewer (. . .) [In *Un chien andalou*] a tuft of hair becomes a sea-urchin, which is transformed into a circular head of hair, to give way to a circle of onlookers (. . .) Buñuel's film maintains the dominant circular shape in the consistently concrete objects that he has following one another through definite cuts. [His early] dream-image obeys the same law: a large circuit where each image actualizes the preceding one and is actualized in the subsequent one, to return in the end to the situation which set it off. (Deleuze 2013, 59–60)

In addition to the previous comments on Buñuel's de/structuring associations, Pier Paolo Pasolini, from whom Deleuze takes his notion of 'free-indirect-discourse', refers to the poetics of *Un chien andalou*, and that of naturalist writers more generally, as one heterogeneous system of relations which breaks with the circular logics of Deleuze's system. By looking at the naturalist tradition in literature, where nineteenth-century writers began to adopt the language of their characters to step out from their own private perspectives, Pasolini suggests that the language of poetry arises whenever an author embraces, and fully participates with, the voices coming from the environment. Similarly, in cinema, free-indirect-discourse appears as soon as the filmmaker immerses into 'the mind of his [or her] characters' and adopts, as in Pasolini's neorealist works, 'not only his [or her] psychology but also his [or her] language' (2001, 44). In referring to *Un chien andalou* as the 'borderline case in which the poetic quality of [film] language is foregrounded beyond all reason' (2001, 43), Pasolini traces one of the first cinematic attempts to subvert the schematism of prose narrative by means of an elliptical, intensive-image. As he writes in 'The Cinema of Poetry':

> Buñuel's *Un chien andalou* is avowedly produced according to the canons of pure expressivity. But, for this reason, it must be labelled surrealistic. And it must be said that, as a surrealist product, it is outstanding. Very few other works can compete with it, be they literary or pictorial, because their poetic quality is corrupted and rendered unreal by their content (. . .) On the other hand, the purity of [Buñuel's] images is exalted rather than obfuscated by its surrealist content – because it is the real oneiric nature of dreams and of the unconscious memory which surrealism reactivates in film. (2001, 43)

The fact that *Un chien andalou* confronts us with images displacing the logical arrangement between sequences, that is sequences being dissolved by the functionality of at least three minds in this film, indicates the poetic excess and heterogenous image proper to Pasolini's Buñuel. This is, in the same naturalist fashion, the intensive-image complex that I am employing to undo Deleuze's movement-image cyclicality of *Un chien andalou*, dominated by the 'circular shapes' and 'definite cuts' of the dream(s). Here, in opposition to Deleuze's solid classification, I suggest that Buñuel's film, which is composed of many dreams at once, expresses the distortions and aberrant gestures of a migratory eye whose trajectories dissolve the shape of the dream, thus leading to a cinematic plane of loss where neither characters nor viewers know where they are anymore. This is, rather, an oneiric universe that follows the free-associative laws of our own dream world, dissolving rationality by its troubling, wakening thoughts.

Take, in this direction, Deleuze's sequence of fixed, circular associations cited above. When it unfolds, we first glimpse a colony of ants coming out from a black hole in the male lover's hand. This leads the philosopher to enunciate the following encircling knots: a tuft of hair in the woman's underarm turns into a sea-urchin, then into an iris shot which subsequently turns into a circle of onlookers in the street (2013, 58). What Deleuze does not account for in this passage is the previous shot annunciating, or rather 'originating', the spherical connections. This is the sequence in which the female character visualises the clothes of her lover (who has just fallen from his bike in the street) and which, quite uncannily, are arranging themselves on top of her bed (e.g. the tie knots itself up). The woman, whose drowsy face is now framed in close-up, turns around in the room and sees her lover standing with one of his hands pointing directly to his eyes (which subsequently leads to the shot opening with the colony of ants just described). The whole sequence then, which is commanded by one of the eyes of the story, stands more specifically for the dream-image of the female protagonist. At other intervals, it is the man who drives the story through his violent (and not necessarily circular) play of visual deformations (e.g. uncovering his lover's breasts to convert them into buttocks; turning books into guns; killing his doppelgänger, etc.). But it is most clearly at the beginning of the film, when the young Buñuel slits the woman's eye with a razor, where the initial dream opens up to a constellation of other dreamers to come. It is as if characters and viewers were all prisoners of Buñuel's sightless game set out from the outset, yet never fixing their vision in a pre-given, transcendental set – which is probably why the film begins in the interior of a closed room and ends at the shores of an open sea. Following this logic, *Un chien andalou* is not governed by the rules of one omnipotent player, or anchored to the subjective pole of one singular character, mainly because there are at least three sets of eyes in this film; that of Buñuel's camera and those of the two lovers. Not even 'God', aka the film director – that 'transcendental' source of all creation – can ensure the results of this game which is rather affirmed by the dice of chance. It is, echoing Borges's famous game of chess, a dream that goes ad infinitum: 'God moves the player, and [s]he moves the piece. Which god behind God originates the scheme of dust and time and dream and agonies?' (1960/1974, 59). Put differently, this migratory nomadism is the expression of an early intensive-image, composed by the shifting eyes of the film's characters, which deterritorialises Deleuze's 'closed circle of onlookers' and, more broadly, his reading of the classical Buñuel. *Un chien andalou* becomes, in this sense, a rhizome-film – a mass of dreamers who bring into play the heterogeneous elements of Pasolini's naturalist poetry.

Buñuel's intensive-image, like Pasolini's free-indirect discourse, is thus taken to inhabit many dreams at once (rather than set off by one 'real' dreamer subsequently actualising other dreamers to come). The filmmaker gets himself into the mind of his characters to see through their own somnolent eyes, somehow combining the *flection* of their bodies with the *reflection* of their minds. Such juncture connecting body and mind, feeling and thinking, is also the synthesis Sarah Cooper arrives at in her article 'Surreal Souls: Un chien andalou and Early French Film Theory' (2013). In looking at the German word for soul [*die Seele*; translated into English from Freud's work as 'intellect' or 'mind'] as well as the French word *espirit*, theorised by early French film critics as 'mental spiritual reality' (2013, 144), Cooper suggests that the collage forms of *Un chien andalou* give Buñuel's 'soul' the status of a mind that is materially manifested in the body – that is, a 'mind embodied' (Varela, Rosch and Thompson, 1991). Here, for Cooper, Buñuel's *espirit* freely portrays oneiric and manifold spaces in which the intellectual activity of his characters (as well as our own cognitive processing) merges with the sensual activity of the body. In her words:

> While the soul attaches itself to thinking, to mind, and by implication spirit, it is also grounded, materially, in the body within [Buñuel's] work and is incarnated on the surface of this film. (2013, 153)

Referencing the same passage commented on by Deleuze, Cooper suggests that the film's decentring of subjectivity – a displacement generated by the intensities of the image – also reveals a free-associative visuality in which neither characters nor viewers can identify with straightforwardly:

> The chain of images [in *Un chien andalou*] does not follow in a linear manner [or, echoing Deleuze, 'in a circular manner']. The chain of dissolves that moves from ants in the hand through armpit hair to sea urchin gesture in so many different associative directions based on vision to start with, but expanding outwards also takes us beyond the development of thinking attached to one thinker. The implication is that both man and woman are seeing this in their mind's eye (. . .) This decentring of subjectivity (. . .) challenges the possibilities of viewing straightforwardly by identification. (2013, 150)

This means that if Buñuel's aberrant bodies activate Cooper's surreal souls, then there is no reason to suggest that *Un chien andalou* should be placed alongside the gravitational centres and rational cuts of the classical movement-image. Liberated from the thinking of one (sovereign) dreamer, or detached from the coordinates of one (originary) source, the poetic language of Buñuel's film expresses the capacity of the visual medium to inhabit many worlds at once. And this is, as I have argued, the intensity-complex proper to Buñuel's naturalist lineage; not the designation of specific cases of solution, but the presentation of migratory eyes that experiment with, and emancipate from, Deleuze's mimetic structure of representation.

A nomadic filmmaker of the spirit then. That is how Buñuel's heterogenous, free-associative spirit is incarnated in his early body of work, in all of those bodies out of joint. This amounts to saying, in conclusion, that if Deleuze's 'cinematic soul' is what puts 'thought into contact with [the] unthought, the unsummonable, the inexplicable, the undecidable,

[and] the incommensurable' (2013, 220), then there is a similar *espirit* in Buñuel's early films that cannot be resolved in thinking – to the extent that his images portray an indecipherable set of dream-relations. Intensity is the concept I propose to use in thinking about this extra-propositional character, and poetic excess, of Buñuel's naturalist vision – a nomadic filmmaker of the multiple who departs from the fixity of Deleuze's originary source. And this sense of *originality*, as the next chapter will investigate, is also linked to another *origin* under the possibility left by a language of beginnings in the figure of the cinematic child.

CHAPTER 3

Human Infancy and the Language of Beginnings: *The Wild Child* and *The Enigma of Kaspar Hauser*

In September 1799, at the end of the French Revolution, a feral child of around twelve years of age was found naked in a southern forest of France. The boy, who had lived in the woods since the age of four or five, was believed to have been abandoned by his parents due to an irremediable malady of the brain. Unable to articulate a word or walk on two legs, the Savage of Aveyron, as he was known back then, was examined by medical experts and diagnosed as mute and suffering from mental idiocy. Doctor Philippe Pinel, the forerunner of French psychiatry and member of the *Société des observateurs de l'homme*, speculated that once examined in Paris, the boy's illness was innate and incurable (the reason why, he presumed, the boy was abandoned in the forest, exiled from society), so that any attempts at rehabilitation were doomed to failure. Younger members of the group, however, sceptical of Pinel's medical hypothesis, suggested instead that a child removed from all human contact since an early stage of life would shed new light on the workings of the human brain and provide relevant insights in unlocking an old metaphysical dilemma: 'to determine what would be the degree of intelligence and the nature of the ideas of an adolescent, who, deprived from his childhood of all education, had lived entirely separated from individuals of his own species' (Itard 1801/1932, 7). Doctor Jean Marc Itard, the appointed physician at the *Institute National des Jeunes Sourds*, the public hospital in Paris where the boy resided, believed that the answer to this question, to a great degree, consisted in showing the capacity of the boy to understand rational ideas. A minister of state, hoping to secure an important scientific discovery for the burgeoning French Republic, decided to entrust the child to the young doctor Itard. First examined at the hospital, and later on at the doctor's private house in the outskirts of Paris, the boy was given the name of Victor by Itard and his housekeeper Madame Guérin, in response to his ability to pronounce the letter 'o'.

A few years later, on the east side of the Rhine River in Germany, another strange boy of around seventeen years of age was found in the town of

Nuremberg holding a letter in his left hand. The document was addressed to the Cavalry Captain of the Fourth Squadron, Sixth Schwolische Regiment, dated 1828, unknown destination. It reads as follows:

> I send to you a boy, who might, as he wishes, serve faithfully the King; the boy was left with me, 1812, the 7th of October (. . .) I have brought him up like a Christian; and have not, since 1812, let him go a step [out] from the house (. . .) I have already taught him to read and write, and when we ask him what he will become, he says he will be a light horseman as his father was. (Feuerbach 1832, 12–13)

In an addendum from the same letter, the identity of the boy is ambiguously described: '[he] is already baptized (. . .) his name is Kaspar [but] you have to give him a name yourself' (Gedmünden 1994, 128). To uncover Kaspar's solitary past, just as in the case of Victor, naturalists and doctors tried to categorise his condition among the taxonomy of animal species as to determine whether or not he could be classified under the rubric of the human genus.

The public interest awakened by the lives of Victor and Kaspar has catalysed into an ongoing intellectual attention in the arts. Adapted many times in the form of novels (Jill Dawson's *Wild Boy*; Jakob Wassermann's *Caspar Hauser or The Inertia of the Heart*); poems (Mary Robinson's *The Savage of Aveyron*; David Constantine's *Caspar Hauser: A Poem in Nine Cantos*); non-fiction books (Harlan Lane's *The Wild Boy of Aveyron*; Jeffrey Moussaieff Masson's *Lost Prince*); opera librettos (Solomon Epstein's *The Wild Boy*; Elizabeth Swados's *Kaspar Hauser*); and theatrical plays (David Holmon's *The Wild Boy of Aveyron*; Peter Handke's *Kaspar*), Victor's and Kaspar's story, along with those of other feral children found in eighteenth- and nineteenth-century Europe,[1] seem to never exhaust the enigma of what it means to be us – the speaking animal who says 'I'. The central question, however, taken up by the intellectual impetus of cinematic thinkers, remains largely the same: Where does the origin of human language reside? Can there be a human subject without the discursive destination of their rational voice?

By examining two New Wave films: François Truffaut's *The Wild Child* (1970) and Werner Herzog's *The Enigma of Kaspar Hauser* (1974), this chapter intertwines Deleuze's pre- and post-war cinemas into one combinatorial intensive-image. This concept, which collapses the separation between cinematic classicism and modernism by maintaining that both

---

[1] An exhaustive list of wild European children can be found in Carl Linnaeus's *Systema Naturae* (1735), Jean-Jacques Rousseau's *Discours sur l'origine et les fondements de l'inégalité parmi les hommes* (1755) and, more recently, in Lucien Malson's *Les enfants sauvages: mythe et réalité* (1981).

image regimes share intensity (that is, a form of sensation originating from images of difference, and of the different), will focus on such juncture in Truffaut and Herzog's films under the figure of the child. Hence, I will locate the power of intensity in Victor of Aveyron and Kaspar Hauser, two historical figures whose identities as 'feral children' problematise the classical, *a priori* definition of humanity as 'being in language' (Kant 1781/2008) in order to account for a more processual understanding of the human entity as 'becoming in a language being' (Agamben 1993/2007). This is a 'straying', intensive figure that, in discussing Barbara Creed's notion of the abject, will be analysed under Victor's and Kaspar's undomesticated life that so often upset the classification of their guardians: 'The stray exists on the border between definitions; her state of being serves to undermine any desire to classify according to strict lines' (Creed 2017, 47).

To address this question then (that is to say, to think about a certain infancy of human language through the lenses of the cinema), I use Truffaut's and Herzog's films to interrogate and break with the rational conventions of the Enlightenment period. New Wave filmmakers both in France (*La nouvelle vague*) and in Germany (*New German Cinema*) represent for Deleuze an important epistemic rupture with previous modes of thinking that he defines, in his cinema books, as the collapse of the Kantian image of *adaequatio*: 'Characters no longer "know" how to react to situations that are beyond them, too awful, or too beautiful, or insoluble' (1995b, 59).

Following the basic outline of Itard's memoir *The wild boy of Aveyron* (1932)[2] and Hauser's writings found in Feuerbach's *Kaspar Hauser: The Foundling of Nuremberg* (1832), I look at both filmmakers' page-to-screen adaptations to rethink this process of language acquisition from the wordless animal that the child represents to the rational speaking subject that humans become in adulthood. To respond to the question of how to treat a young person who is living outside of speech, both films propose, in my view, the possibility of reconsidering the bare experience of our early animal language (*languae*) via a mode of expression that is other than rational or discursive. Because Victor (played by the non-professional actor Jean-Pierre Cargol) and Kaspar (played by the street-singer Bruno S.) are foreigners to these logics of speech, hence no different from other children who remain confined to their self-referential voice, both stories

---

[2] Itard's memoir and subsequent report on Victor (1806) are found in the appendix of Lucien Malson's book *Les enfants sauvages: mythe et réalité* (1981), from which Truffaut is said to have reconstructed the story.

problematise the entry into the symbolic realm of signification by posing, as Giorgio Agamben suggests, 'an experiment with language' (2007, 1). As the characters of Dr Itard (François Truffaut) and Professor Daumer (Walter Ladengast) observe in each film, it seems that the only way for these adolescents to access the realm of reasoning, and thus humanity, is through the acquisition of the language of men. However, as stressed by Truffaut's Itard, crossing this threshold constitutes Victor's biggest despair: 'Now, ready to renounce the task I had imposed upon myself (. . .) I condemned the curiosity of the men who had wrenched him away from his innocent and happy life.' Kaspar, too, symbolises this lamentable position, a person who remains, as Herzog states, 'without concepts (. . .) a yet to be studied kind of human' (quoted in Romney 2000, 25).

Childhood: An Early Field of Intensities

In the nineteenth century, the influence of Kant's epistemology was felt everywhere in European philosophy. In the examinations of Victor and Kaspar, this meant that the prerequisite for being recognised as human was their capacity to acquire speech; the test of whether the wordless child can turn into a fully thinking agent. 'Being in language' was here understood under the Kantian category of the understanding – what the philosopher had described as a 'unitary form of consciousness' which brings about a logic of the environment by way of organising particular impressions into general concepts or categories (2008, 236). Hence, devoid of language, and the faculty of reasoning, the identity of the 'I' would be inevitably disjointed in what Kant calls a chaotic 'rhapsody of perceptions' (2008, 236): sensations and representations that are never brought under a unifying synthesis for a self-identical I, an experience not unlike Kaspar's intuitively lived life is ('nothing lives in me except my life') or Victor's animal gratifications untouched by the instructions of formal education. As Kant notes on his 'Lectures on Pedagogy' (1803/2007), to transcend sensible experience via reasoning constitutes the primary locus of humanity's ontological freedom.

> Savagery is independence from [rational] laws. Through discipline the human being is submitted to the laws of humanity and is first made to feel their constraints (. . .) Thus, for example, children are sent to school initially not already with the intention that they should learn something there, but rather that they may grow accustomed to sitting still and observing punctually what they are told, so that in the future they may not put into practice actually and instantly each notion that strikes them. Now by nature the human being has such a powerful propensity towards freedom that when [s]he has grown accustomed to it for a while, [s]he will sacrifice everything for

it (. . .) Therefore, the human being must be accustomed early [on] to subject himself [or herself] to the percepts of reason. (2007, 438)

For Victor and Kaspar, however, such rational percepts are not necessarily linked to Kant's experience of freedom. In fact, the more they adapt to civilisation, the more they seem to suffer. Victor, for example, who represents an entity devoid of discourse, is never able to master that principle of Kantian reasoning – that is, of decoding the world into words. He remains, as Itard's original report observes, somewhere between 'the precarious life [of an] animal [and] the moral superiority [of] man' (1932, 50). Such a bridge separating animality from 'the human' is nonetheless negotiated, although ambiguously, by Truffaut's Itard, who is shown caressing Victor's hair towards the end of the film, telling him: 'You're no longer a savage, even if you're not yet a man . . .' Something similar occurs to Kaspar, who, trying to retreat from his cultural assimilation, becomes an exotic subject for the adult characters in the film. Herzog's epigraph at the beginning of the story anticipates this drama under Kaspar's discursive rupture: 'Don't you hear that screaming all around us, that screaming men call silence?' Neither Victor nor Kaspar are, in short, full participants of the rational, symbolic field. But doesn't their failure represent an altogether different approach to the question of language and its relation to 'human nature'? Wouldn't it be appropriate to shift from Kant's *a priori* conditioning, like his being in language, to a more processual understanding of the human agent as the 'becoming in a language being' (Agamben 2007, 15–72)? In what follows, and to keep a sense of the philosophical context in which the two real-life events unfolded, I wish to bring into discussion David Hume's *A Treatise of Human Nature* (1739/1888) next to Kant's *Critique of Pure Reason* (1781/2008), two imperative references for Deleuze's model of transcendental empiricism and to my discussion of an early field of intensities in both our childhood experience and the emerging language of film.

The central question informing Deleuze's reading of Hume in *Empiricism and Subjectivity* is to determine how the subject is constituted inside '*the given* of experience' without simultaneously being reduced to 'the *impressions* and *associations*' of that experience (1991, 105–21). Deleuze's connection here is between the phenomenological multiplicity of the world-environment with which we all enter and engage, and the singularity of the self which arises from those relations – that is, a self which cannot be entirely deduced from the accidents and material conditions of that experience. Echoing Aristotle, this would mean, on the one hand, that the whole (self) is more than – and in fact, different from – the sum of its parts and, on the other hand, that Kant's *a priori* reasoning is overturned by a singular, exterior and a *posteriori* experience which Deleuze identifies as the empirico-transcendental principle. In Deleuze's words:

> *The mind is not subject; it is subjected.* When the subject is constituted in the mind under the effect of principles, the mind apprehends itself as a self, for it has been qualified. But the problem is this: if the subject is constituted only inside the collection of ideas, how can the collection of ideas be apprehended as a self, how can I say 'I', under the influence of those same principles? (1991, 31)

Hume provides a response to this difficult question:

> [The mind is] *nothing but a wonderful and intelligible instinct in our souls*, which carries us along a certain train of ideas, and endows them with particular qualities, according to their particular situations and relations. This instinct, this [truth], arises from past observations and experience [impressions]; but can anyone give the ultimate reason, why past experiences and observations produce such an effect, any more than why nature alone should produce it? Nature may certainly produce whatever can arise from habit: Nay, habit is nothing but one of the principles of nature, and derives all its force from that origin. (1888, 179)

For Hume, then, the answer to how the subject transcends the given of experience is by way of habit – that is, the customary effects by which we start to arrange our mind into a daily network of associations and ideas. This behavioural pattern is what endows the early human subject with a unitary form of consciousness which, unlike Kant, is not presupposed to exist outside of experience (*a priori* means, precisely, that which precedes, or does not depend on, experience) but is rather immanent to that experience, hence a form of consciousness that is dependent on sensible encounters. This means that Hume's claim, similar to Kant's, is that knowledge cannot be formed outside of the empirical world (i.e. it is only through the instructions of formal education that reasoning is made possible), but unlike Kant, whose conditions for experience are universal and transcendental, Hume seeks to demonstrate that the mind is rather singular and formed through our external, everyday habits. In this context, the early intensities of childhood would stand for a non-representative, or a not yet qualified image of the environment, that escapes from strict definitions – anything but habituation, anything but the schematisation of sensible impressions into rational ideas. A similarly undomesticated gesture can be derived from Truffaut's and Herzog's films: neither Victor nor Kaspar can organise their world views clearly and coherently, for as long as they are not formed into a unitary ego, as their respective societies want them to be, they will remain in a pre-discursive, intense animal state. Infancy, in other words, can either be read as the Freudian oceanic self or the Lacanian *hommelette* – two psychoanalytical forms of 'perceptual rhapsody', to employ Kant's terms. For Hume, quite similarly, it is *vividness*, or what I call *intensity*, that which signifies the early state of a mind not yet qualified by the ego's habitual associations. These latter terms specify that rather than as preconsciousness, infancy be read as a vital form of the imagination:

> What is happening is that a child looks at the world through eyes like clear windows, really looking outward; then [in adulthood] the individual needs to justify a history that has begun to exist with him, the window silvers over and thickens and thickens and finally we are confronted by a mirror in which we see nothing but ourselves, the affirmation of ourselves over and over again. (Deren 1959/2005)

To summarise: it is only under the effects of *habit* that the imagination adopts the form of reason and the mind stabilises into a unitary form of consciousness to which we give the name of *ego* – the habit of saying 'I'. In Deleuze's words:

> In itself, the mind has two fundamental characteristics: *resonance* and *vividness* [intensity]. Recall the metaphor that likens the mind to a [string] instrument. When does it become subject? It becomes subject when its vividness is mobilized in such a way that the part characterized by vividness (impression) communicates it to another part (idea), and also, when all the parts taken together resonate in the act of producing something new. (1991, 132)

The ego, therefore, appears as the contingent crystallisation of its relations, a kind of external territorialisation within the mind. With this taken into consideration, the intensity of childhood should also account for its own process of maturity and actualisation, the aforementioned habit of saying 'I' – the ground by which the wordless infant[3] turns into a fully speaking subject. However, as regards the cases of Victor and Kaspar, as portrayed cinematically, a question immediately problematises this semiotic/semantic split: How are we to equip the child whose qualities and relations are not exclusively derived from the human environment and its rational habituation? Again, if the subject (the mind) is what transcends the background of its identity relations, how can we define the phenomenological structuring of Victor, whose early life was influenced by animals other than humans? Or the enigmatic consciousness of Kaspar, whose language is still alien to his masters of speech?

---

[3] From Latin infant – 'unable to speak' [*in-* 'not' + *fant-* 'speaking']

It seems to me, at least from Deleuze's reading of Hume, that the answer to these questions relies exclusively on Victor's and Kaspar's early field of relations, that is a differential and instinctive ground constituted outside of the human network; a domain of existence that is not derived from the percepts of reason but from an undomesticated experience of the imagination. This means that if Victor and Kaspar are the product of a customary conjunction with nature, then the way to understand their identities – or self-formations – should be derived from the Humean principle of a mind that, while connected to its environment, remains autonomous in its operations. The question is thus not only to unveil how Victor and Kaspar interact with their immediate environment but also to show how a new type of consciousness (Victor and Kaspar) emerges from this non-human, or 'other-than-human', network. Finally, I would also stress, as I hope to demonstrate in my analysis of the two films, that our id/entity formation cannot be located under the classical rubric of an entity 'possessing language' but is rather of an entity that requires of other humans to be trained into language and thus become, from this ensemble, a rational speaking subject. Human language, as Agamben persuasively maintains, should then be read as a mixture of both our 'endosomatic' inheritance (that is, the genetic make-up that allows us to speak) and our 'esosomatic' or epigenetic experience. In the cases of Victor and Kaspar, there is no doubt that they are well equipped with the first physiological structuring. The problem rests with the latter circuit, where the subject requires of other humans to encircle it with language so as to induce its becoming a fully discursive being. In Agamben's words:

> Certainly, in contrast with what occurs in the majority of animal species (. . .) human language is not wholly written into the genetic code. [Hence], in the human individual, exposure to language is indispensable. It is a fact whose importance can never be overemphasised in understanding the structure of human language that if a child is not exposed to speech between the ages of two and twelve, his or her potential for language acquisition is definitively jeopardized. Contrary to ancient traditional beliefs, from this point of view man is not the 'animal possessing language', but instead the animal deprived of language and obliged, therefore, to receive it from outside himself. (2007, 65)

In what follows, I will explore how Truffaut's and Herzog's film reflect upon this notion of human infancy in their depiction of two feral children who are obliged to enter into civilisation. The claim is that Truffaut's *The Wild Child* introduces discontinuities in the possibility of a boy becoming-man, and that the filmmaker, in his chronicle of the untamed child, is intersected by two image-faces; that of depicting the realities of Victor's infancy or Truffaut's vision of how he wants to portray Dr Itard. Similarly, as regards Herzog's film, it is claimed that Kaspar, too, represents an intense subject who never detaches from his poetic visions which so often 'challenge the dominant point of view embodied in the master discourses of anthropocentrism, history and humanism' (Creed 2017, 18). Hence, in confronting the lessons of their teachers, I argue that both feral children stand for an image of difference and of the different that, echoing Deleuze and Guattari, can be described as a model for cinematic intensity:

> An intensive trait starts working for itself, a hallucinatory perception, synesthesia, perverse mutation, or play of images shakes loose, challenging the hegemony of the signifier. In the case of the child, gestural, mimetic, ludic, and other semiotic systems regain their freedom and extricate themselves from the 'tracing', that is, from the dominant competence of the teacher's language – a microscopic event upsets the local balance of power. (2005, 15)

Truffaut's *Enfants Terribles*

Itard's diaries on Victor are, quite literally, the scripted motion for Truffaut's *The Wild Child*, except that his adaptation is not penned from the perspective of a scientific observer (as Itard's memoire is), but from the gaze of a filmmaker who fuses with his *enfant sauvage* to recover an intense experience of first times: 'I'm never tired of filming with children' Truffaut says in relation to *Small Change* (1976). 'All that a child does on screen, [s]he seems to do it for the first time' (quoted in Insdorf 1994, 145). This is probably why, for Colombian film critic and priest, Luis Alberto Alvarez, 'all of Truffaut's work' is read as a 'search for his lost childhood' (quoted in Codell 2006, 102) – a topic that indeed runs in Truffaut's filmography from *Les Mistons* (1957) to his later productions *The Wild Child* (1969), *The Story of Adèle H* (1975) and *Small Change*.[4]

Similarly, in his feature film debut *The 400 Blows* (1959), Truffaut had already reflected upon this experience of infancy by following the process of a boy who is obliged to enter into civilisation. Antoine (Jean-Pierre Léaud), like Victor in *The Wild Child*, is a wandering teen who not only transits towards the adult domain of human culture but also someone who mirrors Truffaut's own troubled adolescence in France. This is a clear tribute to infancy, and to the birth of the cinema, that Truffaut makes explicit via Antoine's love for the motion picture and Honoré de Balzac.

---

[4] As seen in *The Wild Child* and *The 400 Blows*, this is a recurrent search that intersects and gives continuity to Truffaut's childhood with adult characters who simultaneously stand for his mentoring figures as a child.

But as seen at the film's opening credits, *The 400 Blows* is also a homage that the filmmaker pays to his mentor and close friend André Bazin, represented here by René Bigey (Patrick Auffay). It is a dual relationship between adult-teacher (Bazin) and undomesticated child (Truffaut) that, a decade later, the filmmaker will play again in *The Wild Child*. For it is in the latter film, dedicated to Léaud/Antoine, that the filmmaker stands now for the teacher and the 'father' of his own past: Truffaut's Itard becomes Victor's mentor and Victor subsequently becomes the mirror-image of Truffaut as Antoine. Could this possibly mean, as Julie Codell infers, that the director is split into a double persona here – that is, as a boy in Léaud/Victor and as a tutor in Bazin/Itard? (2006, 110–11). Where can we locate the identity of Truffaut? Is he behind the costumes of a doctor who, by acting for the first time in one of his films, reverses his previous identification with children? Or is he next to Victor who, as an outsider to the realm of adulthood, reconstructs Truffaut's difficult childhood experiences as Antoine? If we claim that his gaze is that of the child, then there is yet another way to reconnect Truffaut's autobiographical infancies as Léaud/Antoine with Victor. (Thus, the preliminary distinction I am suggesting is not between Truffaut's Victor and Antoine, for the director may indeed be both at once in different periods of time, but between Truffaut the filmmaker and Truffaut the actor playing Itard.)

Let's remember for a moment how *The Wild Child* ends. Once Victor has come back to Itard's residence after another attempted escape, he climbs up the stairs with Madame Guérin (Françoise Seigner) ready to have a well-deserved rest. Here, quite stubbornly, the doctor utters a severe sentence from behind (he is downstairs): 'Tomorrow we shall resume our lessons.' That is Itard's final request, and the last image we catch of him on camera. Later on, once the shot cuts to an ascending Victor who stares at the camera with a rebellious gaze, the film closes with an inconclusive iris shot of his face going into black. Similarly, at the end of *The 400 Blows*, the same rigid posture is embodied by Antoine who looks at the camera quite unpleasantly. But unlike Antoine, who has been treated with cruelty and indifference throughout the film, Victor is someone who at least has been looked after and treated with care. As Truffaut declares in one of his interviews: '[*The Wild Child*] responds, ten years later, to *Les quatre cents coups*. We have on the screen (. . .) someone who lacks something essential, but this time there are people who will try to help' (quoted in Codell 2006, 102).

Does this statement mean, as Codell persuasively maintains, that the director has adopted a dual image (in fact, an intensive-image with the feral child at its centre, yet chronicled in a classical 'movement-image' style), or the form of a dual character (as a doctor who loves and condemns and as a child who is no longer free) in *The Wild Child*?

The Reversibility of Truffaut's Face: Looking at and through the Window in *The Wild Child*

From the perspective of the film's *mise en scène*, Truffaut's dual face is akin to a window that is both exterior surface and interior space, simultaneously open upon itself and predetermined as a self-reflexive frame. As many commentators have argued (Andrew and Gillain 2013; Andrew 2013; Elsaesser and Hagener 2010; Insdorf 1994), the window works in *The Wild Child* as a crucial cinematographic prop that juxtaposes the inside/outside tension between Itard, who lacks contact with the open, and Victor, who is unable to leave his early imaginary-state. In one remarkable scene at night, when Itard looks through the window at Victor who is seating next to a fountain in the gardens of his residence, the distance between the two characters – between Itard's civilised enclosure and Victor's natural surrounding – is pronounced visually: while the former, inside the house, holds a candle in his hand, the latter, outside the residence, faces upward towards a moon that is full and bright. So, to come back to the question of where to locate Truffaut's identity in the film, the answer, which is contingent on his adult/infant split, becomes subjected to which side of the window we are looking at. If Truffaut's eyes are identified as those of doctor Itard, then the camera represents a fixed operative frame, hence a film foretold in terms of Deleuze's rational movement-image. It is a viewing position that is constricted and oriented inwardly; as an onlooker who, enlightened by the reason of their own mind, detaches from the exteriority and accidents of nature – that of Kant's 'rhapsody of perception'. On the contrary, if we think of the camera as an open window, one oriented outwardly, then Truffaut's eyes are unavoidably those of Victor's. In fact, it is through the window that Victor always escapes to the forest, or inside the house, the primordial site where he contemplates the outside. Combined with a glass of water, as the doctor mentions through voice-over commentary (another distancing device employed by Truffaut's Itard), the window represents Victor's nostalgia for his lost past. After successfully completing one of his tasks, Itard rewards his pupil with a glass of water and describes how: '[He] stands near the window (. . .) trying to reunite the only things that survived his loss of freedom: a drink of pure water, and the sight of sunlight on the countryside.'

The window – a middle zone between the two protagonists, that is between Truffaut's infant and adult lives – not only helps to reconstruct the opposite angles from which to read the storyline but equally interrogates, and indeed merges, the classical/modern threshold separating Deleuze's two cinemas. As a movement-image film, *The Wild Child* is structured under a firm narrative arc: it starts in the open, in the surroundings of the forest, and it ends in Itard's enclosure, after the boy, who we glimpse through the window, comes back to the villa. As a time-image, the film escapes from its narrative cohesion through Victor's intensity and his open-ended trajectory that resists the capture of the signifier by producing affective 'aftereffects' in the viewer.

Secondly, *The Wild Child* also employs early cinematic techniques to reflect on the infancy of its own language, as if Truffaut were playing a tribute not only to the child Léaud/Antoine but also to the infancy of the cinema more broadly. His film is shot in black and white and its images align quite closely with the *actualité* documentary style of the silent era. It is a classical/modern experiment that, by combining Deleuze's two logics of the image, portrays the potential for the continued vitality of the intensive-image in cinema. Take, as another example of this early cinematic language, the employment of the iris device in *The Wild Child*. As Annette Insdorf observes, the film begins 'with an iris shot [coming] out from darkness' and it ends, in the same fashion, 'with an iris shot going into darkness' (1994, 154–5). It is a black hole that positions the 'classical' filmmaker in proximity with his 'modern', Bazinian spirit. And this reversibility of Truffaut's face is precisely the double gesture projected via his characters who look *at* and *through* the window. As Leo Baudry states, when the camera-window is fixed, as in the case of Truffaut/Itard, the act of seeing is one imposed by 'the perfect coherence of the [screen]-world', but when the window is opened, as in the case of Victor, 'the audience is a guest', thus welcoming the viewer to create 'intense [and] new directions' onscreen (1976, 49). The same distinction is made by Bazin (and Deleuze) in order to split the meanings of classical and modern cinemas. As Bazin writes:

> [If] the neorealist film has a meaning, it is [one] *a posteriori*, to the extent that it permits our awareness to move from one fact to another, from one fragment of reality to the next, whereas in the classical artistic composition the meaning is established *a priori*: the house is already there in the brick. (2005, 60)

But in *The Wild Child*, as I have shown, both artistic traditions seem to resonate under one image with two faces. Victor, on the one hand, becomes here the film's excess, its disequilibrium, the wild boy who goes mad. Itard, on the contrary, stands for the film's signifier, the actor-director who plays the educator-judge of his own past. Hence, Truffaut's film is structured under two conflicting paths; one that eludes domestication, as an image of intensive forces, and another that presupposes an equilibrium, as an image of rational pauses and rests. Truffaut's cinematic eye is thus paradoxically pulled from both directions at once. It is a movement-image chronicle, organically plotted, that nonetheless confronts the commands of the story in the intensity of a boy who problematises his *becoming-man*.

But What is to Become?

Itard's memoirs on Victor are structured by four succeeding aims held for 'the mental and moral education' of the child (1932, 11–51). These developmental stages are also employed by the filmmaker to map out Victor's passage from his 'animal' state in the forest to his more rational behaviour in the doctor's house. Patricia Pisters, in her chapter 'The Taming of the Wild Child', describes Victor's passage as one of 'becoming-human' (2003, 156). She focuses, on the one hand, on Deleuze's 'intensive proximity' that Victor and all children seem to share with the animal world and, on the other hand, on the potential room for 'becoming' that doctor Itard, with his instructive and familial environment, provides to the child.

In the first period, as described by Itard in his memoirs, Victor is a *bêtise* – a wolf-child. Drawing on the work of John Locke and Étienne Bonnot de Condillac, Itard declares that humankind is not free in a state of nature, and that in such a condition 'the individual, deprived of all the characteristic faculties of his [and her] kind, drags on without intelligence or without feelings, a precarious life reduced to bare animal functions' (1932, 47–8). Human freedom is thus perceived as the outcome of formal education, which makes of Itard's 'moral man', like that of Kant's 'rational being', the greatest achievements of civilisation. In *The Wild Child*, the mobilisation of such an image is put forward by the scene in which Dr Pinel (Jean Dasté) examines the boy in the hospital and concludes that while the child's sensory stimuli are able to satisfy bare animal functions, his intellectual capacity is insufficient to embrace the more sophisticated workings of the mind. Pinel, unlike Itard, refers to the boy quite derogatively as an 'inferior being' and a 'naturally born idiot'. Upon these words the film cuts to an image of Victor, swinging in an animal posture under the rain in the gardens of the clinic. Through the windowpane the two doctors watch the child, who, since arriving in Paris, has been exhibited as a scientific curiosity, an ethnographic freak. However, it is also at this moment that Itard declares to his superior Pinel, that he intends to educate the boy in his villa near Batignolles. (Unlike Pinel, Itard believes that the child's abnormality is indeed treatable; that his condition is not the product of an incurable brain malady but the result of a long-isolated sojourn in the forest.)

The second period thus begins, as Itard states in his diaries, '[in] a more pleasant place to stay and learn [with the love of] a patient mother and the intelligence of an enlightened teacher' (1932, 20). The new task set by the doctor is to render the boy's physical strength weaker in order to develop his other senses that have not yet been educated (that of hearing and seeing especially). Truffaut's adaptation follows almost to the letter the recommendations proposed by Itard in his report, from the physical stimulants he utilises to awaken Victor's senses (e.g. Truffaut's Itard gives Victor long, hot showers and dresses him up to make his skin more sensitive to temperature; they play drums together with the boy's eyes covered to develop his sense of hearing . . .), to the more emotional stimulants he deploys (such as Victor's experiences of pleasure and irritation through having or not having a glass of milk) in a bid to awaken his mental functioning. Such methods prove to be effective in the taming of the wild child. As Pisters tells us, Itard and Guérin's enclosure becomes 'the parental site' where the 'human [boy] is born' (2003, 157). Indeed, it is here that Victor gets his name.

The next step is to introduce the child to the domain of rational ideas. In the film, this passage is followed by Itard's highest aim: to awaken the mental operations in Victor necessary to make him speak. To do so, Truffaut's Itard uses a strict system of rewards and punishments that make the boy, from time to time, go mad. He turns 'his only pleasures' as Madame Guérin says, 'into exercises [:] "His tantrums are your fault [doctor Itard] (. . .) he works ten times more than a normal child."' But the doctor ignores Guérin's observations; he is blinded by the fact that Victor is not only capable of activating connections between words and things but is also developing a sense of justice by differentiating what is fair from what is unjust. Itard wants to induce in Victor the judgement of a moral man, and to do so, quite inevitably, his own instructional success relies on his pupil's distress. As Itard's voice-over commentary narrates towards the end of the film, after Victor has bitten his hand in an act of rebellion:

> I wish that my pupil could have understood me at this moment. I would have told him that his bite filled my soul with joy (. . .) I had evidence that what is just and unjust was no longer alien to Victor's heart. By provoking the sentiment, *I had elevated the savage man to the stature of a moral being* by the most noble of his attributes. [My emphasis]

Itard's moral being is thus the becoming man of Victor. But what is it to become? According to Deleuze and Guattari, becomings are always minoritarian, molecular relations rather than molar formations. Becomings express collective singularities instead of individualised forms of being. Like a parliament of owls or a children's pack, they lack a central point of domination, such as that of man: 'Why are there so many becomings of man, but no becoming-man?' ask the authors in *A Thousand Plateaus*: 'First and foremost because man is majoritarian par excellence, whereas becomings are minoritarian' (2005, 339).

In Truffaut's film, as we saw, a clear intersection is revealed between the two characters: there is Dr Itard who follows the road of man, the educator-judge who draws straight lines on the board; and then there is Victor who takes the course of intensity, the wild child who messily draws spirals with his hand. Following this track, it seems to me that the only possible minoritarian encounter in the film is that of Itard becoming Victor and not Victor becoming Itard. However, it is the boy who is forced to learn his teacher's language and the teacher who realises that the boy won't be able to live freely again in the woods. Already habituated to the human environment, Victor has to cope with Itard's lessons in order to enter into society.

Hence, like the language of an adult-child, Truffaut's film combines the vivid intensities of Victor with the narrative cohesion of his mentor Itard. And such a split separating the two modes of existence is also helpful in illustrating the processual ontology of the human entity in its becoming a language being. As suggested earlier via Deleuze's Hume as well as via Agamben, the human subject should not be understood in terms of an entity 'possessing language' but as the entity who requires of other humans to be trained in language, thus becoming, out of this assemblage, a sovereign language being. Following Aristotle, who endorses the capacity of *languae* to all animal species, Agamben indicates that the child is not an entity constituted outside of language (for we are all inside the Aristotelian *animal languae*) but someone who must break with their early voice in order to acquire human speech. This is the moment when our '(in)fancy of experience' (2007, 13–72) can never be reconstituted. Being habituated to mankind is thus to proclaim an 'I' that is removed from its early animal life. 'Man is a distant being', Nietzsche says in a loud voice (quoted in Michaud 2007, 35). Distant not only in relation to the rest of the living species but also in relation to his own animal being. In essence, man is the historical animal who has lost contact with his own beginning. In Agamben's words:

> Imagine a man born already equipped with language, a man who already possessed speech. For such a man without infancy, language would not be a pre-existing thing

to be appropriated, and for him there would be neither any break between language [*languae*] and speech nor any historicity of language. But such a man would thereby at once be united with his nature; his nature would always pre-exist, and nowhere in it would he find any discontinuity, any difference through which any kind of history could be produced. Like the animal, who Marx describes as 'immediately at one with its life activity', he would merge with it and would never be able to see it as an object distinct from himself. (2007, 60)

Herzog's Kaspar: A Man of Beginnings

Such a man – a man united with nature, a man who does not seem to exist – resembles Kaspar Hauser; a person who lives outside of history and who speaks outside of speech. In effect, if humanity begins with history, once the wordless experience of the child has been overcome, then Kaspar is like that infant who never detaches from his beginning, and remains, already in adult form, forever in that beginning: 'I know a story about the desert', he says to housekeeper Katy (Brigitte Mira), 'but only the beginning'. Abandoned early on by his parents, Kaspar, like Victor, enacts another failure to the symbolic realm as represented by his masters in Nuremberg. He is, too, a differential individual who becomes 'a threat to civilized societies' (Creed 2017, 21) and their need to separate out human and animal, mind and body, according to the logic of reason, order and the law. Self-excluded from adulthood, then, Kaspar persists at the margin of what is without meaning; '*un monstre et un chaos*', says Nietzsche (1968, 51) in regards to the nihilist who devaluates the customary values in society. 'Mother, I'm so far away from everything', Kaspar cries holding another weeping baby in his arms, as if confirming the Nietzschean abyss:

> Let us think this thought in its most terrible form: existence as it is, without meaning or aim, yet recurring inevitably without any finale of nothingness (. . .) This is the most extreme form of nihilism: the nothing, Real, eternally! (1968, 35)

Kaspar's abyss then, like that of Nietzsche's, becomes his estrangement from society to live the Real as it is. But what do we see at the film's beginning? Is that the face of Kaspar's mother leaving her baby in the river? Hard to tell really. The image is as blurry as the next shot where Kaspar seems to be arriving at his castle in Nuremberg. Here we see a labourer washing white clothes in the waters of the city. She stares at the camera for a moment, seemingly witnessing something odd, perhaps something miraculous (something like the arrival of baby prince Moses in the river). The film certainly begins with an ambiguous and sublime atmosphere. It imbues the image with the promise of a visionary character to come, like baby Kaspar floating in the river just before entering into the castle where he will remain trapped for many years. It is an overture that, in the words of Thomas Elsaesser, can be described as evoking the sheer expressivity of an instant – an intensive-image apprehending the pure presence of a moment:

> For Herzog an event is never open toward development or a future: it has its end inscribed in its *beginning*, for the first shot already tells it all, and there is very little suspense or dramatic tension between characters. Herzog's concern is with a different kind of *intensity*, a negative one that makes it difficult for him to think of narrative as anything other than an accumulation of isolated moments, running their course, in fact, running down like clockwork and being succeeded by others. (2014, 141–2; my emphasis)

Herzog's overture also brings to mind Deleuze's modern cinema, one producing not only an encounter with intensities that are 'too strange' or 'insoluble' but also an immersive viewing experience in which time runs eternally in the present moment and space is lived without any horizons or constraints. In conversation with Paul Cronin, Herzog recalls a personal experience similarly un-delimited by contours. In describing his childhood days as a ski jumper, he comments that:

> When taking off from a ramp you would hold your head back when falling, but we would thrust our heads forward like when taking a dive (. . .) It is like someone who takes a suicidal jump from a great height, and then regrets his decision when he realizes, midway through empty space, that no one can help him. It is the same with filmmaking. Once you have started, there is no one to help you through. (2002, 101)

In the light of Herzog's aerial vision – as this sort of filmmaking style suspended on air – the coming of Kaspar into the world represents, in the protagonist's words, 'a terrible hard fall'. The fall is, first of all, his own: like most children, Kaspar makes sense of things out of his own intuitive imagination, not quite understanding the categories imposed by the mind of adults. He believes, for example, that apples are conscious entities, but Professor Daumer 'reminds' him that they don't have lives of their own; he solves riddles by means that are not logically deductive, thus mathematicians cannot accept his reasoning; he thinks that to build a tall tower you need an equally tall builder, and that the room inside the tower must be bigger than the building itself, because, as he explains: 'wherever I look in the room there is only room. [But] when I look at the tower, and I turn around, the tower is gone.' Kaspar thus concludes, à la Borges, that the room is bigger than the whole tower. (Recall Borges's short stories 'The Library of Babel' (1941/2005), which describes a vast library containing all possible books ever written, as well as those yet to be written; and 'On Exactitude in Science' (1960/2005), in which a quixotic cartographer sets off to construct the map of the empire on a scale of 1:1 to that of the territory. So, unlike Victor, who is unable to speak, Kaspar already possesses speech. His language, however, does not constitute the ideal syntax imposed by his tutors but instead represents a poetic contestation to their commands. As Nietzsche states in regards to the romantic poet, Kaspar, too, 'raises [his] voice from the bottom of the abyss of being; [his] subjectivity is the pure imagination [of the mind]' (quoted in Deleuze 1969/2015, 144). Like children, then, Kaspar plays a game where language opens up spaces through phonetic actions, and this further complicates the rules of his teachers' lessons. For such reasons, as the viewer may presume, Kaspar is more compatible with those characters who are also foreigners to the film's official milieu: Kaspar gets sick in the house of her highness and is easily disturbed by people 'howling in church'. His friends, on the contrary, are those living outside of the patriarchy, like his young friend Julius, his wooden toy the horse, blind orphan Mozart, or housekeeper Katy. In sum, Kaspar's 'hard fall' into this world represents the inadequacy of a poet who, as expressed in the circus of Nuremberg, becomes 'the greatest riddle of all'.

The second hard fall, however, is that of Herzog's film descending into a solid narrative plot. *The Enigma of Kaspar Hauser*, as Kaja Silverman remarks, imposes a coherent formula – unusual in Herzog's cinema otherwise – to tell a story that clearly 'exceeds that coherence' (1981, 88), thereby contradicting Herzog's own anti-narrative fantasies (in the character of Kaspar) with a film that partially follows a cause-and-effect logic. In her words: '[The film] does make some preliminary gestures in the direction of a non-narrative cinema', but for its most part, she continues, 'it adopts the format of a chronicle, a format in which casual and linear values play an especially conspicuous role' (1981, 92).

A Classical/Modern Continuum: Origin qua Originality

Herzog's chronicle, like that of Truffaut's *The Wild Child*, paradoxically tells the story of a boy without a chronicle; its protagonist is a person of becomings rather than a man of history. Such a portrayal of alterity, quite common among New Wave filmmakers, brings us an image of the childpoet who, in resisting the meanings imposed by his society, is nevertheless trapped in a chain of narrative events on-screen. As in the case of Truffaut's film, Herzog too produces an image lingering between 'the two ages of the cinema' as described by Deleuze; one classical that gives consistency to the plot via careful arrangement of actions, and another modern that escapes from the film's organisation through Kaspar's enigmatic visions. The German director, like his French contemporary, not only chooses to impose a rational formula to portray a boy whose marginalised life emancipates him from the film as a whole, but at the same time he identifies with a character whose intense visions have become his own: 'What constitutes poetry, depth, vision and illumination', Herzog says in regards to those films that 'stun' him, 'I cannot name' (Herzog quoted in Ambrose 2013, 1).

Herzog's twofold formula underlined by Silverman in 1981 is presumably leading Deleuze to place the filmmaker in both of his cinema books in the years to follow. In *The Movement-Image*, Herzog is described as 'the most metaphysical of [all] cinema directors' (2005, 189) and his films represent a special case of the model action-situation-action (ASA') – namely, 'an inverted sensory-motor-schema' where the situation, which is not given, is revealed by the action, and depending on what is revealed about the situation, the character performs a second action. This is a system where Herzog's action-image, according to Deleuze, necessitates a visionary character who 'seems to be the only one capable of rivalling the milieu in its entirety' (2005, 188). In *The Time-Image*, quite similarly, Herzog's cinema assumes the form of a crystallised space with overlapping – rather than unified – perspectives. Deleuze describes such image in terms of a 'crystalline narration [where the] anomalies of movement become the essential point instead of being accidental' (2013, 134). This is, in sum, a direct time-image that subordinates itself to the expression of the sublime instead of the sublime being subordinated to the ASA' model.

But following the premise of the intensive-image, it is possible to claim that classicism and modernism coexist in Herzog's and Truffaut's film, and this is because they both share the ruptures of difference, and of the different, within their movement-image chronicles. Here, as in Truffaut's *The Wild Child*, Herzog too counter-actualises the aprioristic meanings of Deleuze's classical era by means of an inactive, 'helpless character' who 'crystalizes the great abyss of the Universe' (2005, 189). It is a poetic, *original* gesture that not only stands for the usual artistic meaning we assign to the notion of *originality* but also as an image that is situated near to, and maintains a close relationship with, its cinematic *origin* (Agamben 1994/1999, 59–67).

Kaspar's relation to origins, as we know, derives from his own stories about beginnings. But as we saw with the case of *The Wild Child*, such '(in)fancy' can also be reflected through the cinema, for it is in borrowing conventions from the early grammar of film that Herzog puts forward his origin/al language and perspective. In the case of Truffaut, this was observed in his choice to shoot the film in black and white, with an extensive use of the iris device, and in a documentary style similar to those early *actualité* films. In the case of Herzog, the hypnagogic memories and hallucinatory dreams of Kaspar are also reminiscent of those evocative landscapes from the early cinematic period. Fading, flickering and with cinch marks on the colour film's footage, his visions are no doubt akin to those 16 mm pictures from the beginnings of film.

At the climax of Herzog's chronicle, while on his deathbed, Kaspar is finally allowed to share one of his elapsed stories. It is a vision about the desert that takes us back to the beginning of his/story: 'I see a large caravan coming through the desert, across the sands. This caravan is led by an old Berber tribesman, and this old man is blind.' Through voice-over commentary, Kaspar concludes his prophetic fable accompanied by the hypnotic tunes of a flute:

> The caravan stops; some of them believe that they are lost because of the mountain in front of them. They look at the compass but it's broken. Then their blind leader picks up a handful of sand, turns his face towards the sun, and tastes it as if it were food. 'My sons' says the blind man, 'you are wrong. Those are not mountains in front of you, it's only your imagination. We must continue northward.' And so they follow the old man's advice, and reach the city in the North. That's where the story begins, but I don't know the rest . . .

The Enigma of Kaspar Hauser and *The Wild Child* can be thought of as two cases of the intensive-image which merges the beginning of the cinema, its early language, with the deterritorialising forces of a modern Deleuzian act. It is an *ars combinatoria* in which the *old* and the *new* come together by reconnecting with the *origin*ality of an early voice. This is, in fact, the open possibility left by Truffaut's and Herzog's film and their infant characters. Language was here understood not as the unlocking of meaning in reason, or its promise – through education – in finding our freedom, but quite the opposite, freedom as the site where human language is rooted and the place where every intensive, minoritarian encounter is experienced. The question, accordingly, incessantly goes back to the intensity of a beginning; as in Herzog's Kaspar who endlessly remains where he began and Truffaut's Victor who becomes an outsider to signification by resisting the loss of his being in meaning.

CHAPTER 4

In Between Modernities and the Contemporaneous

What is the intensive-image? As I have argued in the previous chapters, intensity stands for an image which associates, rather than separates, Deleuze's two ages of the cinema under its differential movement that intensifies *in* and *with* time. It is thus a bridging image in that it unifies Deleuze's pre- and post-war eras under unresolved forms of difference – that is, as an image of sensation and becoming that gathers force in films from the classical to the modern and the contemporary periods. As discussed earlier, the intensive-image creates a sensuous synthesis of the viewer's experience of the film, linked to the uncertainty of grasping the image's totality in its affective meanings without (yet) signification. Its formal characteristics, although specific to each of the films analysed in this book, are defined by the flowing and heterogeneous character of thermodynamic intensity, described by Deleuze as a property that does not exclude excess, transformation or disproportion, precisely because intensity *is* what differentiates: 'The expression "difference of intensity" is a tautology (. . .) Every intensity is differential, by itself a difference' (Deleuze quoted in Bertetto 2017, 795).

Hence, like a metastable system which changes its modalities over time, intensity represents here an image that is multiphased yet singular, not double, or if it has two terms, as in Deleuze's case, it corresponds to the same 'heterogeneous image', one that prolongs cinema's past into its present moment and towards a yet-to-be-actualised future. It is, therefore, an image of topological continuity – the type of nomadic distribution that problematises Deleuze's thesis on pre-war cinema, as it questions the sensory-motor-equilibriums embedded in his critique of quantitative time. This false conception of movement according to which time is only conceived mechanically or indirectly in classical films is thus blocking the deterritorialising forces of early intensive-images that, among other examples, I have described next to Buñuel's naturalism operating 'according to the canons of pure expressivity' (Pasolini 2001, 43). In this capacity, and following Susana Viegas's assertion that the theories of Deleuze on early film culture are 'archaeologically and historically inadequate' (2016, 236), I have suggested the importance of looking for a more revisionist approach to Deleuze's cinema(s) by 'understanding film modernity even before [his] modern cinema, thus dislocating Deleuze's "emancipation of time" into another perception of 'aberrant movement"' (2016, 248) in early intensive-images.

In this train of thought, I clearly support David Rodowick's observations when he states that '[early] time-images do persist from the very beginnings of the cinema' (2010, xvii), which is to say, as Deleuze himself mentions – quite vaguely though, or at least without sufficient empirical proof in his cinema volumes – that time-images and movement-images can coexist in the same historical plane. In fact, at the end of *Cinema 2*, while discussing the silent films of F. W. Murnau and Sergei Eisenstein with the modern 'read image' of Jean-Marie Straub and Danièle Huillet, Deleuze seems to account for this rather spiralling structure of the history of cinema by moving back and forth between the movement-image and the time-image periods, suggesting for instance that the readability of modern cinema 'was closer to silent film than it was to the first stage of the sound cinema' (2013, 252).[1] However, instead of merging the time-image and the silent film into one differentiating trajectory, as the intensive-image aims to do, Deleuze decides to break with the early works of German expressionists and the Soviet school of montage in order to account for a 'new [modern] aesthetic' in which the image, after the Second World War, 'becomes legible for itself, assuming a power which did not generally exist in silent cinema' (2013, 253).

According to this logic, where the cinematic image would develop through a continued adherence to an evolving artistic difference, Deleuze not only accounts for a philosophical preference towards the 'modern' sequence of the time-image, but also for an aesthetic bias towards its European, post-war artistic emergence, thereby suggesting that the shift from one epoch to the other represents the fulfilment or realisation of the cinema's artistic destiny. Consequently, if Deleuze's 'soul of the cinema' is what the time-image may only become in its 'potential evolution', as Claire Colebrook remarks in her *Deleuze: A Guide for the Perplexed* (2006),

---

[1] 'Not only because', as he continuous, '[the modern time-image] sometimes reintroduces intertitles, but also because it proceeds with the other means at the disposal of silent film, the injection of scriptural elements in the visual image (notebooks, letters and, constantly in Straub, lapidary or petrified inscriptions, "commemorative plaques, monuments to the dead, the names of streets . . ."') (2013, 252).

then what allows for its inventiveness, 'creation or time in its true sense' (2006, 14–15), is a cinematic style (such as that examined under Buñuel's surreal time-image) that subsequently intensifies (differentiates) across history.

In this capacity, Deleuze's cinematic 'essence' and the intensive-image share the same notion of *durée* as developed by Bergson, for it is in his conception of time as 'hesitation or inventiveness' where the image becomes and 'continuously elaborates what is new' (1998, 93). However, under the concept of intensity, Bergson's notion of duration as qualitative time must necessarily be opened to the potentialities and divergences of the past. Because it is always in connection to the past, in repeating and recognising what the cinema was, the problems that it once opened and occluded, that the new image will arise and differentiate constantly – past and future continue each other in an endless flow. A theory of intensities is thus always bound up with the question of time, becoming, multiplicities and the problematic.

This emancipatory form of time is what informs, in this chapter, the 'in-between modernities' of Deleuze's cinemas. What I suggest, therefore, is not a break between two different ages of the image, but one deterritorialising tendency – that of the intensive-image – compressing both sequences of Deleuze's film-art. This is, although ambiguously, what the philosopher also sets to investigate in his pre-war period under 'a direct time-image of thought which has always been breaking through [in cinema]' (2013, xii).

Put differently, and next to Bergson's idea of qualitative time as informed in *Creative Evolution*, I do not speak of two opposite images but of one and the same intensive-image that transforms itself into more complex degrees of difference – its being or *durée* is alteration as such. This indivisible continuity is brought about by an image of affection and displacements that has developed in complexity and in the frequency of its appearance over time.

Consequently, if intensity is understood as difference, and difference is what enacts the fissure in the image and the 'crack' (to use Deleuze's terminology) in life, or the shock, the unthinkable excess that awaits the thinker, then the visual analysis I am proposing is similarly approached from an intervallic, more incongruent angle. This is a filmmaking style that privileges the gap, or the indifference of a viewer's gaze that is lost viewing a landscape, allowing for screen detours leading nowhere, or everywhere except the main plot. This means, quite contrary to Bordwell's analysis of *intensified* continuity of the North American mass-audience film, that if 'intensity' is what 'speeds up' a certain tradition of cutting in the US studio system, then the type of filmmaking – and editing – that the intensive-image proposes is said to slow down that speed of the action thrill, e.g. by means of images and shots connected sensuously through montage, rather than by the 'action-sequence' model of the commercial studio film (Bordwell 2002, 16–28; Purse 2011, 56–75). Consider, in this direction, the Japanese school of editing, with directors such as Yasujiro Ozu and Kenji Mizoguchi reducing the speed of action – and the movement of the camera – to a minimum. It is a poetic cinematic style that can also be thought of in terms of those realist images Bazin dreamt about in 'The Evolution of the Language of Cinema' (1958), and which contemporary filmmakers such as Béla Tarr, James Benning, Ming-liang Tsai or Lucrecia Martel, are imbuing with intensity, that is: '[by composing films] of ninety minutes [or more] of the life of a man [or a woman, a cyborg, an animal, or a landscape] to whom nothing ever happens' (Bazin quoted in Nagib 2015, 28). This is, in brief, a form of audiovisual intensification that confronts the logic of action and entertainment in favour of a logic of contemplation which allows the viewer to linger around images with more than sufficient time to perceive them. Such is the intensive-image-complex that results not from successive association of events but from an imperceptible power of imaging that is not yet grounded in the subject-signifier.

In this chapter, I will describe the 'in-between modernities' of Deleuze's cinemas under the deterritorialising tendencies of intensity, an image which I argue manifests the breakdowns of representation and action as accounted for by Kant's experience of modernity. However, and in order to account for such an evolving trajectory of the intensive-image across Deleuze's film periods, it is necessary to examine first his (post-Kantian) place in the history of ideas and grasp the meaning of modernity for a philosopher writing on film.

Here, if we were to follow Deleuze's logic of the classical movement-image exactly, one populated by characters who orient themselves according to the commands of reason and towards the resolution of action, what we find is not only the Bergsonian schemata informing his critique on the artificiality of time reduced to a series of 'immobile sections' in 'abstract succession' (2005, 11), but also an image of the understanding that, in philosophical terminology, represents the Enlightenment, or the Kantian modern. It reads as an image of *adaequatio* that produces Deleuze's sensory-motor alignment between character, action and setting, or to put it in a Kantian fashion, an image of transcendental thinking that is represented in the triad of the subject, resemblance and world. Hence, when Deleuze states in *Cinema 2* that 'There is always a time, midday-midnight, when we must no longer ask ourselves, "What is cinema?" but "What is philosophy?'" (2013, 280),[2] the question of 'what is', which is the question of ontological essence and the univocity of Being, is determined, or at least conceived, by the 'when' and 'where' of a Kantian inquiry that confronts the previous essentialism of ancient philosophy. As Foucault reflects on Kant's modern metaphysics in contrast to Descartes's classicism:

> When in 1784 Kant asked, *Was heist Aufklarung?*, he meant, What's going on right now? What's happening to us? What is this world, this period, this precise moment in which we are living? Or in other words: What are we? As *Aujkldrer*, as part of the Enlightenment? Compare this with the Cartesian question: Who am I? I, as a unique but universal and unhistorical subject? 'I', for Descartes, is everyone, anywhere at any moment. But Kant asks something else: What are we? In a very precise moment of history. Kant's question appears as an analysis of both us and our present. (Quoted in Huyssen 1987, xi)

Modernity 1. The Age of Reason and the Emergence of the Subject

So, let's begin with the equation *Modernity 1 = Cinema 1*. Here, Deleuze's movement-image introduces a Kantian image of thought which organises the dynamics of time and space under the *a priori* of a consciousness, what Deleuze translates (via Bergson) into his classical sensory-motor-schema. Kant's epistemology is one that explains how the physical and spiritual worlds are understood by the thinking rational subject. It is a transcendental form of consciousness, that presupposes and thus predetermines our relation to experience by conceiving of the understanding as an *a priori* conception. (A priori means, precisely, that which precedes, or does not depend on, experience. Consequently, a transcendental form of consciousness is equivalent to a universal attribute that is not dependent on sensible encounters.) In the movement-image, this pre-given movement of the intellect is similarly located by Deleuze's 'classical cinematic consciousness' and his clairvoyant heroes who signify the things of this world under a unified – and thus rational – logic of perception. However, here to say

---

[2] The relation between cinema and philosophy is further elaborated by Deleuze in an interview on *The Time-Image* for the magazine *Cinéma*, when stating: 'It's true that philosophers haven't taken much notice of cinema, even though they go to cinemas. Yet it's an interesting coincidence that cinema appeared at the very time philosophy was trying to think motion. That might even explain why philosophy missed the importance of cinema: it was itself too involved in doing something analogous to what cinema was doing; it was trying to put motion into thought while cinema was putting it into images. The two projects developed independently before any encounter became possible. Yet cinema critics, the greatest critics anyways, became philosophers the moment they set out to formulate an aesthetic of cinema. They weren't trained as philosophers, but that is why they became. You see it already in Bazin' (Deleuze 1995, 57).

'consciousness' or 'subject' is something of a reality that is entirely modern, in the sense that it implies a spatio-temporal dynamic that is always in reference to, and interpreted by, an agent who controls it or dominates it. This is, in philosophy, the place of modernity – the Enlightenment, the rational paradigm, the sovereign subject. In the case of Kant or Hegel for instance, this is a form of idealism that can be illustrated under the romantic painting by Caspar Friedrich, *The Wanderer Above the Mist* (1818). Like in Deleuze's movement-image 'stars' who dominate the film's universe from a transcendental angle, Friedrich's man on top of a hill is also elevating this self-reflective spirit of the modern subject by representing the things of this world through reasoning and meaning – that is to say, in a form of recognition that transcends the very condition of the sensible and which Deleuze defines as the 'dogmatic image' in Plato's *Theaetetus*: 'This is a finger, this is a table, Good morning Theaetetus' (2014, 138).

However, contrary to Friedrich's wanderer above the mist, which pairs Kant's transcendental consciousness with Deleuze's celestial characters of the movement-image system,[3] classical philosophy praises a radically different, and quite opposite, reality; one in which the things of this world exist independently of a subject who signifies them, so that instead of a world rendered visible by an agent (as in Deleuze's classical hero) the ancients were concerned, for their most part, with the determination of the thing in itself – what medieval scholastics used to call the essence of being. *Verum est ens*, says St Thomas Aquinas: truth is not contained in the things we see or name, but in the essence that the thing is in its very being, namely its substance (that is, an independent reality that does not depend on anything else in order to be conceived or be what it is). This could mean that the philosophical modern emerges in a displacing movement of thought that replaces the Thomist reference to being (the thingness of the thing) for a subject who transfers his or her intellect onto the thing itself, so that truth is no longer located on the side of *being* but on the side of a *subject* who experiences the things of this world via reasoning. Thus, Kant's motto: *adaequatio intellectus ad rem* [truth is the accommodation of intellect to thing] and not *verum est ens* [truth is being] as informed by the theologian Aquinas.

---

[3] Visual references to Friedrich's *Wanderer Above the Mist* have also reappeared in various contemporary films, such as *Under the Skin* (Glazer 2013) where a man (Jeremy McWilliams) stands on top of a hill to demonstrate and signify his dominant power over the female alien (Scarlett Johansson); or in the more experimental film *The Trouble with Nature* (Jacobi 2020), an eighteenth-century road movie based on the philosopher Edmund Burke who searches for the meaning of the 'sublime' in the immensity of nature but who can't get to grips with the aesthetic concept he himself invented when contemplating the world on top of a mountain.

Hence, one could also claim that if Deleuze's movement-image characters represent the promise of reason under Kant's transcendental schemata, then the failure in language and the breakdown of narrative in the modern image is conversely said to portray that ancient univocity of being, in the sense that Deleuze's time-image characters perform a 'form of thinking' that, according to the philosopher, 'happens to things themselves' (2015, 185). Echoing Bruno Latour's return to *Gaia*, this could mean that 'we-have-never-been-modern', as it is in the representational crisis of 'modern' cinema that Deleuze substitutes his rational Kantian subject for the ontological immanence of classical being – that is, in his inactive characters who live *in* and *with* the time of this world instead of *against* and *out* of it. Put differently, and following Levi Bryant's 'onticology', we can state that in Deleuze's time-image modernity there is a return to the inner life of things, as his objects/subject characters are also performing 'a subterranean volcanic core with which [their] virtual being is haunted' (Bryant 2011, 281). This 'virtual domain', as Bryant suggests:

> is like a reserve or *excess* that never comes to presence. It is not simply that objects [or subjects] are, in themselves, fully actual and only withdrawn for other objects [/subjects] relating to them, but rather that objects [/subjects] are withdrawn in themselves. (2011, 282)

Wouldn't this Deleuzian 'excess' not only be Bergsonian but also Kantian in its virtual withdrawal of being?

Modernity 2. The Age of Art and the Fracture of the 'I', or the Inhumanity of Deleuze's Cinema

If we take this path, and claim that Kant's transcendental spirit could also be regarded as this passive subject/object who interacts with other subjects/objects in the world and who is simultaneously affected by them as a passive recipient of affection, then there is a second modernity announced by Deleuze's Kant, or rather, by the Kantian reversal in philosophy revisited by Deleuze's Bergsonian account of time. As mentioned in Chapter 1, this reversal consists in taking time not as an external function of movement – that is, as a fixed time subordinated to a series of movements in space – but internal to a movement that is in itself present and shifting. This is, as I argued, the essential point of Deleuze's modern characters who are resolutely moved *in* and *by* time, which is to say by this Kantian 'form of everything that changes and moves [in time]' (Kant 2008, viii). Deleuze's new cinema, therefore, no longer equates with indirect representation of time but with direct creation, which is the site where his time-image ontology, and the bridging concept of the intensive-image, emerges. Recall Deleuze's reading of Bergson's *Données immédiates* (1889/2015) when he states: 'Duration is what differs, and this is no longer what differs from other things, but what differs from itself. What differs has itself become a thing, a substance' (2004a, 25). As the philosopher concludes in this same paragraph: 'Bergson's thesis could well be summed up this way: *real time is alteration, and alteration is substance*' (2004a, 25; my emphasis). His modern cinema, in other words, gestures a return to things themselves in its classical apprehension of a substance. And this recollection of the past – a matter of the very old that is making us who we are today – is precisely the task of the intensive-image which transforms itself under its spiralling relationship between classicism and modernism. Such trans-temporal vocation of the image, discussed in the next section of this chapter under the idea of the contemporaneous, will be said to inscribe eternity in the history of film under the general movement of intensity – an accumulation of cinematic experience that changes without ceasing.

In this regard, it is also important to consider Deleuze's Kantian experience of temporality. In his book on *Deleuze, Cinema and the Thought of the World* (2019), Allan James Thomas similarly observes that this 'great Kantian reversal', employed initially by Bergson and then reworked by Deleuze, 'can only take place with the elimination of the human subject as a centre of perception and action [in the movement-image]' (2019, 216). He goes on to suggest that:

> This terror [introduced by Kant] is precisely the experience of time as change, as transformation. The doubling or duality of 'self' [in the Kantian notion of time] as 'the affection of self by self' presents this 'experience' in the form of a fracture or crack in thought and in the 'I' which thinks. (2019, 216)

So, what happens if we reframe this Kantian reversal in terms of the equation *Modernity 2 = Cinema 2*? Kant's experience of time as terror and transformation – a time which converts the transcendental subjects of the movement-image into wanderers who remain in a perpetual state of powerlessness[4] – similarly constitutes Deleuze's second great foundation of the cinematic modern. The latter is one that is based on Nietzsche's nihilist position and the critique of enlightened reason as developed by both post-war French intellectuals and the Frankfurt School of thought (the latter becoming hegemonic in Germany from the 1950s and later in

---

[4] Take, for example, Antonioni's trilogy 'on modernity and its discontent'; Herzog's Kaspar Hauser, Rossellini's Edmund, or my reading of Buñuel's kids in *Los olvidados*.

the USA under the name of Critical Theory).[5] It is, as Thomas suggests, a dual breakdown of humanity's centring in history and consciousness that Deleuze's modern characters advance. The focus, then, is on the fracture of the subject and the traumatic experiences associated with the loss of absolutes, or the *a priori* consciousness inherited from the Enlightenment. But these breakdowns of representation and failures in action proper to Deleuze's post-war characters are also distinctive of a human decentring that, as Freud spoke of in his lecture on the fragmentation of the sovereign human consciousness, belongs to three previous historical displacements: that of Copernicus in astronomy; Darwin in biology; and his own in the workings of the psyche. As E. Ann Kaplan and Ban Wang summarise it in their introduction to *Trauma and Cinema* (2008), the decline of Deleuze's God-like subjects in the movement-image can be traced back in history with:

> the discovery that the earth, the homeland of humans, is but 'a tiny fragment of a cosmic system of scarcely imaginable vastness', a humiliating blow associated with the name of Copernicus. The second is the devastating knowledge that God-like and God-creating humans are but descendants from the monkeys.[6] The third blow comes from the [psychoanalytical] revelation (. . .) that the ego is not the 'master of its own house', but must content itself with whatever little it can glimpse from the depths of itself. (2008, 3)

From a world-theological and world-theoretical perspective, the 'inhumanity' of Deleuze's modernity falls into an evolutionary tendency towards the lost centre and the experience of the unthinkable that the philosopher only discusses with the emergence of post-war films around 1945. It is only at this stage that the previous scientific decentring of human consciousness in Europe begins to take place in his modernity of the time-image. As Deleuze states:

> [The] revolution that took place in philosophy over centuries from the Greeks to Kant [that of time no longer being subordinated to movement, but movement being subordinated to time] (. . .) was achieved by the cinema under faster conditions (. . .) The movement-image of so-called 'classic' cinema was replaced after the war by a direct time-image (. . .) Time ceased to be the measure of normal movement; it increasingly appeared for itself and created paradoxical movements. (1988/2007, 356)

---

[5] For further discussion, see Adorno and Horkheimer [1947] 2002.
[6] Actually, Darwin did not say this. He said that humans and chimpanzees shared a common ancestor, and that they evolved differently (that is, they 'differentiated') from this common mother-ape. Moreover, all apes and monkeys shared a more distant relative, which lived about 25 million years ago.

Perhaps for these reasons, some critics have also regarded the classical/modern binary set up by Deleuze as an artificial 'new point of departure' that helps him, as well as Bazin and the critics of *Cahiers du cinéma* before him, to make 'the fragmentary and the open' an almost exclusive 'French post-war invention' (Losilla 2012) – thus disregarding the previous breakdowns of narrative in supposedly classical films by Keaton's 'comedies of the mind' (Perez 1998, 92–122), Minnelli's 'ars poetics' (Rancière 2014, 71–84), or Buñuel's 'nomadism', as discussed in Chapter 2.

The concept of the intensive-image, which does not divide but runs through and brings together the pre-war/classical and post-war/modern, is one that certainly takes its cues from this critique. It is an image that affirms the nowhere, this increasingly infinite outside from which the experience of modernity began in science, and which so affectively has displaced the ordinary viewer of cinema from the centre to the margin. Here, 'by thinking of cinema this way', as Schefer reflects on early film culture, 'all I've learned is this':

> In the midst of all that is *solid* in the world, and of all images, a new substance becomes *sensible*. This substance grips me, not through the suggestion of actions, or through the repetition of movements, but because it affects the sight – the entire responsibility of the visible – of all the phenomena and the events the thought of which is characterized by their prior-body and their preliminary, incomplete figure. Here, the [cinematic] visible is new because it constitutes an act of thinking rather than an object of thought. Such matter, taken up in a new movement retains the tremor of an inchoative thought but not its product. (2016, 207)

El Sueño de la Razón Produce Monstruos[7]

Along with Kant's dual experience of modernity – that is, in the transcendental subject (*Cinema 1*) whose fractures occur within the self, in the 'I' which thinks (*Cinema 2*) – the notion of the modern has also been predicated by other philosophers upon the emergence of the Enlightenment.[8] Max Weber, for example, also sees modernity as a world that orients itself towards secular actions and scientific reasoning, hence as a reality that displaces the 'great enchanted garden of religion' for a disenchanted form of rationality that, as he says, befits the 'iron cage of the modern[s]' (1922/1963, 166–83). It is, to express it in a biblical manner, the swapping of the God of St Thomas Aquinas – an omniscient creator – for

---

[7] 'The Sleep of Reason Produces Monsters', Francisco de Goya.
[8] Enlightenment is understood here as a rational consciousness that distances itself and the subject from the univocity of Being proposed by the Aristotelian triad of the Truth, the Good and the Beautiful.

the laments of Job in his theodicy, someone who, being perplexed and confronted with a world that no longer has any sense of universal justice, asks God: Why if I do right, things go wrong? Why do bad things happen to good people? In Weber's post-religious era, the individual is led, quite inevitably, to think and to act upon a world that is radically contingent and cruel: why are things no longer the way they used, and *ought*, to be?

As a cinematic counterpart to Weber's disenchanted form of modernity, Tarkovsky's *Andrei Rublev* (1966) portrays a similar traumatic loss of classical certainties and religious absolutes. Based on the metaphysical quests, ethical dilemmas and aesthetic struggles of the Russian icon, the filmmaker obscures the medieval journeys of his character, who, being at once philosopher, monk and artist, is incapable of connecting with the Truth, the Good and the Beautiful, as in Aristotle's Being. In episode V, *The Last Judgment*, Rublev is unable to complete his religious fresco, mainly because of the uneasiness of his state of mind; or in the subsequent episode *The Raid*, after killing the Russian soldier to save his orphan friend, he decides to give up painting and takes a vow of silence for more than a decade. Also in episode VI, while envisioning a conversation with his dead friend Theophanes the Greek, Rublev utters a lament that in many regards echoes that of the book of Job: 'Why is there so much evil in mankind and in my own soul?' The film closes with an epilogue in colour (the previous episodes were all shot in black and white) depicting some of Rublev's most iconic artworks; all masterpieces that were nonetheless incomplete and unresolved in Tarkovsky's adaptation due to the confused visions, and spiritual fractures, of his protagonist.[9]

---

[9] Another philosopher who clearly brings this sense of disjointedness and terror in the modern industrial era is Karl Marx. He is probably the thinker who most strongly showed the irrationality of reason under his critique of capitalism – namely, the individual's loss of control over their own productive activity. For Marx, there are three interconnected inversions that put the rational paradigm of the Enlightenment, and thus the modern subject, to work against itself. The first two, both related to the phenomenon of consciousness, are those of alienation and fetishism. Alien means, precisely, foreign, a state of estrangement, a form of consciousness that cannot identify its own presence in reality. Alienation, therefore, not only in relation to a specific mode of production but more critically in relation to the very condition of humanity that is put at risk by such an economic activity. Hence, the famous Marxist distinction (never made by Marx himself though) between *homo faber* – the rational agent who takes control of their own destiny – and the *animal laborans* that the impoverished proletariat becomes in the industrial monetary landscape (Arendt 1998). The second inversion, which also designates a reified form of consciousness, is that of Marx's commodity fetishism: exchange-value over use-value; material relations among people and social relations among things. And from this follows the most critical and general of his inversions, which is that of the modern monetary economy. Because if capitalism is based on exchange-value and commodification, then such an activity necessarily requires of an equivalent or general measure to trade its products, so that things are no longer compared to other things in the marketplace but to the one and only thing that is stripped of all its use-value, namely money. For Marx, therefore, the

For Deleuze, however, such a crisis of the Enlightened subject is rather celebrated by his (post)modern artists who expand the means of what is possible in life. It is a sensible overturning of the paradigm of reason that many French thinkers writing in the second half of the twentieth century were developing, including Jean-Paul Sartre's existentialism, Guy Debord's situationism and Jacques Derrida's post-structuralist critique. However, it is probably next to Foucault's and Deleuze's views on madness and the arts that the whole principle of rationality starts to be 'shattered from within'. Influenced by the artist-philosopher who went mad in Turin, Foucault's and Deleuze's questions surrounding the relationship between philosophy, insanity and the arts can be echoed by Nietzsche's nihilism: '[If] we philosophers should become sick, surrender a while to sickness, body and soul – and as it were, shut our eyes to ourselves' (Nietzsche 1974, 34).

So, what is this relationship between madness, philosophy and art? Certainly, as in Foucault's deviant subjects which I will further investigate in my reading of *The Lobster* in the next chapter, Deleuze's 'mutant characters' of the time-image are also confronting the rational paradigm of *modernity 1* by way of a creative difference or insanity that is able to de-schematise reason. It is a subjective, nihilist position that both authors share and which threatens the hegemonic status of Truth by means of art. In the case of Foucault, such a critique is heard from the epistemic possibilities that the mentally ill entail for his theory of knowledge, especially in regard to his analysis of bourgeois society in eighteenth-century Europe. This is a period of vast exclusions and confinement in which not only madmen are thrown into asylums, but also criminals into prisons and homeless into refuges. Here, to say that deviance is marginalised and made invisible means basically that the very condition of humanity starts to be defined by the principle of rationality itself, so that everything and everyone that falls outside of the rational paradigm becomes, *stricto sensu*, delegitimised. Francisco de Goya's paintings *Casa de locos* (1812–19) and *Corral de locos* (1793),[10] or his series of prints *Caprichos* (1797–8) and engravings *Disparates* (1815–24), are some of the visual representations accounting for Foucault's modern paradigm: 'Through Sade and Goya', he says at the end of *Madness and Civilization* (1961/1988), 'the Western

primary evidence of modernity is not the fact that the earth goes around the sun, as in Copernicus's discovery, but that money goes around the earth. His modern terror, as in Kant, is one that dislocates the rational subject as the centre of social and productive relations (i.e. the principle of *adequatio*) for a universal God-value that fetishises and misfits their reality.

[10] *Yard with Lunatics* is, in fact, the cover image for the new English edition of Foucault's genealogy of madness, *History of Madness* (2009).

world received the possibility of transcending its reason in violence, and of recovering tragic experience beyond the promises of the dialectics' (1988, 285).

On the side of Deleuze, on the other hand, madness and the arts transcend reason in characters who see the milieu differently and in its entirety. Art, in this sense, becomes for both a mode of thinking that deconstructs the premises of Western rationality by means of sensible encounters with intensities – the differential in thought. However, what interests Foucault in his genealogical approach to deviance is not so much the artistic genius behind Deleuze's mutant characters but the complete nihilistic position of the mentally ill, as the lunatic who turns every encounter into one of misrecognition: *This is not a finger, Theaetetus, but an elephant!* In both of these cases, then, what gets inverted is the principle of Kantian *adequatio*, as it is this sovereign rational consciousness that is no longer corresponding to those objects it apprehends. 'Thinking', says Deleuze in reference to Foucault 'means reaching non-stratification. Seeing is thinking, speaking is thinking, but thinking itself takes place in the gap, in the disjunction between seeing and speaking' (1984/2007, 258). This gap is the split in thought and in temporality itself that announces the emergence of the time-image. Drawing on Astruc as well as on Blanchot, Deleuze suggests that the fissure in the thinker is the primary novelty of modern cinema:

> It is not a matter of following a chain of images, even across voids, but of getting out of the chain or the association. Film ceases to be 'images in a chain (. . .) an uninterrupted chain of images each one the slave of the next', and whose slave we are. *It is the method of BETWEEN*, 'between two images', which does away with all cinema of the One. *It is the method of AND*, *'this and then that'*, *which does away with all the cinema of Being = is*. Between two visual images, between two sound images, between the sound and the visual: make the indiscernible, that is the frontier, visible. (2013, 185; my emphasis)

As I have argued previously, such failure in language or irrepresentability of thinking in Deleuze's post-war cinema is also manifested in the gaps, or incongruencies, of pre-war intensive-images. This image, which claims to undo Deleuze's organic associations of the classical 'cinema of Being = is', is also one that affirms the interstice, or the 'in between two images', in a form of difference that is freed from solid measure, thus incorporating the cracks of the Nietzschean thinker into a previous sequence of the modern. This is, precisely, the decentring of human consciousness that can also be found in the workings of the psyche (Freud), secular culture (Weber), industrial society (Marx) and the work of art (Foucault and Deleuze). It is, to put it simply, an image that confronts thought in virtue of all the indeterminacy that thinking is, and in so doing, intensities that create doubts about the reality we perceive onscreen. Cinema, in this sense, becomes the modern art par excellence – that is, the 'art of the fragment', to employ Perez's terms:

> The fragmentary view characteristic of our modernity has been, Raymond Williams says, especially characteristic of film. Film is indeed an art of the fragment: a painting is a whole, a theatre stage is a whole, but on the movie screen we see merely a part, a piece of a larger field extending indefinitely beyond our view. (1998, 302–3)

In what follows, the notion of cinematic intensity which bridges Deleuze's divide between the two periods will be examined under a classical/modern image that simultaneously looks backward and forward in time. This is what Nietzsche calls the 'untimely' and which I will discuss under the notion of the 'contemporaneous' as developed by Deleuze, Godard and Lacan.

The Intensive-Image and the Idea of the Contemporaneous

Is not Deleuze's method of 'in between' also the type of intervallic image developed by Aby Warburg in 1924 – the surrealist art historian who, overcoming a severe psychosis in Germany, set the foundations for a new theory of knowledge by interconnecting classical and modern ways of seeing? Warburg's (unfinished) *Mnemosyne Atlas*, which I previously associated with Buñuel's nomadic vision, sheds new light here in thinking of the intensive-image as a continuous succession of breaks, in the sense that it opens up the interval as the displacing operation common to both the classical movement-image and modern time-image and not just as a method specific to the later new system. It is, similar to Foucault's *History of Madness* (1961/2009), a genealogical approach to deviance that deepens through time, and which Foucault describes in terms of a 'heterotopic space' that questions official truths by its 'disruptive and intense' faculties.

Connecting Warburg's heteronomous atlas with Deleuze's time of *Aiôn*, which is an encompassing temporality that goes beyond the historical (that is, a time of becoming rather than the ages of the world), the image theorist Georges Didi-Huberman, while thinking about intensities, similarly describes Foucault's heterotopia as those:

> uninterrupted area[s] of crises and deviance, [as] concrete arrangements of incompatible places and heterogeneous times (...) actual machines of the imagination that create a space of illusion which accuses all real space, all locations inside which human life is compartmentalized, as being far more illusory. (2011/2018, 55–6)

Such a site of the mismatched stands here for the intensities generated by Warburg's (and Deleuze's) method of the interval – as in Foucault's peripheral worlds within official spaces that upset dominant orders and texts, ranging from his gardens of antiquity to his marginalised brothels in the modern West. Heterotopia, in Didi-Huberman's reading, is thus akin to those 'incompatible places and heterogeneous times' populating Deleuze's cinemas under what I call the intensive-image. This is a rebellious image upsetting (b)orders, one which, echoing Warburg comments in his speech of 1912, may be said to 'range freely, with no fear of border guards, and can treat the ancient, medieval, and modern worlds as a coherent historical unity [als zusammenhängende Epoche]' (quoted in Didi-Huberman 2000/2017, 328). So, if Warburg's method is at all needed in this book it is because his *Mnemosyne Atlas* portrays a similar 'way of visually unfolding the discontinuities of time throughout all of history' (2017, 311); thus, as I have argued, an image that breaks with the dogmatic thinking about the cinematic past instead of making a break with such a past. It is, in other words, a differential movement that reintegrates those heterogeneous elements of Deleuze's time-image system into the rationalism embedded in his previous 'classical' act.

Warburg's iconology of the interval thus presupposes a theory of the intensive-image that recognises or is rather constituted by a time that is in itself intervallic and heteronomous. Echoing Borges's short story 'Death and the Compass' (1956/1962), we can think of the intensive-image as that 'singular straight line' which is 'labyrinthic and everlasting,'[11] and which Didi-Huberman connects directly to Deleuze's temporality of *Aiôn*:

> By adjoining the paradoxes of Borges and the Stoic idea of temporality, Deleuze succeeds in making us understand something essential in the idea of [Warburg's] atlas that I am hoping to construct here: What happens in the paradoxical space of the different 'tables of Borges' is possible only because a paradoxical time affects all the events that happen to it. This time is neither linear, nor continuous (. . .): Instead, it is 'infinitely subdivisible' and is 'to be parceled out'. This time is the Stoic *Aiôn* placed by Deleuze in opposition to measurable *Chronos*: time 'at the surface' – or at the table – of which events are, he says, 'gathered as effects'. This is how 'each present is divided into past and future, ad infinitum', according to a 'labyrinth' whose forms Borges would invent. (2018, 58–9)

Stoic *Aiôn*, or what Deleuze calls the 'untimely' and the 'contemporaneous', is defined by the philosopher as an 'empty present' (2015, 66) that

---

[11] 'I know of a Greek labyrinth which is a single straight line (. . .) The next time I kill you. Along this line so many philosophers have lost themselves that a mere detective might well do so too (. . .) I promise you the labyrinth made of the single straight line which is invisible and everlasting' (Borges 1962, 82).

is infinitely subdivisible between 'that which has just happened and that which is about to happen, but never that which is happening' (2015, 8). Of course, in its colloquial usage, contemporaneity comes to represent almost its opposite, namely, the manifestation of a presence in the present, like two events happening in the same historical 'now'. From its Latin etymology, contemporaneity reads 'together with' [*con*] plus 'time' [*temporaneous*] which I take to affirm rather than negate Deleuze's conception of *Aiôn* as an empty form of the present (as much as *Aiôn*, following the Greeks, is understood as 'timeless being', meaning 'vital force' or intensity). Here, Deleuze's notion of the untimely qua contemporaneity, which is a singular temporal line that never dies, is also informing those unlimited mutations of Nietzsche's becoming in the work of art that I have been referring to in this book. Indeed, it is in his 'return to Nietzsche' – a philosophy that is neither dialectical nor historical but *creative* – where Deleuze discusses contemporariness as that trans-temporal dimension of thought which operates by virtual presence (*Aiôn*) rather than by measurable actual presents (*Chronos*).[12] And this is the reason why, I believe, the untimely thinker must confront an 'always limited present' (2015, 64) by means of art.[13] As Deleuze explains in an interview conducted in 1967, it is through Nietzsche's resistance to the present that the philosopher-artist reinterprets the world and 'announce[s] an exodus from today's desert':

> The masters according to Nietzsche are *the untimely*, those who create, who destroy in order to create, not to preserve. Nietzsche says that under the huge earth-shattering events are tiny silent events, which he links to the creation of new worlds: there once again you see the presence of the poetic under the historical. In France, for instance, there are no earth-shattering events right now. They are far away, and horrible, in Vietnam. But we still have tiny imperceptible events, which may announce an exodus from today's desert. Maybe the return to Nietzsche is one of those 'tiny events' and already a reinterpretation of the world. (1956/2004c, 130)

To resist the present thus means not only to confront the actual historical time in which we live but all the times of dominant history. This

---

[12] Referring to his Stoic conception of temporality, Deleuze reminds us in his 'Tenth Series of the Ideal Game' that: 'We have seen that past, present, and future were not at all three parts of a single temporality, but that they rather formed two readings of time, each one of which is complete and excludes the other: on the one hand, the always limited present, which measures the actions of bodies as causes and the states of their mixtures in depth (Chronos); on the other, the essentially unlimited past and future, which gather incorporeal events, at the surface, as effects (Aion)' (2015, 64). For further reading, see *Logic of Sense* (2015, 61–8).

[13] See, in this regard, Goya's painting: *Saturn Devouring His Son*. Saturn, as we know, is the Roman name given to the Greek myth of Titan Cronus, the youngest of the divine Titans who represented in antiquity the measuring of time.

is, in philosophy, the heterotopic discourse of Judith Butler today, or Foucault in the previous century. They become untimely archers who send their (Nietzschean) arrows towards the darkness of our feverish world: 'Nietzsche opposes history not to the eternal but to the sub-historical or super-historical: the Untimely which is another name for haecceity [and] becoming' (Deleuze and Guattari 2005, 295). Or as expressed by Nietzsche himself in the *Untimely Meditations*:

> This meditation is itself untimely, because it seeks to understand as an illness, a disability, and a defect something which this epoch is quite rightly proud of, that is to say, its historical culture, because I believe that we are all consumed by the fever of history and we should at least realize it. (Quoted in Agamben 2009, 40)

Such a creative force of the untimely, its disconnection or out-of-datedness to the present, is another term to designate the non-representative drive of the intensive-image in cinema. As a poetic language which unfolds the differential gestures of cinematic classicism and modernism, intensity comes to represent a category which disturbs closed sensory-motor arrangements in a movement that becomes incommensurable – that is, an experience of the unthinkable that produces the intensive shock in the viewer. This caesura in the image and in temporality itself which Deleuze claims is specific to his modern regime of art is what I have traced back to the early days of the moving image (and the vividness of infancy), thus establishing a certain continuity among Deleuze's *ante* and *post* periods under the permanency of cinema's affective powers. The intensive-image, which I have described earlier under different film texts, is one that consists precisely in seeing classical and modern periods as one continuous iconology of the interval, very much in the style of Warburg's *Mnemosyne Atlas* where the author interrelates Antiquity and Renaissance's avant-garde objects in a dismantling (and renewing) pictorial manner.

Being contemporary, in this differential and originary (new) sense, is thus establishing a close relationship with origins. A 'classic', after all, represents in philosophy the permanence of a question in history (e.g. the idea of Being, or the Aristotelian question of 'What is?') as much as its original posing in a specific time and space (e.g. the era of *theoria* launched by the ancient Greeks). In cinema, quite similarly, a classic, which never dies, not only stands for those pioneering filmmakers working in the early days of the medium, but more broadly includes all of those creators who have brought, at various intervals of its history, the new language of film. This is the case, among others, of Dreyer's intense close-ups and disconnected spaces in *The Passion of Joan of Arc* (1928); Peixoto's ellipses in *Limite* (1931); Deren's choreographic movements in *Ritual in Transfigured*

Time (1945–6); Godard's archeological montage in *Histoire(s) du cinema* (1989–99);[14] or Costa's poetic obscurity as seen in his most recent film *Vitalina Varela* (2019) – no doubt a future classic.

In this line, Jacques Lacan's definition of contemporariness is probably the closest to my own definition of an origin in cinema. 'In order to be contemporary', as A. J. Bartlett, Justin Clemens and Jon Roffe suggest in relation to Lacan, 'it is necessary to return to the origin' (2014, 9). That origin, for a psychoanalyst, bears the name of Sigmund Freud: 'albeit not so much to the latter's key propositions, but to the new fault-lines – "problems"? "questions"? – that those propositions at once open and occlude' (2014, 9). Similar remarks are highlighted by Martin Heidegger who states that the problem of Being in philosophy (or the problem of the Real in Lacan) always repeats itself by revealing the primordial possibilities contained in the original question, so that Being represents at once the revelation of an origin (hidden in the initial question), as well as its transformation via the line of the problematic. In analogous terms, the intensive-image, which is based on Nietzsche's thermodynamic power to metamorphose, is similarly said to return (eternally!) to that primal source or energy,[15] so that intensity is what preserves, while mutating, the inherent problems contained in the original cinematic *phántasma*.[16]

Put differently, it is next to the origin or the archaic that the contemporaneous connects to the original and the new. It is a fleeing trajectory that, while looking forward, is also glimpsing backward in time, very much like Walter Benjamin's reading of the monoprint by Paul Klee *Angelus Novus* (1920), which the philosopher describes in terms of a contemporary artwork whose face 'is turned towards the past [while also looking] into the future' (quoted in Sennett 2018, 311). As Giorgio Agamben suggests in *What is an Apparatus?* (2006/2009):

---

[14] It is precisely Godard, our 'contemporary', who once said that 'in cinema the *present* never exists, except in bad films' (quoted in Deleuze 2013, 38; my emphasis)

[15] On the topic of clothed repetition and the origin of the question, Deleuze quotes Heidegger and claims that, in this point, he has become a Nietzschean: 'By a repetition of a fundamental problem we understand the disclosure of the primordial possibilities concealed in it. The development of these possibilities has the effect of transforming the problem and thus preserving it in its import as a problem. To preserve a problem means to free and safeguard its *intrinsic powers, which are the source of its essence and which makes it possible as a problem*. The repetition of the possibilities of a problem, therefore, is not a simple taking up of that which is "in vogue" with regards to this problem ... The possible, thus understood, in fact hinders all genuine repetition and thereby all relation to history...' (2014, 263). For further discussion, see Chapter 4, 'Ideas and the Synthesis of Difference', in Deleuze, *Difference and Repetition* (2014, 223–92).

[16] This is the Greek word calling upon the appearance of the image; a phantom, apparition or ghost that becomes the true life of intensity.

> Contemporariness inscribes itself in the present by marking it above all as archaic. Only [s]he who perceives the indices and signatures of the archaic in the most modern and recent can be contemporary. 'Archaic' means close to the *arkhē*, that is to say, the origin. (2009, 50)

To summarise what has been argued so far, which combines Deleuze's notion of the untimely with Lacan's return to (an original idea in) Freud, contemporariness paves its way not so much in direct relationship or at ease with an actual cinematic present, or in mere belonging to a specific historical past, but in proximity or immediacy with a gigantic cinematic atlas which moves, and is formed, by the intensive coexistence of all its parts; the old – archaic – parts that allow for the new in the image, and the new – modern – parts that repeat and subvert the original act (by intensifying the unequal hidden in the previous sequence). This is, in short, the task of contemporariness and the intensive-image: to collect and recollect what has been lost, or effaced, and renovate it into something new – a singular straight line which never dies. As a mathematician would probably have it, the intensive-image is one that transforms itself by manifesting a topological continuity along its path, bending and stretching through time, and yet, this sense of plasticity or multiplicity is localised, every time, in the singular intervals of its trajectory, classical *and* modern.

This is, in similar terms, the type of intensities of the infinite established by Alain Badiou in *L'immanence des vérités* (2018), his third and latest volume of *Being and Event*. The aim of Badiou's book, recently translated into English, is to take us from the 'constructable universe' that we live in into the absoluteness of a larger 'non-constructible infinite' which stands for the class of all sets of his 'V' (the mathematical image for 'Vérité'). Here, what Badiou does is to rework his cumulative hierarchy of axioms-truths under the V of set theory to suggest that each of the sets within this figure (our constructable universes or actuality) touches on a certain notion of infinity, thus allowing us to re-index the different sets or ages of the world according to a principle of absoluteness, intensity or eternity.

In this capacity, like the movement of the intensive-image differentiating from the silent film period to the present, Badiou's movement also gathers force from the smallest (local) infinity at the bottom of his V0 to the largest (generic) infinity at the top of the V, thus making up the whole structure of his notion of the 'Absolute'. His V, as in Bergson, represents here a virtual and inverted cone that connects all of the sets through its singular points in the curve, that is a 'Whole that changes and never stop changing' (2018, 51–75). In discussing "the gigantic memory' that makes up the entire schema of Bergson's thesis on *Creative Evolution* and *Matter and Memory*, Deleuze illustrates a similar 'geometrical cone' to suggest that each of its sections, all virtual parts, incarnate the singular 'divergent lines' that make possible the actualisation of the different sections of the cone (2014, 276). In this way, and whether we take Badiou's mathematical V with its multiple axiomatic *vérités* or Bergson's inverted cone with its various *virtual* sections, what both models suggest is an image of intensity that differentiates precisely by preserving and prolonging the past into the present, hence an image that gets more complex from the first phase of modernity in *Cinema 1* to its second 'set' or period in *Cinema 2*.

In a sort of audiovisual counterpart to this intensifying continuity, we could also trace the virtual points outlined by Bergson in Jean-Luc Godard's last two film periods; that is to say, in his first militant period, at the moment when he gets involved with the Marxist collective group (the Dziga Vertov group, around the mid-1960s and early 1980s), and his second – more essayistic – period, which commences, roughly speaking, in the mid-1980s, a few years before the publication of his book and video essay *Histoire(s) du cinéma* (1988–98). In the former, as Deleuze mentions, Godard's preoccupation is mainly concerned with the political transformations of his post-war age. On the topic of *Two or Three Things I Know About Her* (Godard 1967), which is a dramatised *vérité* film that mediates on the Vietnam War and the turbulent situations in the streets of Paris during the 1960s, Deleuze claims that Godard intends 'to observe [political] mutations' and further adds that his cinema 'become[s] completely political, but in another way' (2013, 20). Deleuze's approach to the 'politics of the modern image' is well known. His interest relies on transforming the truthful world of Platonic representation into the falsifying functions of a Nietzschean philosophy – that is, a cinema of purely optical and sound situations devoid of rational, sensory-motor associations. And these are, in Deleuze's words, the 'huge [political] forces of disintegration' (2013, 19) released by the French filmmaker. In fact, as Godard himself mentions in relation to his characters in *Band of Outsiders* (1964): 'These are people who are real and it's the world that is a breakaway group. It is the world that is making cinema for itself. It is the world that is out of synch' (quoted in Deleuze 2013, 177).

Now, what exactly happens with Godard's more reflective second period if we claim that his previous (New Wave) phase had already established this kind of Nietzschean cinema under his political forces of disintegration? What happens to his (or Deleuze's) 'method of between'? Here I suggest that it is in the image-gaps of Godard's latter phase that his cinema becomes intensified in a more essayistic method, one that develops from *Histoire(s) du cinema* onwards, including *Film Socialism* (2010), *Goodbye to Language* (2014) and *The Image Book* (2018). This method is achieved by means of an archaeological montage-technique that combines old and new media as well as the cinema's intrinsic relationship to the other arts. And in revealing such a composite structure of the moving image, as Badiou would probably suggest, what Godard does is to *take* a bundle of statements and conventions from the previous arts, in the sense that he orchestrates and makes explicit references to the world of literature, painting, photography and music, all of which help him to create a deep trans-historical mediation on the status of art and the filmic image: 'a retrospective and prospective mediation on what cinema is and what the image is' (Badiou 2013, 167).[17]

Such intertextuality of Godard's method, bears direct resemblance to Warburg's *Mnemosyne Atlas*, which is a similar archaeological technique of cinematic arrangement that brings anew classical and modern images by way of their combinatorial potential. Commenting on Warburg's approach to Antiquity and the Renaissance period, Dimitros Latsis suggests that Godard's *Histoire(s) du cinéma* portrays a similar overall vision on the history of cinema in connection to the previous arts:

> [*Histoire(s) du cinéma*] is laid out in episodic format and in it Godard compiles clips of old films and newsreel, photographs, stills, reproductions of paintings, new footage, music, narration and commentary, primarily by him (we also see him at his typewriter 'orchestrating' the whole enterprise) and superimposed titles, all manipulated and edited with wipes, superimpositions, crosscuts and every other technique imaginable. The historian-artist deals with a wide variety of subjects from film and politics to globalization, memory, genocide, art and God. Treating the screen like a page or a canvas Godard creates an end-product that is both dazzling and bewildering and which aims, according to Raymond Bellour, to incorporate in a singular articulation 'the creation of film, the creation of the world, [and] the history of the creation of cinema'. (2013, 778)

Such a genealogical montage-technique put forward by Warburg's and Godard's visualisations of history through the work of art, shares the same trans-temporal connections of the intensive-image. By creating a temporal line based on the fractures, missing links or hidden gestures of the image, both 'historian-artists' are showing the intensities of an

---

[17] Badiou would probably agree here that in Godard, Deleuze's division between artificial time and real *durée* reaches a creative synthesis combining the two different conceptions of time and the image, for as Badiou would say in in relation to Murnau's films, especially *Sunrise* (1927): 'In the greatest films you can absolutely show how moments of pure duration are inscribed within the "assembled" construction of time (...) In the final analysis, what cinema offers, and I think it is the only art that does so, is the possibility of the presence of pure duration within temporal construction, which can really be termed a new synthesis' (2013, 213).

avant-garde, cinematic reflection throughout its audiovisual elements that mount the dissimilar into a combinatorial 'series of series'. As this sort of gigantic cinematic method which is arranged under specific heterogeneous signs, the intensive-image and its differential tendency equally leads to the virtual coexistence of all its parts: the archaic preserved in the modern, and the modern incorporated in the classical. Thus, as this chapter has argued, the concept of the intensive-image presupposes a theory of the cinema that treats 'old' and 'new' sequences in terms of a crystalline or intervallic unity that intensifies throughout history. This image, which in itself constitutes the differential – or what Warburg calls the 'the interval' – will be discussed in the following section under contemporary filmmakers, and their works, which have expanded upon the indeterminate potential and dynamic nature of the concept of intensity.

Section Two

The Politics and Poetics of the Intensive-Image in Contemporary Cinema

CHAPTER 5

Resistance in *The Lobster*: Mapping an Intensive-Image in Contemporary Popular Film

The film *The Lobster*, a surreal comedy that satirises the ideological formation of the couple, portrays three different spaces to represent the conformism of romantic and political alliances in contemporary culture. This tripartite structure, used to present a dystopic parody of the notion of coupledom, is composed in the film by a city-space, a hotel-space, and a forest-space, all of which I investigate under an oppressive programme of events which varies, ideologically, according to the specific rules of each of the film's spaces.

Firstly, following *The Lobster*'s itinerary, the city appears as the central space, not just because it is in here that the story opens and ends, but also because it is from here that the whole action of the film will be dominated and shaped. Early on in *The Lobster*, we discover that an urban edict enforces David (Collin Farrell), the main protagonist, to move to a policed hotel in the countryside. This space works as a reformatory-like institution set up exclusively for matchmaking and to punish single individuals – that is, all of those who are single, widowed or divorced. Like David, a middle-aged man who has recently been abandoned by his wife in the city, Singles are obliged to look for a partner in the hotel within forty-five days or be turned into an animal of their own choosing. Here, individuals who appear without a companion are policed and turned into an animal that, as the manager-in-chief (Olivia Colman) informs, 'no one would like to be'. The partner must be someone who shares a key characteristic as oneself such as a nosebleed or a passion for skiing or studying social sciences. Coupledom, in this way, becomes juridically determined by an urban edict that is administered by the fortress-like resort.

In mapping such an alliance, the connection between the two spaces will be drawn under the issue of surveillance as developed by Foucault; a route that, as I hope to show, will link his (modern) disciplinary institutions within the normalising powers of Lanthimos's dystopic society. Lastly, the third zone to be analysed in this map, one that works as an 'outlaw' community run by fugitive Loners in the forest,[1] will express a political detour from the previous ensemble by imposing an opposite yet equally despotic prohibition – that placed on romantic relationships of any kind. Unfortunately, for David, who escapes from the hotel to the wilderness after failing to stay up to date with the villa's regulations (once his concubinage with the heartless woman (Angeliki Papoulia) comes to a bloody, violent end) he will fall in love with a Loner in the forest where everything is permitted except for love and sex. His destiny, once again, will put him at odds with the oppressive practices of an alternative, fugitive regime. Rachel Weisz, who plays the role of David's short-sighted lover and who also delivers the film's voice-over commentary, summarises this sense of ideological oppression in a similar way:

> I think the movie is about the way we live sheep-like following rules and ideologies without questioning them, and even the people in this story who rebel against the dominant ideology end up building their own rules, so I think it asks the question how do you live originally, how do you live thinking outside of the rules that are prescribed to us[?] (Quoted in Bradshaw, 2015)

The geopolitical map proposed in this chapter will thus be determined via three spatial and extensive parts: the city at the centre of the story, the hotel in one axis and the forest in its opposite other; the latter two being micro-segments of the city that, by way of antagonistic ideologies, are placed 'in war against each other' (Zoro 2017, 3). This is the closed Pythagorean triple that Javier Zoro develops in his article '¿Qué es lo que me hace decir te amo?'[2] to envision the possibility of an emancipatory 'politics of lovance' through the act of resistance in the film. By mapping these controlling spaces, Zoro reads David's becoming not as his chosen 'lobster metamorphosis' that the film's title seems to be suggesting, but more interestingly as the possibility of finding in love, in *blindly* loving someone, that original and reciprocal law which questions and goes beyond any other social contract. His approach, which connects the fervent sentiment of loving with its own incorporeal capacity to transform (David chooses to become a lobster if he fails), equally reveals the poetics and politics of the intensive-image under an alternative displacing map – that of the two lovers' secret relationship and their 'maritime-becoming' while living in the forest. Such a map will look in greater depth at those unforeseeable gestures put at play by the film's main couple; that is a potential 'line of flight that will carry [them] away, across the segments (. . .) towards a des-

---

[1] The word forest comes from the Latin *foris*, meaning outside; e.g. outside of the city walls.
[2] 'What is it that makes me want to say I love you?'

tination that is unknown' (Deleuze and Parnet 1988–9/2002, 125). This is a cartographic reading that will be echoed once again by the thermodynamic significance Deleuze and DeLanda give to the concept of intensity: 'a zone which is marked not by spatial limits but by critical thresholds [of intensity]' (DeLanda 2010, 116); a poetic and political displacement that upsets order, sameness and control.

In playing its role as the differential, the intensive-image will be identified as the act of resistance against the film's spatial norms. Such an act will be understood in two complementary ways: one that resists the political threats in the film (e.g. the quest of characters to escape from their ruled, despotic spaces); and another that confronts *The Lobster*'s narrative structure by opening the story as a whole through visuals and their soundtrack. Put differently, *The Lobster*'s intensive-image works as a twofold displacing movement: it stands for the unknown destination of the two main lovers, as well as for the potentiality of an image that remains hidden, or blinded, for the look of both characters and viewers. As director Yorgos Lanthimos declares in regard to the film's overture (it is a rainy day in a rural background and we see a woman shooting a donkey from the windshield of her car), this is an image of mental relations that signals some of the unresolved actions of the story to come:

> I like starting the film like that – you set the tone but you don't explain or go back to it. When the film finishes, the viewer can return to the beginning (. . .) and give their own sense or interpretation. (Quoted in Strickland, 2016)

Just after this uncanny moment where an equine creature lies dead on the ground, *The Lobster* opens with a back shot of David who is sitting on a sofa next to Bob, his dog-brother who years ago didn't make it at the resort. Off-screen, his wife tells him that she is leaving him for another man: 'Does he wear glasses or contact lenses', the short-sighted husband asks. The doorbell rings and the shot cuts to a frame of the city where David and Bob walk escorted by two guards in the direction of a white minibus, or ambulance, or patrol. At this moment, we start listening to Beethoven's String Quartet in F Major, Op. 18, No. 1; *Il adagio affettuoso ed appassionato*. The score plays over an as yet unidentified female voice who informs us that David has been left by his wife in the city and thus removed to the hotel where Singles are obliged to find a new partner. The woman's voice, as Sarah Cooper observes, is that of David's short-sighted lover 'who exists in excess (. . .) albeit in the wrong place and at the wrong time according to the laws of the different spaces he inhabits' (2016, 164). Beethoven's *Adagio*, which is inspired by the burial-vault-scene of

Shakespeare's *Romeo and Juliet* (Act 5, scene 3), when Romeo is exiled from the city and put to death by the authorities, clearly resembles and anticipates this love story unfolding later in the film, when the two lovers finally meet in the forest and the viewer realises that 'love is blind, and lovers cannot see' (*The Merchant of Venice*, Act 2, scene 6). And it is also here, next to Beethoven's musical piece, that the first displacement of the geopolitical map comes to fruition; a change of physical location (David's transition from the city centre to the hotel-axis) imposed by the despotic metropolitan command. So, by extending the rule of the *polis* to the rural territory, the hotel will display all of its programmatic agenda to correct and 'normalise' the structure of relations of single individuals.

The Hotel: A Coercive-Administrative Ensemble

In the manner in which Foucault depicts the treatment of delinquency, madness and sexuality in modern regimes of surveillance, the hotel is a disciplinary institution that polices and controls the conduct of its guests. On arrival, the conditions are explicitly set for David, who can stay no longer than forty-five days in a single room. If everything goes well and he finds a partner within this time frame, he will be transferred to a double room for two weeks, then to a yacht for another two (honeymoon) weeks, and finally brought back to the city in the company of his new partner. Coupledom thus becomes the villa's main institutional aim, and the staff will do everything in their power to achieve and safeguard the romantic quest of its guests.

Such is, for example, the rationale behind the coercive mechanisms employed by the manager-in-chief who, after handcuffing David in his room 101 (the same room number as in George Orwell's *1984*, a prison chamber in which citizens' worst fears are manifested and used against them) says to him: 'This is to show you how easy life is when there are two rather than just one'; or when, in the middle of the cafeteria, she burns the hands of lisping Robert (John C. Reilly) with a toaster to show everyone in the hotel the consequences of engaging in compulsive acts of masturbation. It is a visible mechanism of torture – a physically localised relation of power – that represents the archetypical monarch of Foucault's classical period. The villa's manager stands here for the sovereign Queen,[3] who has 'the right to take your life or let you live' but whose physical authority, nonetheless, is largely dependent upon 'what is seen, what is

---

[3] Olivia Colman will literally become the Queen of England in Lanthimos's later film *The Favourite* (2018), and be celebrated for her remarkable performance.

shown, and what is manifested [in the public sphere]' (1977, 55). In other words, since the manager incarnates the Law in *The Lobster*'s society, to violate her orders translates into a direct attack on the city-state. However, as Foucault also declares in *Discipline and Punish* (1977), this public punishment aiming to create fear and restore order among the population, is highly reliant on the visibility of the monarch's body, so that its effects on the whole of society are rather limited, dependent on the presence of the sovereign. That is why, as Foucault goes on to argue, to truly achieve an omnipresent controlling gaze, the modern State[4] sets off to replace the previous 'horrifying spectacles of public torture' (1977, 9) for a more sophisticated disciplinary technique. This is a policing method that substitutes the presence of – and fear towards – the classical ruler for the more invisible procedures of Foucault's panoptical modernity. Here, the philosopher defines the panopticon as a disciplinary, vigilant gaze based on Jeremy Bentham's architectural model for prisons, a space designed to watch the convicts in confinement without them knowing they are being watched. More generally, panopticism becomes for Foucault that modern surveillant apparatus which goes beyond the prison's walls in order to inhabit and 'normalise' the entire functioning of his disciplinary society:

> The judges of normality are present everywhere. We are in the society of the teacher-judge, the doctor-judge, the educator-judge, the social worker-judge; it is on them that the universal reign of the normative is based; and each individual, wherever he may find himself, subjects to it his body, his gestures, his behaviour, his aptitudes, his achievements. The Cerebral network, in its compact or disseminated forms, with its systems of insertion, distribution, surveillance, observation, has been the greatest support, in modern society, of the normalizing power. (1977, 304)

To a fictionalised degree, one could also speak of the villa's administrative ensemble as a panoptical system that supervises, regulates and modifies the conduct of its guests. By exploring 'the things that [visitors] take for granted, the rules that [they] follow and nobody questions', as Lanthimos reflects in one interview (quoted in Johnston, 2015), there is a similar disciplinary principle that could be extracted. Certainly, in *The Lobster*, it is the hotel's staff who normalises the behaviour of its visitors and habituates them into a system of punishment and self-control: 'a type of power that presupposes a closely meshed grid of material coercion rather than the physical existence of a sovereign' (Foucault 1979/2004, 36). This is, on the whole, Foucault's hyper-administrative network operating behind the daily activities run by the resort's team. 'Man eats alone' (where a man

---

[4] Emerging in seventeenth- and eighteenth-century Europe.

chokes on something and dies) and 'woman walks alone' (where a woman is raped at night) theatrically displays the horrors of being single, while 'man eats with woman' (the same man is helped by his wife and survives) and 'woman walks with man' (the same woman walks peacefully next to her lover) reinforces the benefits of being a couple. Nightly dances and sexual intercourse with the villa's maid are also organised by the staff members to motivate their visitors' search for a new partner, and since their match must be based on the principle of resemblance (which is another command imposed by the metropolis), the hotel will do everything it can to help them identify similar characteristics in others that they could match (for example, by running public events such as biographical speech sessions). And finally, a whole list of benefits is outlined (from exclusive hotel facilities to special couple therapies) for those who have successfully paired. This being the case of the limping man (Ben Whishaw) and his nose-bleeding wife (Jessica Barden) who, after facing some marital problems, are given a child in adoption to help them relieve their stress.

In navigating such an ideological structure – a space of daily routines producing docile individuals – it becomes clear, as the film's reviewer Yonca Talu suggests, 'that this is no ordinary Holiday Inn but a severely administrated open prison' (2016, 69). The fact that in arrival visitors are stripped of all their personal belongings and given a uniform set of garments clearly echoes a place where personal expression is not only denied (they all dress the same) but also measured and objectified under the careful watch of a vigilant sentinel. This time, however, the hotel not only epitomises Foucault's modern State as a space of confinement but more broadly integrates Foucault's other policing institutions, such as the hospital, the school and the family unit, to effectively portray his idea of panopticism. 'The clinic' says Foucault, 'owes its real importance to the fact that it is a reorganization in-depth, not only of medical discourse but of the very possibility of a discourse about disease' (1975, xix). The same separation between the norm(al) and what deviates from it is examined under the conjugal family site and its Christian discourses on sexuality, what Foucault calls not only the formative locus of heterosexual desire but also the very 'framework of modern European sexual morality' (quoted in Lenoir and Duschinsky 2012, 20). In either case, whether it is next to the gaze of the doctor, the heterosexual couple or the sentinel, 'society', as Foucault ironically mentions in one of his lectures at the *Collège de France*, 'must be defended':

> You can see that all of these cases – whether it is the market, the confessional, the psychiatric institution, or the prison – involve taking up a history of truth under

different angles, or rather, taking up a history of truth that is coupled, from the start, with a history of law (. . .) This law is nothing other than a prohibition, and the formulation of the prohibition is, of course, an institutional reality. (2004, 35; 254)

At the level of *The Lobster*'s sexual administration, what truly threatens the hotel's regulations and procedures is not so much the dichotomous trajectory of a homosexual/heterosexual body as the polymorphism located on its bisexual queerness. When requested upon arrival to specify his sexual preference, David indicates he likes women. Although, after recalling a homosexual experience he once had in college, David asks whether there is a bisexual option to mark. Straightforwardly, the receptionist of the villa replies: 'I'm afraid you have to decide right now whether you want to be registered as a homosexual or heterosexual.' Forced to answer within the limits of the hotel's 'either/or' structure, David finally checks in as a heterosexual. Minutes after registration, when asked about his shoe size, he is again made to realise that queer, indeterminate states of being will not be tolerated. Being forty-four and a half, David must decide whether to wear shoe size forty-four or forty-five, because, as the villa's maid (Ariane Labed) informs him: 'There're no half sizes in the hotel.'

Whereas for film critic Zoro this rejection of David's 'amorphous body' fits perfectly in the Platonic myth of Aristophanes – whose split identity finds its missing half in the couple/other – for Sarah Cooper, on the contrary, the hotel's dual structuring 'being either/or rather than both/and' (2016, 166) corresponds to the learned functioning of gendered behaviour that is imposed upon us by normative heterosexuality and which Judith Butler questions under her performative sexual body: 'Gender reality is performative which means, quite simply, that it is real only to the extent that it is performed' (1988, 522). Interestingly for Butler, who draws on Foucault's juridical systems to suggest the normalisation of a sexual desire that subsequently individuals 'come to represent in society' (1990, 2), the queering of a body-complex gets *troublesome* as soon as the fluidity of its gender emancipates from those heteronormative frameworks imposed by the Law. It is, as represented in the film, the ab/normal or the differential corpus that must be supervised and 'brought back' into the norm.[5]

---

[5] Lanthimos's filmography, and especially *Dogtooth* (2009), can also be read as a mockery illustration to such a normalising gaze. *Dogtooth* is about a conservative Greek family – a dystopic disciplinary institution – where its over-protective parents isolate their (adult) children in a fenced-off house that they can only leave once their dogtooth falls out. The offspring's world view, as a consequence of this confinement, becomes the expression and extension of their parents' commands. The same rule-bounded structure, reinforced by a different panoptical network, is perceived in *The Lobster*'s hotel administration; it is deviance, once again, that must be examined and normalised under the city-command.

Put differently, it is sameness that is the basic principle for the normative functioning of Lanthimos's and Foucault's society. In the case of *The Lobster*, it is the principle of resemblance which becomes mandatory for the union of couples. This means that matching, the general rule that citizens must obey and follow, necessitates likeness as its specific feature to legitimise any romantic endeavour. Once again, Lanthimos satirises coupledom throughout the film: whether characters share a love for skiing or a similar passion for the social sciences; whether they have a nice voice or a nosebleed, all that matters is to find a suitable partner to bind conjugality in its dominant ancient scheme – that of sameness or Aristophanist familiarity, to some degree: 'If, then, you two are friendly to each other, by some tie of nature', Plato writes in *Lysis*, 'you belong to each other' (quoted in Derrida 2005, 138). Because 'for the man who keeps his eye on a true friend', as Cicero proclaims in *Laelius de Amicitia*, 'keeps it, so to speak, on a model of himself' (quoted in Derrida 2005, 5).

Such an ideal self-image contained in the being of the other, predominant among the ancient Greeks, is also what motivates Cooper to link 'Narcissus and The Lobster' (2015) in her article of the same name. Derrida, who more broadly examines this mythological gaze of the Greeks in his *Politics of Friendship* (2005), similarly deconstructs the philosophical premises of a Western 'true relationship' based on the social bonding between male friends. For Derrida, the fact that in most discourses about friendship – and by extension love – the idea of brotherhood is what informs our filiation with the *polis* (e.g. the oligarch male citizens of the Greek Republic) or with the Modern State (e.g. the Declaration of the *Rights of Man*) not only signals this reciprocal union between male political friends but also, and for the same reason, it is what excludes the female-other from dominant society:

> Fraternity requires a law and names, symbols, a language, engagements, oaths, speech, family and nation (...) Do you not think, dear friend, that the brother is always a brother of alliance, a brother-in-law or an adoptive brother, a foster brother? – And the sister? Would she be in the same situation? Would she be a case of fraternity? (2005, 149)

By the same token, it could be suggested that Lanthimos's tale operates according to a similar code of patriarchal associations; one that by requiring 'a law and names' creates a network of homo-political filiations. This is, however, a difficult hypothesis to sustain. There are at least two reasons for this latter claim. On the one hand, and following the Greeks' phallogocentric model, one rapidly observes that it is mostly men, and not women, who acquire a proper name in the film. It is David, and not his short-sighted partner, his heartless woman or his city-wife, who bears a name. There is even a name for his dog-brother, Bob, his lisping mate, Robert, or his limping friend, John, but no names for their mothers, lovers or female friends. In any case, and however marginal to the story this may be, there is at least one female name to acknowledge there; that of little girl, Elisabeth – John and nosebleed woman's daughter, who happens to appear fleetingly in the film twice. So, properly speaking, the hegemony of the name remains on the side of men. And naming, as Derrida maintains, prevails as an important political oath in the Greek 'democracy of [male] friends' (2005, 306). It is naming then that enacts the minimum condition to perform what he calls a *speech* – that is, to have a voice in the public sphere; it is the *symbol* of equality among the citizens-brothers of both Lanthimos's fictional society and Derrida's ancient Greeks. Not naming would thus signify the exclusion from such a politics of friendship, what I previously linked to the marginalisation of the deviant subject (via Foucault) and which now Derrida locates on the side of the sister-other as the excluded friend from the *polis*-state.

But here is where, on the other hand, the modern Greek filmmaker complicates this political alliance of the traditional friend. Let's pretend, for the sake of the argument, that the female character is indeed someone who remains excluded from the film's political relations – thus, in Lanthimos's society, by not naming the sister, the male character remains faithful to Derrida's model of the canonical friend. But if that were the case, and the sisters were omitted among the citizen-brothers, how come women, and not men, personify the ruler in *The Lobster*'s regimes? Why is it the female character, and not the male, who plays the role of political leader in this seemingly European Empire: one being British (the chief manager in the hotel) and the other being French (the Loners' leader in the forest)? Or could this perhaps signify another form of women's patriarchisation – a kind of 'toxic femininity' – dominating Lanthimos's political filiation in his *polis*? A non-becoming woman of women? A female subject internalised into Foucault's official-judges or Derrida's male-regulated democracy?

The Internal Resonance of Resistance: A Case for the Intensive-Image

The dissymmetry of this operation expresses an aporia of relations that Lanthimos puts at play in his classical/modern fable. Hence, by not cohering its pieces under a firm logical schema, *The Lobster* proposes an internal opposition that questions, on the one hand, the political filiations described under the motto 'only men are brothers in the [W]est' and, on the other hand, the very politics of the film's narrative based on likeness as the principle for love and fraternity. This means that if the basic premise of the storyline is that of matchmaking via resemblance, then what Lanthimos does is to set a counter-movement, or an act of resistance, that is internal to itself.[6] This is what the intensive-image generates in film, and which Giorgio Agamben defines in terms of an unactualised tendency that in itself contains a power to resist: 'If the potentiality that the act liberates is internal to the act, [then] in the same way, resistance must be internal to the act of creation' (2014). The word *resistere*, which in its Latin etymology stands for the act of withstanding or standing still, expresses for Agamben the virtuality of a movement that remains inoperative in its 'impotence' – that is to say, in the potentiality of an image not to be in actuality [*dynamis me einai*]. Hence, what Lanthimos creates under his unresolved, differential images is that their intensity never really enters into the extensive/actual [*energeia*] but remains suspended in the indeterminacy of its internal resistance [*adynamia*]:

> In the potentiality to be, potentiality has as its object a certain act, in the sense that for it *energhein*, being-in-act, can only mean passing to a determinate activity [this is why Schelling defines the potentiality that cannot pass into action as *blind*]; as for the potentiality to not-be, on the other hand, the act can never consist of a simple transition *de potentia ad actum*: It is, in other words, a potentiality that has as its object potentiality itself, a *potential potentiae*. (Agamben 1993, 35–6)

Such a concept of potentiality qua intensity or virtuality,[7] however, does not always assume an absolute – unmediated – suspension in *The Lobster*. At times, it also enunciates a concrete or 'actual' image which anticipates itself in future scenarios, hence cancelling its unresolved difference or impotence in images to be [*dynamis*]. This can be grasped towards the second half of the film, when we finally get to 'see' the short-sighted woman who has been narrating the story, or when, already in the forest,

---

[6] The screenplay was co-written with his Greek collaborator Euthymic Filippo.

[7] In philosophy, the notion of the virtual, as derived from the Aristotelian conception of potential as *dynamis*, generally designates the passage from one possible state of matter to an actual state of itself – thus linking the virtual event to its concrete future reality or form. Deleuze's virtually, on the contrary, does not account for such process of actualisation, because the virtual, '*qua virtual* (...) possesses a full reality [of its own]' (2014, 275). In this sense, Deleuze's conceptualisation of the virtual, like Agamben's idea of *adynamia* taken from Aristotle, finds in its non-actualised tendencies a common opposition to the possibility of something to be: 'If the real is opposed to the possible', Deleuze suggests in *Difference and Repetition*, then 'the virtual is opposed to the actual' (2014, 275).

we realise that punishment may descend upon her and her lover (after the Loners' leader finds out about their prohibited, and well-hidden, romance). In both cases, as in other episodes of the film, the passage from perception to action revokes, in all its indeterminacy, the internal resonance of intensity. To paraphrase Deleuze's comments on Hitchcock's mental-operations, which is a cinema that similarly goes from a virtual state of perception to actual events on-screen, viewers in *The Lobster* are also caught up in a system of temporal (dis)connections introduced by a shot that is double: 'the one turned towards the characters in movement, and the other turned towards a whole which changes progressively as the film goes on' (2005, 207).[8]

However, what is new about the mental operations introduced by *The Lobster*, that is, the trajectories of an image that remain unanswered in the development of the story, is that the temporal instability introduced by the shot, as in Deleuze's reading of Hitchcock, not always transforms itself into an actual – foreseeable – event on-screen but it could also remain virtual in the unresolved potential of the intensive-image. Here, and closer to the poetic act described by Agamben, the internal resistance of *The Lobster*, its intensity or potentiality, will move up towards a vaporous destination that is destabilising all possible links between events. (This is, as we will see shortly, the secret language of the main couple who are escaping from the forest to embrace an unknown destination next to the sea.)

This sense of unactualised potentiality can preliminarily be mapped in the film's overture and closure – in an opening sequence that remains endlessly suspended and in a final shot that violently cuts across our vision. In the first case, when the story opens, there is a woman who shoots a donkey who we do not see again in the film. Neither do we know why she was killing that particular animal and not the others of the same kind: Was the donkey her ex-husband? Did she get the right animal? Was she, by any chance, David's city-wife, who in the next shot we *hear* but not *see*? Such a beginning, which anticipates the intensity of the story to come, represents the internal resonance of an image that remains inconclusive until the last

---

[8] It is also important to observe the common technical aspects and thematic operations that Hitchcock and Lanthimos share. One of them is the primacy of the couple and their interest in showing 'how love is at work' (Bonitzer 1992, 24) in narrative stories that, most of the time, remain suspended in the mind of viewers. Another common thread is the use of music and its role in adding tension through audiovisual overlapping and juxtapositions. In *The Lobster*, for example, the score of Bernard Hermann used alongside the façade-framing visual of the hotel – a score widely known for its appearance in the shower scene of Hitchcock's *Psycho* (1959) – works as a dramatic element that, as Lanthimos suggests, 'adds something other than what the scene is doing itself, something that might be in the exact opposite direction of the scene' (quoted in Strickland, 2016). For further discussion, see Bonitzer (1992, 15–28) and Strickland (2016, 135).

moments of the film. And also, at the end of the story, in the restaurant scene, the viewer does nothing but confirm the film's initial fabulation. At this time, after we see David holding a steak knife in the toilet next to his right eye, the frame cuts to a visual of the restaurant where his now blinded (ex-short-sighted) partner awaits. Right after, the final credits appear over the black screen and the viewer remains uncertain whether this is the end of the story or, hypothetically, the next shot in which David has already taken out his eyes on-screen – hence, a completely blinded visual produced by David's subjective point of view that we viewers can't either see or recognise. I'll come back to this point when discussing Sophia Loren's song musicalising this tale of mad love with the final credits of the story: *S'agapo, s'agapo, s'agapo. Ti'ne afto pou to lene agape? Ti'ne afto, ti'ne afto* . . . (I love you, I love you, I love you. What's this thing called love? What is it? What is it?) For now, and to summarise the internal resonance of *The Lobster*'s politics of lovance, I suggest that the non-actualised tendencies of the film, which begin when the image does not yet have a clear, foreseeable meaning but a full potential towards its unknown destination, does speak to the 'suspension of language' (2014) that Agamben associates with poetry, and which, in discussing the intensive-image, I have argued the Greek director is also covering over, or 'suspending', in accordance to his virtuous – and virtual – style.

The External Resonance of Resistance: Tactics, Pass-Words, Counter-Attacks . . .

In addition to Agamben's comments, and more in line with Lanthimos's story of blind lovers, I also take the resonance of resistance to be an external political act, that is to say, as a set of tactics that the film's characters employ to mock the 'order-words' (Deleuze and Guattari 1988/2005, 126) imposed by their sovereigns (that being the case of the main couple who try not to be subjected to the imperatives of the city-Law). This is the initial – and most elemental – meaning of the notion of resistance that Agamben derives from Deleuze's lecture on 'What is the Creative Act?': 'Resistance as opposition to an external force (. . .) resistance to the society of control and the paradigm of information' (2014). Resistance, in short, as the refusal to comply with a system of directions or *communiqués*.[9]

As Deleuze mentions, quoting Foucault, such a control-society is no longer defined by the physical presence of a sovereign (e.g. classical

---

[9] As in school *communiqués* or police *communiqués* – namely, the order-words of a society of control.

torture), neither by the confined spaces of modernity (e.g. disciplinary society), but by a new system of information organised under the logic of 'order-words': 'When you are informed, you are told what you are supposed to believe (. . .) Informing means circulating an order-word' (1987/2007, 327). In *The Lobster*, such a modality of subjection is contained in both of Foucault's epochs, the classical *sovereign* and the modern *disciplinary*, so that besides the public tortures enacted by the traditional queen/administrator in the villa, or the tyrant-leader in the forest, there is a panoptical ensemble effectively put at play by the gaze of the city-hotel ensemble. However, in Lanthimos's society there is a new informational network that can no longer pass through Foucault's classical punishment or modern confinement exclusively, but through a broader system of communications that Deleuze defines, quoting William Burroughs, as 'control society':

> [Foucault] clearly thought that we were entering a new type of society. He clearly said that disciplinary societies were not eternal (. . .) Control is not discipline. You do not confine people with a highway. But by making highways, you multiply the means of control. (1987/2007, 326–7)

This is what Foucault calls, in his late lectures at the *College de France*, 'biopolitics' – the interiorisation of an external command into the very body of individuals. Here, as Deleuze remarks, any person can now move 'infinitely and freely without being confined while being perfectly controlled' (2007, 327). And this is, as we know, the juridical sentence that goes unquestioned, reproduced and internalised in *The Lobster*'s controlling spaces; an effective (and surreal) form of communication that can transform the body of individuals from citizens to convicts, or more oddly, from human to non-human animal. This means, in other words, that to pose the question about external resistance next to the film's dystopic reality is less a matter of escaping from the city-Law as it is to find the zones less striated in it; less a matter of becoming 'outlaw' (as the Singles do in the forest) as to avoid the impact of the Law in the very body of individuals. Resistance, in short, as the 'practice of the weak' (De Certeau 1984, 17), as represented in all those screen characters who mock and deconstruct 'order-words' to find 'pass-words' lying underneath. In Deleuze and Guattari's view:

> Order-words bring immediate death to those who receive the order, or potential death if they do not obey, or a death they must themselves inflict, take elsewhere (. . .) There are *pass-words* beneath *order-words*. Words that pass, words that are components of passage, whereas order-words mark stoppages (. . .) It is necessary [therefore] to transform the compositions of order into components of passage. (2005, 126; 128)

Tactics, pass-words, resistance. The tactic is a pass-word performing a resistance to the external command. Resistance to what, though? To the hell of a situation that the film's characters are trapped in. As described by Italo Calvino in his *Invisible Cities* (1972/1997), there are two ways so as not to suffer this hell. The first, which is 'easy for many' is to become such a part of hell that you no longer see it. That, simply put, means to accept the rules and follow the orders imposed by *The Lobster*'s metropolitan Law: find a partner within forty-five days or become an animal of your own choice. The second, which is 'riskier' and more uncertain, demands the ability to recognise, within this hell, those spaces that 'are not hell', hence to look for a more affirmative place to dwell:

> The hell of the living is not something that will be: if there is one, it is what is already here, the hell where we live every day, that we form by being together. There are two ways to escape suffering it. The first is easy for many: accept the hell and become such a part of it that you can no longer see it. The second is risky and demands constant vigilance and learning: seek and be able to recognize who and what, in the midst of the hell, are not hell, then make them endure, give them space. (1997, 74)

Either way, whether we look at Calvino's hell or Lanthimos's film, it seems that life is always captured by the official structures of a molar power. To resist, once again, would be nothing but to dissemble *within* this capture or, more actively, to struggle *against* its systemic interiorisation, for as Foucault suggests: 'Where there is [dominant] power, there is also [subaltern] resistance' (1978/1990, 95). Let me explain how the characters of the film enact this political, intensive struggle.

At a basic level, resistance represents a purely instrumental act; a tactic that pretends to follow the commands imposed by the city-Law while disobeying its premises. Visitors in the hotel assume different coping strategies, all of which thwart the juridical order by faking its matchmaking principle. John, for example, who declares to prefer a nosebleed from time to time rather than be converted into an animal that will, later on, get eaten by a bigger animal, beats himself about the head to pair with a nosebleed woman and, in this way, remains *all too human*. Or David, who thought that it was more difficult to pretend to have feelings when you don't than to pretend not to have feelings when you do, mistakenly chooses to match with a partner whose coldness of heart he cannot put up with: after having suspicion about David's emotional character, she kills his dog-brother Bob and confirms, once she spots David crying in the toilet, that he has built their relationship on a lie. When David weeps next to his dead brother lying on the floor, this also reminds him of the hotel's punishment for such a misconduct – a severe penalty that he will try to avoid at all costs.

Threatened by his partner's accusation to the manager-in-chief, David rebels against her betrayal and, in an act of desperation, takes justice into his own hands; he shoots the heartless woman in the back and turns her, in his words, into 'the animal that no one wants to be' (an animal, moreover, that no one else will recognise onscreen, except for him). Also, the villa's maid who has helped David to accomplish this crime, and whose loyalty (as we are now starting to realise) belongs not to the hotel's manager but to the forest-leader, marks a passage that replaces the previous form of resistance indicated above (an instrumental resisting act that copes with the hotel's orders while cheating its premises), to a more subversive act that rejects the order to follow the hotel's commands. In this capacity, David's escape to the forest, which exhausts the city-hotel administrative apparatus, reverses the previous instrumental strategies of those characters who prefer to survive in the hotel for a more active counter-attack. In short, our protagonist is transforming 'order-words' into components of a passage.

What You Hear Above All is Loving: The Forest, the City and the Two Maritime Lovers

The transition from the hotel to the woods is marked cinematographically by the door device as threshold space. After David stuns the villa's maid with a tranquilliser gun in the abdomen (to feign that she wasn't part of his escape) he drags the cold-blooded body of his ex-partner to the room where the animal transformation will take place. Once we see the door closing with both of them on the inside, David reappears in the next shot running towards a destination that is yet unknown to him. The short-sighted woman who narrates this episode, musicalised again by Beethoven's *adagio*, indicates David's second change of geopolitical location. This time, however, by employing the metaphor of the door, David's transition from the hotel to the woods not only marks his entrance into a new physical realm but also, as Thomas Elsaesser and Malte Hagener suggest, into a new ideological and ontological domain: 'The door [in cinema] not only signals the crossing from one physical space into another but also (. . .) the transport from one ontological realm to another' (2010, 50).

After having slept beside a tree in the forest, David is found by a Loner who takes him where the runaway Singles live. At first, this encounter seems to open a brighter future for him. Framed from a relatively high angle shot, with a tender voice, a poncho and a messianic look, the Loners' leader (Léa Seydoux) informs David that he can stay indefinitely in the woods, asks him if he is a doctor who could help around in the commune and invites him to live there peacefully and happily as a Single. David feels thankful, and the new ruler hugs him wholeheartedly. Unfortunately, though, this is also the moment when the door to heaven turns into another despotic inferno for him: 'By the way', she adds, 'any romantic or sexual relations between Loners are not permitted and any such acts are punished. Is that clear?' David is confined once again by an authoritarian sovereign who, although permissive in appearance, is as oppressive as the previous manager in the villa. Or to paraphrase Hannah Ardent, even when the Loners seem to be a group of 'radical revolutionaries', in reality, and after their revolution against the hotel is over, they become nothing but a bunch of 'conservative individuals' (1970).

The forest's ideological mandate is therefore understood as an opposite repressive programme to that of the film's canonical society (Zoro 2017): if masturbation was prohibited in the hotel, such an act is now allowed; if the villa's manager hosted ballroom dances to form couples, Loners will perform solitary dances with earphones in the woods; if the hotel's administration rewarded and gave extra days to those who hunted Loners, Singles will party every time they conspire against couples. In short, if the issue back in the hotel was about an intimacy with *the self*, the problem in the forest is about an intimacy with *the other*. Taken to an extreme, this is also why Singles must dig their own graves and the reason why they receive cruel punishments for their romantic offences (e.g. the red kiss for flirting and, what is worse, the red intercourse for sex). David, once again, runs the risk of defying the norms of his new political space: by desiring to match with someone he loves and whose astigmatism he perfectly matches, he decides to transgress the order-words of the forest where neither sex nor love-alliances are allowed.

David's drive to resist – a displacing movement that unsettles the organisation of any dominant regime – clearly manifests the deterritorialising forces of the work of art, and of what I call the intensive-image in cinema, by interrogating what is commonly accepted in the public sphere. Being an architect himself – thus a creator of spatial habitation – David is someone who enacts an unsettling political power 'capable of overturning orders (. . .) in order to affirm *difference* [intensity] in a state of permanent revolution' (Deleuze 2014, 67). Quite contrary to the sovereigns of *The Lobster*'s society then, whose missions are that of Arendt's 'conservation' or Deleuze's 'prolongation [of] an established historical order' (2014, 67), David represents that 'artist-stranger' (Karalis 2012)[10] who defies the

---

[10] The hero as stranger has been discussed by film historian Vrasidas Karalis to designate a current audiovisual language in Greek cinema in which characters, within and outside Greek limits, are

molar identity of the spaces he inhabits to open up a process of minoritarian-becoming instead. That is the reason why he and his short-sighted partner decide to move away from the forest and live secretly together at the riverside. As Weisz's voice-over commentary tells us, it is next to this 'smooth', open territory, where they create a hidden language of gestures that can only be read through their bodies:

> We developed a code so that we can communicate with each other even in front of the others without them knowing what we're saying. When we turn our heads to the left, it means 'I love you more than anything in the world', and when we turn our heads to the right, it means 'watch out, we're in danger' (. . .) The code grew and grew as time went by, and within a few weeks, we could talk about almost anything without even opening our mouths.

'Gesture', the key element of Deleuze's modern cinema according to Agamben (1995/2000, 54), stands in this fable as the non-legible component of the two lovers' spatial habitation. It is a hidden, *passing* language that rejects the forest's official mandates and which they develop in proximity to a boundless sea. Such an 'oceanic feeling' (a concept Freud may employ to describe their impulsive love event), not only signals here the couple's opposition to the rules of the forest but it also points to their intense maritime-becoming unfolding next to the waterside. Take, for example, David's choice of a lobster-becoming in case he had been turned into an animal back in the hotel. Among the reasons he gives to the manager-in-chief, he declares to 'like the sea very much'. The same rationale goes to his short-sighted partner who wants to visit the ocean for vacations. As she writes down in her diary, intersected later by one of the forest-leader's followers: 'Portofino: Italian fishing village. Beaches nearby: Paraggi beach, Camogli, Chiavari, and Lavagna. Serifos: Greek Island located in the western Cyclades . . .' Finally, as we have already anticipated, it is also their love relationship – a maritime-becoming – that has been formed in proximity to the waterway. Here is where, among other things, they practise a dance together as to develop their body language; where they kiss each other and realise they're a perfect match; or after she has been blinded by the forest's ruler, where they prepare their escape to the city in a coded language that no one (not even viewers) can understand: 'I raise my left foot' says David to her, 'I bring my elbow to my knee and tap it twice. I bring my foot to my knee, and tap it three times . . .' David is determined to go ahead with this secret plan, but by the expression on his

manifesting a radical sense of displacement in regard to those spaces they inhabit. For further discussion see Vrasidas 2012 and Cooper 2016.

partner's face, and the dubious tone of her answer, the viewer *senses*, rather than *foresees*, the dreadful actions to come: 'Are you sure you're prepared to do that?'

The potentiality of this gesture – no longer a visible sign – thus expresses the intensity of an image which remains indiscernible throughout the film: Was David suggesting in the above sentence to take his eyes out so that they could perform a 'sightless match' in the city? If so, why not claim their common passion towards the ocean instead of going blind? Is this perhaps a case of Shakespearean love becoming where passionate lovers can no longer see? Certainly, their tactics against the forestry-decree not only alter the rigidity of their confinement as it also opens up an alternative intensive-map which goes beyond the metric spaces of the film. So, and to return to this double form of resistance discussed previously, the couple's 'pass-words' represent, on the one hand, the *external* refusal to cope with the commands imposed by the forest-leader and, on the other hand, the *internal* resonance of an intensive-image that remains unactualised – that is to say, 'impotent' or 'blinded' to the look of viewers. In the former case, their language becomes what Deleuze calls, concerning the work of art, an act of 'counter-information': 'A work of art does not contain a bit of information (. . .) Counter-information is only effective when it becomes an act of resistance. [And] the act of resistance is also the act of art' (1987/2007, 327). In the latter case, their bodily gestures portray what Agamben calls, with regard to the act of poetry, a 'suspension of language', thus an image that uses those secret passing-words lying underneath order-words. This is the type of intensive-map, or 'smooth, non-metric intensive space' (Deleuze quoted in Rölli 2009, 46) that the film creates in connection with its oceanic landscape, in contrast to the extensive-map or 'striated spaces' subordinated to the film's ruling metropolis.[11] In Deleuze and Guattari's words:

> Smooth space is filled by events or haecceities, far more than by formed and perceived things. It is a space of *affects*, more than one of properties. It is *haptic* rather than optical perception. A Body without Organs instead of an organism and organization (. . .) In contrast to the sea, the city is the striated space par excellence; the sea is a smooth space fundamentally open to situation, and the city is the force of striation that reimports smooth space. (2005, 557–60)

---

[11] As Marc Rölli rightly asserts, in *A Thousand Plateaus* Deleuze and Guattari discuss the whole problem of intensive and extensive magnitude under the rubric of smooth (the ocean) and striated (the city) space. In Rölli's words: 'A smooth space is a non-metric intensive space, "one of distances, not of measures", whereas a striated space is an extensive space, with a closed parceled out or measured surface' (2009, 46).

Following this intensive trajectory, the lovers' maritime-becoming can also be heard in a 'key musical note' (Langer 1977). During the final credits of the film, once the screen turns black, we listen to Sophia Loren and Tonis Maroudas's '*Ti'ne afto pou to lene agape?*' ('What's this thing called love?'), a song that originally played in *Boy on a Dolphin* (Negulesco 1957), which is another film set by the sea.[12] In Cooper's view, their score 'brings the male and female voice together in ways that the imagery of *The Lobster* kept separate in its final sequence' (2016, 173), the reason why, for Zoro, their romantic destiny is *heard* rather than *seen* at the end of the film: 'An important clue is the song heard at the end, beyond the end, towards the final credits of the story' (2017, 1; my translation). Indeed, Loren and Maroudas's musical composition echoes the 'haecceities' of 'this thing called love', a question that is of primary importance for Cooper and Zoro's readings of *The Lobster*. However, what the authors do not mention in their musical analysis of the film is the oceanic breeze and the waves crashing on rocks that we listen to over the black screen once the song in Greek has finished – that is, a purely aural space which I take as another sonic clue gesturing to the lovers' maritime-becoming towards the end of the film's credits.

Thinking more generally about *The Lobster*'s amorous politics then, this question of love and its various types of partnership play, in different episodes of the story, to the ear – under the film's *sound-tracks*. First, during the ballroom dance in the hotel, the chief manager and her partner (Garry Mountaine) sing 'Something's gotten hold of my heart', an ardent feeling that 'keeps your soul and senses apart' and which 'cuts its way through my dreams like a knife'. (It is, no doubt, another key note musicalising David's fervent deed at the end of the story when eventually slicing his eyes in the restaurant's toilet.) In their performance, however, the song clearly negates this passionate 'politics of lovance', as the hotel's managers sing it emotionlessly, without that burning sentiment heard from the song's lyrics. To the question: What to do when love ceases? the duet seem to offer a rather average, mediocre response: if love is no longer there, just strive to find someone with whom to share your life and spend the rest of your days. And that is precisely the type of instrumental alliance examined previously when looking at the matchmaking tactics employed by the hotel's guests – a relationship based not on *virtue* or common attraction but on *necessity*; what the ancient Greeks used to call a 'useful relationship' (Derrida 2005, 203).

Secondly, in opposition to the hotel managers' show, there is also the song by Nick Cave and Kylie Minogue 'Where the wild roses grow', a

---

[12] The film is set in the Greek Aegean Sea.

melody that the two lovers play together by the river (the song is hardly heard by the audience as the couple plays it on their earphones) and which later on David sings *a cappella* in the forest. This song, which is all about mad lovers and a love that kills, about roses that grow 'sweet and scarlet and free', clearly expresses this loving-excess of the main couple. It indicates both the radicalness of their alliance as well as the violence of their hidden romance ending in potential death. It is a song of intense and disproportionate desires; it invites the viewer to listen carefully to their union as one of pure fervour and erotic exchange. Remember what the female lover imagines in her sleep: 'That night, I dreamt that we lived in a big house together in the city (. . .) I was wearing dark blue trousers and a tight green blouse, and he took my clothes off and fucked me up the ass.' This sexual urgency is also one that David performs at the end of the story, when (supposedly) cutting his eyes with a knife. It is an ardent, uncontrollable feeling that not only 'cuts through his dreams like a knife'[13] but also an image of intense desire akin to that of the god, Cupid, who out of his burning love stabs a sharp golden dart into himself.

Put differently, isn't their wild and fiery love another musical note suggesting that true lovers, as Cooper observes (2015, 172), must confront the trial of death? In *The Lobster*, as we saw, most characters fake their romance with one another, thus couples avoid death by showing more concern for their own private lives than for the lives of their loving others. Personal death is thus denied in the story by at least two operations: by faking resemblance (as in the case of the limping man who lies to his nose-bleeding partner to stay human); or by killing your partner before dying for him/her (as in the case of the hotel manager's husband who decides to shoot her instead of killing himself first). This means that to think about death with an open heart – that is, beyond any measures or rationale – the loving presence of the other must take complete possession of one's self. Or conversely, passionate death can occur from despair in the absence of a loving partner, meaning a person's soul has never had the experience of loving another or of having had a love affair. The latter case is illustrated in the film by the biscuit woman who ends up throwing herself out of the window in the absence of a suitable partner to love and to have sex with. Her song, if any, would be that of the first hunt scene in slow motion, when Danae Strategopoulou's '*Apo Mesa Pethamenos*' (Dead Inside) evokes a similar solitary lament, one of suffering, renunciation and despair: 'You

---

[13] This is also a rebuke to Buñuel and Dalí's *Un chien andalou*, whose eye-slicing scene, as commented previously in Chapter 2, heralds the confirmation of the couple's bloody romance.

wonder, they tell me, how my heart still goes on. But aren't there lots of people like me – *dead inside and alive on the outside*?' Now, in regard to the main two lovers, which is the converse image of a *life inside* and (potential) *death outside*, affection 'seems to consist more in loving than in being loved', as Aristotle once said (340 BC/1998, 12). For example, in their first trip to the city, just after David realises his partner is also short-sighted, they feign matrimony in the apartment of their leader's parents. Here, David kisses his wife and publicly declares his love to her: 'I love my wife so much [that] I could die for her. That's how much I love her . . .' Previously in the forest, the short-sighted woman had already saved his life (while putting her own at risk) by sticking a knife in the lisping man's leg before shooting him. Grateful for her heroic action, David will hunt and marinate rabbits for her to eat, or as it happens at the end of the film, kill the forest-ruler who has impeded the fulfilment of their astigmatic love. Death, in all of these expressions, becomes the true trial for the two lover-friends. In Derrida's words:

> In all good sense, what you hear above all is loving; you must hear loving (. . .) it is, therefore, an act before being a situation; rather, the act of loving, before being the state of being loved. An action before a passion (. . .) Someone must love in order to know what loving means, then, and only then, can one know what being loved means. (2005, 8)

An action before a passion. Better still, an action that is driven by a blind, intense passion. That's how much the main couple love each other and the reason why they don't find any other suitable match while preparing their escape to the city: 'Do you like berries? Can you play the piano? Do you speak German?' David asks her persistently: 'No, no, no!' She replies, without any hope of finding feasible criteria to pair. How about: *Do you like the sea? Why don't we stay together forever on the beach . . .?* No, as for the lovers who do not see, the zeal of passion demands a certain disproportion.

* * *

That night, when I watched *The Lobster* at one of Melbourne's cinemas, I was waiting for one last image to come, waiting perhaps for that moment of certainties and answers through which the eye, so rejoicing and expectant, transforms the intensity of an image into a fully readable sign. Such an episode, however, never arrived – the visuals were not actualised. Remember, said the forest-leader to the short-sighted woman in the forest: 'When someone goes blind the other senses are heightened.' The same words were pronounced to David before taking out his eyes, and there I was also experimenting with a similar blindness in-sight, looking at this vanishing sequence that no light could illuminate – for in that moment in the movie theatre, when the screen went black, I was, too, already blind.

CHAPTER 6

Zama and the Method of Dramatisation: From Di Benedetto's Novel to Martel's Film

Lucrecia Martel's *Zama* opens with a visual and the sound of a river. It also ends around there, in a canoe up the creek. At the start of the story, we see Don Diego de Zama (Daniel Giménez Cacho) standing upright at the centre of the frame, on the riverbank, while in the background of the image there is a group of Indigenous children voicing unintelligible words in local dialect. Here, Zama awaits impatiently (as the viewer will realise later in the film) for a royal letter that will eventually grant his return to the place where his wife Marta and his two children await. However, by the end of the story this Magistrate of Indians – an eighteenth-century functionary of the Spanish Crown born on South American soil – won't have moved at all. With his arms severed lying in agony in a boat poled by the Indigenous, Zama will be floating downstream just like another conquistador did before him on-screen – that of Werner Herzog's Aguirre in *Aguirre, Wrath of God* (1972). Martel's finale is predicted from the film's beginning, at the moment when the slave announces to the functionaries of the Spanish Crown that 'there is a fish that lives all his life struggling to remain in the river, because water rejects him, water doesn't like him'. Once we listen to these words uttered by the subaltern being punished in the Magistrate's office, the film's title appears over the black screen, followed by a river fish swimming underwater (this is the only underwater shot we see in the film, setting the atmosphere for a narrative that itself liquifies, becoming porous). Zama, delivered unto nothingness, is presumably one of the fish-characters destined to wait endlessly in a liquid territory that doesn't want him and where he doesn't want to stay either. Zama is, like the viewers inhabiting his deliriums, a character out of place, lost in himself and in the environment he inhabits.

This chapter will focus on Martel's politics of script adaptation and her intensive-image of *Zama*, a contemporary film commanded by her disruptive and polyphonic aesthetics which not only enlarges the elliptical nature of Di Benedetto's book of the same name but also the modernity of Deleuze's cinema towards more diffuse screen scenarios. Her off-screen work, acoustic design and page-to-screen detours will constitute some of the formal characteristics of this intensive-image that de-visualises, or 'dramatises', the literary referent, for as Perez argues in *The Material Ghost*: 'nothing is dramatic in a realm where everything is visible (1998, 169). This dramatising method, which is entirely consistent with Deleuze's philosophy of difference and with my concept of the intensive-image, will be a key element to account for Martel's process of intensification and her capacity to problematise what is materially visible in the image, as it is through the absences and partial views of her protagonist Zama that such intensity will hide, more than it will reveal, what is seen on the surface of the film.

Based on the novel written in 1955–6 by Antonio Di Benedetto, *Zama* is dedicated, as the book informs us in its epigraph, 'to the victims of expectation' (2016, i). In the film, Di Benedetto's statement is accentuated by one of Martel's favourite metaphors – that of water, a whirlpooling mode of sensation. Once we see the river fish appearing in the film, the voice-over commentary by Ventura Prieto (Juan Minujín) tells us that:

> these long-suffering fish, so attached to the element that repudiates them, must devote all their energy to conquer lastingness. You will never find them at the centre of the river, but always and only along the banks.[1]

Zama is, in this regard, one of the fish; and in the next shot he appears looking at the river from its bank. Clearly, Martel's preference for the liquid environment not only dominates the atmosphere of her film *Zama* but more broadly the tactility and landscape of her entire cinematic career. In *La ciénaga* (*The Swamp*, 2001) and *La niña santa* (*The Holy Girl*, 2004) for example, there is the swimming pool that conveys the inaction of both the bourgeois families sunbathing in the former and the teenage girl wandering around the hotel in the latter – not to mention the high-pitched sounds of the irrigation ditch in *La mujer sin cabeza* (*The Headless Woman*, 2007); an aural space that attracts the attention of viewers and simultaneously renders the image more phantasmagoric, via 'sound[s] that wander the surface of the screen, awaiting a place to attach to' (Chion 1994, 4).

In the case of *Zama*, as this chapter argues, it is the element of water that intensifies the storyline and the bodily decline of Don Diego de Zama, in the sense that the film transposes the novel – which is already composed of highly elliptical passages – into more diffused affective sce-

---

[1] 'Estos sufridos peces, tan apegados al elemento que les repele, emplean todas sus energías en la conquista de la permanencia. Nunca les vas a encontrar en la parte central del rio, sino en las orillas.'

narios. Water thus becomes another motif that reinforces not only Martel's non-syntagmatic editing and acousmatic filming style but also a wavering viewing experience that we must struggle with to piece together the spatio-temporal layers of Martel's first literary adaptation and period piece. It is a *mise en abyme* that stages new relations within and between the sequences of Di Benedetto's text in order to dramatise its images into more indiscernible screen events. This is a process that, as Martel comments while referring to her page-to-screen adaptation, 'contaminates' the visuality of Di Benedetto's universe in virtue of the open landscape that the book presents to her as a reader: 'It's not interpretation, it's not translation but infection, contamination. [Reading and adapting the novel] is like a disease' (Marchini 2018a, 45). This contagion, as this chapter will argue, is the contagion of intensity. It is the intensive-image that haunts Martel's screenplay and gives a new body to her cinematic *Zama*:

> Why make a film about *Zama*? Because very few times in life you can undertake such an exquisite and irreversible excursion between sounds and images to a definitely new domain. (Martel, 2017)

How does Martel create this metamorphosis, rather than a metaphor, to dramatise the misfortunes and failed promises under which the literary Zama awaits? Can the film withdraw from, and as it were 'infect', the images of the original text? These are the questions concerning my analysis by looking at Di Benedetto and Martel's *Zama* in connection to what Deleuze calls 'the method of dramatization' (2014, 223–87; 1967/2004, 94–116). First, it will be argued that instead of finding *solutions* to adapt Di Benedetto's book in an orthodox or conventional way – that is to say, by being 'faithful' to the original referent – Martel's film will rather follow the line of the *problematic* to stress the paradoxes, disparities and incongruities already contained in the text. Dramatisation, or 'the differen*c*iation of differentiation' (2014, 281–7)[2] as Deleuze calls it, will thus offer a new means to describe the intensive-image and its process of intensification by looking at the mutations from book to film. In this sense, dramatisation, which is a method entirely consistent with Deleuze's philosophy of difference, will visualise the plasticity or becomingness of an intensive-image which is said to change constantly through time and space – that is to say,

---

[2] For further discussion on the concept of 'differen*c*iation' with the '*c*' and the notion of intensity, see the chapter 'Ideas and the Synthesis of Difference' in *Difference and Repetition*, where Deleuze claims that 'the idea is precisely real without being actual, differentiated without being differenciated, and complete without being entire (. . .) Why is differenciation differentiated along these two complementary paths? Beneath the actual qualities and extensities, species and parts, there are spatio-temporal dynamisms. These are the actualizing, differenciating agencies' (2014, 278).

a type of spatio-temporal dynamic that is moved by the virtual 'drama' dominating Deleuze's world-theatre:

> The world is an egg, but the egg itself is a theatre: a staged theatre in which the roles dominate the actors, the spaces dominate the roles and the ideas [the 'dramas'] dominate the spaces. (Deleuze 2014, 281)

Once again, it is by using the analogy of different water states, as expressed in Section One of this book, that I will account for Martel's intensification of Deleuze's cinemas at yet another level of intensity. At times, I will speak of a vaporous, gaseous-image – put forward by Martel's highly sensorial aesthetics – when discussing her de-visualisation of the literary *Zama*. It will be argued that her screenplay not only dramatises the sequences of Di Benedetto's book but also the time-image modernity of Deleuze's cinemas. In the second part of this chapter, I will reiterate that the nature of Deleuze's two film volumes, taken as a virtual whole or an open field, is destined to intensify constantly. Finally, based on Martel's tactile approach to filmmaking and to *Zama*, I will look more closely at her film transposition and its whirlpooling plot line to propose a third interconnected drama; one that focuses on the bodily and mental decline of her protagonist, the Magistrate Zama. He begins by standing upright at the riverbank, and then goes on to spy on a group of naked women mud-bathing nearby, and is seen at end of the story lying on a boat in agony with his arms severed and his eyes shut. (In the novel, the amputation is only limited to Zama's fingers and its execution is not described. Martel, on the contrary, elaborates on this passage and shows us both of his arms being hacked off with a machete at the waterside.) Here, Martel's Zama will be said to move from a body that starts at the pinnacle of action and pleasure, almost like a replica of Mulvey's classical voyeur, to suffering the violent affects described by Antonin Artaud in his theatre of cruelty, when introducing, as the film does, his reflections on fish-being and suffering in 'Petit poème des poissons de la mer':

> L'Être est celui qui s'imagine être
> Être assez pour se dispenser
> D'apprendre ce que veut la mer . . .
> Mais tout petit poisson le sait!
>
> (Artaud quoted in Marks 2015, 119)

So, to summarise these interconnected dramas, this chapter will seek to convey a differentiating intensive-image locally integrated into one topological space – that is, a movement that flows from the literary fluctuations of Di Benedetto's text to the de-visualising operations of Martel's *Zama* and its dramatisation of Deleuze's cinematic modernism.

First Drama: From Di Benedetto's Novel to Martel's Film

In the preface to her English translation of the novel *Zama* (2016), Esther Allen situates Di Benedetto's text alongside the literary landscape of realisms populating the Latin American scenery of the second half of the twentieth century. However, she also makes sure to elude the general label of 'magical realism' (one dominating most of the international reception of Latin American literature) to describe the psychologically driven type of realism characteristic of Di Benedetto's prose. This singularity, according to Allen, has to do with the influence of Kafka:

> In Di Benedetto's first book, *Mundo animal*, which concerns all sorts of transactions and transmutations between human and [non-human] animal, the profound influence of Kafka and particularly of *The Metamorphosis* seems much in evidence, though Di Benedetto would claim that he didn't read Kafka until 1954, the year after *Mundo animal* came out, the year before he wrote *Zama*. (2016, xix)

Di Benedetto's Zama is, no doubt, a claustrophobic character similar to Gregor Samsa in *The Metamorphosis* (1915/2016), but as the reverse image of him. (In fact, when read in Spanish, Samsa and Zama sound almost the same.) As Allen suggests, Zama becomes the 'negative image of Samsa', someone who is trapped not 'in home and family but (. . .) in exile, away from home and family' (2016, xix). Her remark is a telling one, in that Kafka's writings are relevant to illustrate Di Benedetto's psychological realism alongside other realisms of the Latin American writers of the twentieth century, from Borges and Cortázar's *lo real fantástico* – the former also being one of Kafka's first (mis)translators into Spanish – to Rulfo's *lo fantástico terrible*, or Bolaño's more recent *realismo visceral*. In fact, it is probably with the latter, or more specifically with Bolaño's short story 'Sensini' (2011), where the Kafkaesque influence on Di Benedetto's *Zama* is made manifest. Based on his encounters with the (fictional) Argentinean writer Luis Antonio Sensini – presumably Antonio Di Benedetto's alter-ego – Bolaño begins the story by describing a written work that his friend sends to a literary contest in Spain and whose critics interpret as 'very Kafkaesque'. In Sensini's tale, Bolaño explains, a son of his called Gregor[3] 'dies constantly', but whether that happens or not 'remains unclear', as Sensini's 'style of writing is very claustrophobic (. . .) [There you get]

---

[3] 'An unconscious homage to Gregor Samsa', adds Bolaño in his tale.

these great geographical spaces that all of a sudden shrink, to the point of reaching the size of a coffin' (2011, 50). This description of Sensini's style of writing as claustrophobic is exemplary of the type of landscapes populating Di Benedetto's novel, such as the 'great geographical space' that begins the book, with Zama waiting for a ship at the riverbank, and which progressively 'shrinks' to the point of reaching 'the size of a coffin', as when Zama agonises in a small wooden canoe next to the blonde kid in the creek.

Beside this claustrophobia, Di Benedetto's novel is also composed in an elliptical and episodic way, ever widening horizons and detours. And it is this dialectic that I'm interested in examining with regard to Martel's film. The intention, therefore, is to suggest that the correspondence between the audible and the visible in the film renders the literary images of the Mendocino writer even more gaseous or intense – that is, an intensive-image accentuating the cuts, the confusions, the claustrophobia of the novel that precedes it. But how can this overturning occur, especially after considering Di Benedetto's elusive style of writing?

The correspondence between literature and cinema is certainly not new to the humanities. As old as the film medium itself, this connection has been subjected to debates and discussions by filmmakers and interdisciplinary scholars who have looked at the various effects – narratological, semantic, epistemological, archeological, 'dramatic' – between the two art forms (see, in this respect, Harris Ross's introduction to cinema's relationship to literature (1987)). Maya Deren, for example, who was one of the first avant-garde filmmakers seeking to free the language of film-poetry from the grammar of literature, insisted upon the autonomy and even 'superiority' of the filmic medium to communicate sensible experience, henceforth disapproving of the development of cinematic language from the perspective of 'pictorializing literature' (1946/2005b, 29) – that is, under its schematic, storytelling logic. Similar views had Andrei Tarkovsky, who, himself being the son of a writer, searched for a new poetic language of images that would escape or at least confront the verbalisation of the written work. Or as Ruiz has so lucidly put it in his *Diario*, if literature represents that art which grants visibility to the blind person (in the sense that its images are created by the reader's imagination instead of directly captured by their eyes) then cinema would represent an art which has the potential to blind the seer (as long as its images express, in material and poetic ways, those invisible, affective aspects of reality):

> Can it be said that cinema, as an art form, lies at the antipodes of literature – in the sense that literature is the art which grants visibility to the blind person whereas cinema is the art which blinds the seer? (2017, 524)

This blindness or de-visualisation of the literary work in film is precisely the type of intensity that I will explore in connection with Martel's 'contamination' of Di Benedetto's *Zama* – a subtraction of the excessive visual imagery that the novel presents to her as a reader, a movement of the imagination that goes beyond its own powers.

In responding to such a long-standing relationship between the domains of literature and cinema, my analysis in this section mainly draws on Rancière's *Les écarts du cinéma* (2011) and his chapter on '*Mouchette* and the Paradox of the Language of Images' (2011/2014, 41–67) to better illustrate this sense of subtraction, or 'de-visualisation' that Martel's film creates in her script adaptation.

The starting point for Rancière is to state that the cinema arises 'not *against* theatre but *after* literature' (2014, 43), though not in the sense of claiming that what cinema does is to translate written stories into audio-visual events but that in the very *corpus* of the novel you already find a form of visuality (*imagéité*) and a motion that is properly cinematic:

> Literature is not simply the art of language that would need to be put into plastic images and cinematic movement. It is a practice of language that also carries a particular idea of 'imageness' and of mobility. (2014, 43–4)

So, how can cinema respond to, and as it were, overturn this form of visuality that precedes it in the novel? According to Rancière, this is a process that withdraws from 'the excess' of *imagéité* contained in the text for a more sensuous imagery that 'de-visualises' its narrative on-screen, hence a visitation to the world of literature that pushes its images towards 'higher levels of cinematic abstraction' (2014, 46).

Such 'literary cinematographism' is exemplified by Rancière with regard to Georges Bernanos's *Nouvelle histoire de Mouchette* (1937) under what he calls the 'sequentialized tempo [of the novel]' (2014, 49), a movement that is subsequently intensified, or de-schematised, by Robert Bresson's film *Mouchette* (1967). According to Rancière, what Bresson does to the literary referent is to fragment its tempo and motion into a language that would remove the 'concrete sensations [of the story]' (2014, 49) for a space connected haptically via three de-visualising techniques: that of Bresson's intuitive hand or 'feeling-image' (2014, 50); that of the film's *mise en scène* and its 'haunting screenplay' (2014, 54); and that of the role of the actress in *Mouchette* (Nadine Nortier), whose performance is described by the philosopher not only as 'one of the most astonishing in the history of cinema' (2014, 59), but also one that displays a theatrical 'talent for opacity' (2014, 61). These three elements combined,

Rancière concludes, make up the quintessential, and paradoxical, language of cinema:

> The 'language of images' is [thus] not a [pure] language. It is a compromise between divergent poetics, a complex interlacing of the functions of *visual presentation, oral expression and narrative sequencing* (. . .) What comes after literature is not the art of the language of pure images. Nor is it a return to the old representational order. Rather it is a double excess which pulls the literary datum backwards on one side and ahead of itself on the other. It is what I have suggested elsewhere might be called a logic of the [thwarted] fable.[4] (2014, 66; 67)

In light of Rancière's logic, to say that cinema arises '*after* literature' is thus only partially correct, in the sense that it is also from theatre (the oral expression of the actress) and painting (the visual framing of the story) that his reading of *Mouchette* interlaces a mixture of divergent poetics. After all, and for precisely these kinds of reasons, cinema has been named 'the seventh art', as it is from the previous six that its images interlace an impure, heterogeneous poetry. Cinema, echoing Alain Badiou, would thus be defined as 'the art of taking' (2013, 88–93; 202–32).

This means, following Badiou's writings on film, that what is properly cinematic is the take itself: cinema is nothing but a mass – a very specific summation – of takes (in the same way that the take is a mass of images and the image is a mass of light). To say that cinema 'takes' also means, quite literally, that its elements are 'taken' from the previous arts – that is, cinema as the 'plus one of the arts' (2013, 88–93). So, in the light of Badiou's definition of the seventh art as this sort of borrowing, thievery activity, we can also read Rancière's divergent poetics as a visitation that is at least triple, not single (e.g. to literature), in the sense that Bresson's *Mouchette* takes its language from the world of theatre (the performance of Nadine Nortier); painting (the panoramic visuality of the film); and literature (the film's narrative sequencing). That is, I believe, how Bresson's film carries Bernanos's novel towards 'higher levels of cinematic abstraction', according to Rancière. It is a poetic intensification that unleashes the expressiveness contained in the written work– in a character, in a gesture, or in a visual landscape – by virtue of a movement that displays the intrinsically indeterminate nature of the image. And what I call the intensive-image here, following Rancière's reading of Bresson's film, is precisely that haptic transposition favouring rhythmic editing over denotative meanings. It is, essentially, a differential movement that accentuates the tactility and indirectness already contained in the novel: 'a structure

---

[4] See Jacques Rancière's prologue for *Film Fables*, 'A Thwarted Fable' (2001/2016, 1–19).

that wants to be another structure', as Pasolini refers to his works of adaptation (quoted in Martin 2020, 349). Cinema, in this sense, and the intensive-image most particularly, would thus be described as an art of relations: a divergent poetics placed in proximity to the previous arts (and to the cinema's artistic past) by virtue of a movement that 'dramatises', or intensifies, its signs. So again, if 'literature is the art which grants visibility to the blind person', then cinema would be 'the art which blinds the seer', as noted by Ruiz.

By the same token, I also want to explore how Martel's film de-visualises Di Benedetto's *Zama* by pushing his literary images towards higher levels of poetic intensity. The first and most general subtraction – a process of 'contamination' according to Martel; 'de-visualisation' according to Rancière; or, as I will argue shortly, 'dramatisation' according to Deleuze – would thus have to deal with the politics of adaptation itself. As it has already been noted, to authentically adapt a novel you do not need to be faithful to the narrator's voice in the text, but on the contrary, as Martel does, to infect its images by following your own intuitive thoughts as a reader – the reason why adaptation represents for her a form of para-doxy, or following Robert Stam's 'Beyond Fidelity: The Dialogics of Adaptation', 'a plethora of possible readings [produced by] an ever-shifting grid of interpretation' (2000, 57). *Contaminatio*, which is the term the ancient Romans employed to incorporate and transform previous Greek materials into their own cultural texts (such as plays or myths), stands here for Martel as the method illustrating her audiovisual transformations emerging out of her encounters with the text. It is, in this way, by infecting Di Benedetto's novel that Martel's (and Rancière's) 'cinematographism' adds more sensation, which allows for her *Zama* to be felt more intensely:

> Now that I've made a film based on a novel, I realize how many stupid things are said about the relationship between cinema and literature. Now that I've lived it, I understand it better (. . .) A novel is cinematic when its language permits you to create your own; when its grammar, its words, lend themselves to the creation of a [new] audiovisual language (. . .) In ancient Rome they did something called *contaminatio*. *Contaminatio* was the way in which the Romans reworked ancient Greek literature, incorporating the same basic elements into their own cultural setting, which was very different. [In a similar way] I find [in] Di Benedetto's language [something] thrilling, it's like a whirlwind of *déjà vu*, and I felt that the rhythm of the novel was a rhythm I could translate into a film. (Martel quoted in Marchini, 2018a, 45)

So, how does Martel contaminate Di Benedetto's novel? Firstly, she does it by politicising the colonial past in which the story is rooted. Of course,

Di Benedetto's Zama – a Kafkaesque *criollo* settler – is already embedded in this elliptical reality of Latin American writers whose characters problematise European notions of progress and history under their unresolved mestizo identities. (Take, for example, the musician-narrator in Alejo Carpentier's *Los pasos perdidos* (1953/1998),[5] who finds his authentic, primordial voice on a trip he makes to the inner jungle; or the question about Latin American identity in Octavio Paz's essay *El laberinto de la soledad* (1950/2000).[6]) Quite similarly, in Di Benedetto's book we also trace the lost steps of a character, who, willing to go back with his Spanish family, has to wait in vain, by a foreign river that rejects him, because 'water doesn't like him . . .'. However, instead of deepening the protagonist's relationship to his locality in the Viceroyalty of the Río de la Plata, or of complicating his identity in connection to this land which gave birth to him, Di Benedetto concludes his novel with a character reaffirming his own European heritage by looking at a blonde boy who epitomises the ideal image of himself as a teen: 'It wasn't an Indian', Zama says at the very end of the tale, 'It was the blonde boy. Filthy, in rags, still only twelve. He was me, myself before me' (2016, 198).

Martel's finale, on the contrary, supplants such a westernised image of Zama by introducing the black (local) inversion to his mestizo identity: she replaces the literary ending with an image of the Indigenous kid who asks Zama whether or not he wants to live, while another local rows the canoe in the creek. As Edgardo Dieleke and Álvaro Fernández note in their film analysis of *Zama*: 'Martel complicates the question of [Latin American] identity by giving voice to the subaltern [Indian boy] at the end of the story.' In this way, they continue, the filmmaker 'proposes an image that not only reinterprets the life of [Di Benedetto's] Zama but also inverts a dominant historical time and its representation by giving voice to a different narrator' (2018, 3; my translation).[7]

As a result of this hegemonic overturning, Martel's film effectively stresses the political presence of those marginalised bodies long erased from the European writing of Amerindian history. (See, in this regard,

---

[5] In *Los pasos perdidos*, Carpentier's protagonist is a metropolitan music lover who finds the origin of his 'inner voice' in a trip he makes to the Venezuelan jungle, where, at the end of the novel, he decides to stay, thus deepening his relation to an Indigenous identity that he had forgotten.

[6] In this essay, the poet Paz revisits the Mexican (and by extension Latin American) ethos embedded in that violent encounter between the Indigenous woman and the (white) European settler, from which the mestizo self and their identity is born.

[7] 'Martel complica la pregunta sobre la identidad, y a la vez da el poder del cierre del relato a una voz subalterna. Así, este marco planteado por la película puede pensarse como una mirada o una interpretación de una vida, la de Zama, circular, pero también, como una revisión del tiempo histórico y su representación, respecto a quiénes narran y a cómo lo hacen.'

Michel De Certeau's description of Amerigo Vespucci who, like Cristoforo Colombo after him, arrives from the Atlantic to baptise his naked, 'Latin American' land (1988/1992).) Here, quite contrary to the Spanish settler who confidently pens his Western desire on a blank body to be written, the Magistrate Zama is rather confused by his hallucinatory visions, probably because, as the film tells us, he lives all his life struggling to remain by a river that rejects him. However, Martel's attention to the river where the fish must struggle to stay alive is also a metaphor that applies to viewers who are puzzled by the film's aesthetics and thus must also work to stay in the swim. It is, as Dieleke and Fernández state, via Martel's 'alternative explorer' – a mestizo character – that the audience gets access to those multiple subaltern bodies lost in the annals of Latin American history: 'Diego de Zama makes you see, hear, and feel about a world that is lost, but that centuries later keeps resonating next to our contemporary relations of race, class, and gender' (2018, 3; my translation). Politicising the colonial past in which the novel is rooted thus means to denaturalise the hierarchies organising local history by virtue of a voyeur who grants us access to those minor voices populating all corners of the screen, yet not the literary piece. In many respects, as Iain MacKenzie and Robert Porter suggest in their 'dramatising' of Deleuze's modern artist by looking at the work of Kafka, these are also the intense political effects caused by the deterritorialising powers of Martel's screenplay in *Zama*:

> Thanks to art, instead of seeing a single world, our own, we see it multiplied, and we have as many worlds at our disposal as there are artists, worlds more different from each other than those that spin through infinity (. . .) In Kafka, to take but one other example, [Deleuze and Guattari] insist that his fiction dramatizes 'a deterritorialization of the world that is itself political'. Time and again, they locate various aesthetic forms at the heart of their philosophy of difference, and they attribute to these forms a particular power to dramatically effect movements in thought. (2011, 47–8)

Although this is Martel's first feature film centred on a male protagonist (as well as her first film shot in digital and historical piece), it is nonetheless via Don Diego de Zama that the viewer is immersed into those marginalised bodies so distinctive of Martel's filmography – from the lunatic lady in *The Headless Woman* to the wandering teen in *The Holy Girl*, or Isabel in *The Swamp*, that family servant who is unfairly accused of stealing from her mistress. In *Zama*, quite similarly, women and children are also those who interrupt the journeys of the male explorer: e.g. Indigenous kids appear in the background of the image while Zama is at the centre of it; they make unintelligible sounds which often deepen our viewing attention; they hear and see adults without them noticing; in short, children see while 'the adults are blind' (Di Benedetto 2016, 188). In a passage borrowed from Di Benedetto's book, when Zama is called to the shores of the river to welcome Indalecio (Germán de Silva) from Montevideo, his son (Vicenzo Navarro Rindel) makes an uncanny remark which completely decentres the colonial positioning of the Magistrate.

In the novel, however, the boy seems only to celebrate the royal standing of Zama as in the following:

> Don Diego de Zama, the forceful executive, the pacifier of Indians, the warrior who rendered justice without recourse to the sword. Zama, who put down the native rebellion without wasting a drop of Spanish blood, winning honours from his monarch and the respect of the conquered. (2016, 15)[8]

The child's description, which is included in the film's scene commented on above, is preceded by another utterance that changes the dynamic of Di Benedetto's sentence completely. Out of focus, Indalecio's son, who is being carried in a chair on the back of a black man, looks in the direction of the sun while whispering a mysterious revelation about our 'forceful executive': 'Don Diego de Zama is a god who was born old and can't die. His loneliness is atrocious.'[9] Immediately after, the Magistrate asks the boy whether he is talking to him or not. Then, as Eleonora Rapan remarks, Martel employs for the first time in the film the Shepard tone that will accentuate Zama's inner delirium.[10] And it is at this point – via the film's descending and decentring sonic effects – that the viewer cannot guarantee any longer whether these words are being uttered by the boy or fantasised about by Zama. Put differently, what the filmmaker does here, at the moment when Indalecio's son offers his auspicious descriptions of the *Corregidor*, is to contaminate the ideal image of the literary protagonist by intensifying his mental perplexity, as it is in this passage borrowed from Di Benedetto's book that the kid's sentence no longer synchs to the words coming out from his lips. Such uncanniness put forward by Martel's audiovisual labyrinths, described by Rapan as a combination of

---

[8] Zama, quite proudly, later adds in the novel yet not in the film: 'I was that Corregidor: a man of the law, a judge (. . .) A man without fear, with the vocation and power to bring an end – to crime, at least . . . This boy, Indalecio's son, demanded that of me with all the force of his admiration' (2016, 16).

[9] 'Don Diego de Zama es un dios que ha nacido anciano y no puede morir. Su soledad es atroz.'

[10] As Rapan remarks: 'In Zama, Martel applies various audio novelties for the first time, among them the use of Shepard tones. As explained by sound designer Guido Berenblum (2018), Lucrecia Martel was at the early stages of the pre-production when the idea of introducing the Shepard tones was developed. Since Don Diego de Zama is waiting for a transfer that never comes, a wait that is beyond the normal, a wait with a metaphysical dimension as in Beckett or Buzzati' (2018, 138).

both the film's 'immersive sonic landscape' and 'the uncanny use of the off-screen space' (2018, 138) is also commented on by Adrian Martin in similar terms. Referring to the same passage described above, Martin states that:

> An incident from the book is faithfully staged and recreated, yet at the same time it is approached and rendered obliquely: the choice of angles, the atmospheric sound design, the ellipses, and the decisions to push so much of the action into either off-screen space or blur, all serve to constantly redefine and transform the nominal 'center' of the action. Not to mention those sudden swerves from reality to fantasy – two realms that are never quite distinct, anyhow, right from the film's opening moments (. . .) Lucrecia Martel's *Zama* is, alongside everything else that can be said about it, an extraordinary work of adaptation (. . .) While following the basic outline of the book, she takes the usual liberties involved in page-to-screen adaptation: characters are subtracted, events are condensed, interior monologues are transposed into exterior dialogues. But Martel has allowed herself a far greater margin of freedom in this genuine 're-imagining' of the novel. (2018)

Martel's adaptation thus favours an enigmatic *mise en scène* that metamorphoses the literary connections between characters and spaces in a process that Martin describes as 're-imagining the novel'. This is, most clearly, a baroque method that opens the story out in a non-totalisable arrangement of perspectives and events, allowing the filmmaker to contaminate the literary referent by blending the real and the imagined in a reservoir of virtual images which never really activate a stable form of identity:

> What characterises the baroque most of all is an emphasis on the fragment over the whole and a resulting complexity in which there are multiple levels coexisting within the same work, which are not reducible to an overall scheme or perspective. (Goddard 2013, 6)

In addition to these observations, Martel's film is also able to de-visualise Di Benedetto's book and its protagonist by cutting most of his monologue, in the sense that Zama remains an almost speechless character throughout the movie, while in the novel he is our first-person narrator. But as I have already argued, Di Benedetto's Zama in many respects represents the type of elliptical and introspective character that Martel had in mind for her film, except for the fact that by silencing his voice, in addition to her elusive cinematic techniques, Zama's mental delirium is rendered more intense and obscure for the viewer to engage with. Hence, if what defines Di Benedetto's protagonist is his incapacity to escape from his own inner voice (a sort of Kafkaesque character trapped in the labyrinths of his own world), then what makes Martel's film more 'gaseous' or intense is precisely that lack of a solid first-person narrator guiding us through the story. This means, echoing Rancière, that the *imagéité* introduced by Di Benedetto's novel is being mobilised towards higher levels of cinematic abstraction under Martel's intensification of the text – a visual indeterminacy that prevents the intensive-image from ever reaching a solid, unitary form of solution.

In this sense, Martel's film is equally enacting a temporal subtraction that erases the chronological ordering of the book, further complicating the viewer's capacity for orientation. But again, time in the novel is more elastic than linear, closer to Zama's existential crisis than to the three periods in which the story is rooted; 1790, 1794 and 1799. However, the fact that Martel eliminates these historical breaks from the book makes of her film and its protagonist an even more ethereal form of psycho-logic. It is as if past, present and future were transformed into another mode of temporality that no longer responds to chronological orderings, but to a cyclical pattern. As Jonathan Romney writes: 'Time itself liquefies', and the motif of water in *Zama* reinforces this sense of 'temporal porousness' (2018, 32). Hence, what we experience in the film is a sense of 'becoming-ness' that frees the intensive-image from its rigid time-form in order to give birth to a different mode of temporality, one that Deren refers to as 'the time-quality of a woman's body' (2016, 9).

In short, I suggest that Martel's film is capable of intensifying the literary *Zama* by means of three interconnected subtractions: that of politicising (and dramatising) the colonial past in which the novel is rooted; that of silencing the narrator's voice in the text; and that of withdrawing from the book's historical breaks to announce an even more elastic form of cinematic temporality. This is, as a whole, the type of de-visualisation that is played out not only in relation to Rancière's passage from literature to film but more broadly, in relation to the different levels of 'dramatisation' that Deleuze describes at the end of his fourth chapter in *Difference and Repetition* – a method that is further developed in his other books and talks, as in *Nietzsche and Philosophy*, his dissertations for the French Society of Philosophy in early 1967 and his seminar for *Doctorat d'Etat* in early 1969. This method of dramatisation, which according to Deleuze is the only one 'adequate to Nietzsche's project' (quoted in MacKenzie and Porter 2011, 42), of transforming philosophy via more affective and genealogical inquiries, is thus akin to the emergence of different levels of intensity that I put forward in my analysis of the intensive-image as it is manifested in the classical, modern and contemporary periods. It is a dramatising movement that, as Deleuze infers in his 1968 masterwork, is always staging new relations between actors, spaces and ideas in a world-stage that intensifies constantly:

> Intensity is the determinant in the process of actualisation. It is intensity which dramatizes. It is intensity which is immediately expressed in the basic spatio-temporal dynamisms and determines an "indistinct" differential relation in the idea to incarnate itself in a distinct quality and a distinguished extensity (. . .) The aesthetic of intensities thus develops each of its moments in correspondence with the dialectics of ideas: the power of intensity (depth) is grounded in the potentiality of the idea. (2014, 320–1)

Second Drama, or the Drama of Deleuze's Cinema(s): From One Level of Intensity to Another Level of Intensity

Dramatisation, like any method, presupposes at least a principle and a path – a sense of direction. In the case of Deleuze, such a principle is referred to as difference or intensity, while its destiny, always virtual, is defined as differentiation, actualisation or intensification. Here, what Deleuze calls dramatisation is the underlying process through which the idea (that is, the 'drama') is revitalised in extensity, so that every time an idea becomes actual *in extension* (i.e. in a concept) it simultaneously *différencie* ['differenciate'][11] itself *in intensio*, which means that Deleuze's drama is always on the move towards an actual infinity – an ideal Leibnizian continuum: 'There are two labyrinths of the human mind: one concerns the composition of the continuum, and the other the nature of freedom, and both spring from the same source – the infinite' (Leibniz 1679/1973, 83). In Deleuze's words, this continuity expresses 'the differenciation of differentiation' (2014, 281); this is the reason why I argue that in his two cinema volumes there should be an early drama – an intensive-image already at play in the classical period – which later on intensifies and thus transforms itself into another (modern) drama. So, rather than two isolated logics of the image placed in opposition against each other, there should be one interconnecting image, the intensive-image, that places Deleuze's two film ages into one differentiating continuum. Here, one of the conditions Deleuze sets for this method is that the drama itself has to be operative, and yet hidden underneath, every concept or image, so that by accounting for an early intensive-image I have suggested that Deleuze's 'modern'

---

[11] In the translator's preface of *Difference and Repetition,* Paul Patton refers to *différencier* ('to make or become different') as 'differenciate' with the '*c*', a term of art in English that is used to distinguish it from 'differentiate' or *différentier* in French, which is restricted to the mathematical operation. For further discussion on the term 'differenciation', see Chapter 4, 'Ideas and the Synthesis of Difference' in *Difference and Repetition* (2014, 223–92).

system is what pushes the previous 'classical' sequence towards higher dramas, all the way up until reaching an unprecedented level of intensity today by which the initial difference is integrated or 'differentiated' into a new drama. In Deleuze's words: 'Ideas are dramatized at several levels, but so too dramatisation of different orders echoes one another across these levels' (2014, 285). 'This continuity', he also explains in 'The Method of Dramatization' while referring to Leibniz's ideality, 'is defined not at all by homogeneity, but by the coexistence of all the variations of differential relations, and of the distribution of singularities that correspond to them' (2004, 101).

Put differently, and whatever cinematic epoch we are looking at, the concept of the intensive-image suggests that there is an initial 'drama' associated with its own differentiating trajectory, very much like the point made above regarding Rancière's paradoxical language of images, when asking: 'What can cinema do with the literary "cinematographism" that precedes it?' (2014, 45). The answer, as we saw, was given by the dramatic movement between the two Zamas – a process of de-visualisation that Martel puts at play in her reimagining of the novel. Henceforth, I argue that dramatisation as a method is not only useful to describe Rancière's movement from literature to film, or Deleuze's movement from classical to modern cinemas, but also one that further differentiates Deleuze's time-image modernity into higher levels of intensity today.

This observation has already been made in my book. In Chapter 1, for instance, Deleuze's intensification of the time-image was said to reach a differentiated (gaseous) state of perception in contemporary filmmaking practice. Scholars have referred to this heightened form of audiovisuality in various – although not always equivalent – terms: 'ex-centric cinema' (Harbord 2016); 'cinematic boredom' (Ruiz 2013; Quaranta 2020); 'slow cinema' (Flanagan 2012; Ciment 2013; de Luca and Nuno Barradas 2016); contemplative cinema (Martin 2020); or '*adynamic*' cinema (Agamben 1993). The latter term signifies here an image of 'impotence', or the potential of images not to be, which I have discussed next to the Aristotelian notion of *adynamia* as reworked by Agamben in my analysis of *The Lobster*. In all of these cases, I have argued that the significance of the intensive-image also relies on the way it turns on-screen reality into a purely expressive and affective phenomenon. It expresses, as accounted for by Pedro Costa's aesthetics of *temps mort*, a porous form of visuality, or a 'gaseous intensity', that is freed from mimetic concerns. Here, by looking at one of Costa's early films on Cape Verdean Ventura, I examined a de-framed, or un-framed form of perception that encourages the viewer, echoing Deleuze, to have an on-screen 'encounter with pure intensive difference' (2014, 140). *Colossal Youth* was, in this sense, another film connected haptically through feeling rather than meaning, one in which its sequencing is devoid of any sensory-motor links thereby composing a highly poetic displacement. But Costa's sensorial aesthetics in this film is also indicative of his larger cinematographic oeuvre. Taken as a unity, his entire filmography becomes a singular continuum that glues independent pieces together as sequences of one and the same film – that is, an intensifying drama narrated by his various characters (Tina, Vanda, Ventura, Vitalina . . .) who are surpassing the viewer on all sides and in relation to all meanings.

Similarly, in Chapter 4, I also looked at Godard's two film periods to suggest a differentiating trajectory in what Deleuze's Bergson calls an 'image-tendency.[12] The intention there was to connect the director's different modern phases, with a first political phase associated with the French New Wave, or with Godard's commitment to the 'method of between', according to Deleuze; and with a second more reflective phase dramatising the previous act by means of an archaeological montage-technique that I associated with his essayist, post-New Wave period. In Gilberto Perez's words:

> From the beginning critics would describe Godard as more of an essayist than a storyteller, but it was near the end of his New Wave period that he really began to make cinematic essays, inquiries into a situation, explorations of a scene. (2019, 171)

According to Perez, Godard's second phase appears, roughly speaking, with *Masculin féminin* (1966) and *Two or Three Things I Know About Her* (1967), although it is clearly with *Histoire(s) du cinéma* (1989–99) that his cinema starts to shift towards a more reflective political phase. In this sense, Godard's filmography, like that of Costa, can also be said to manifest an intensive, 'dramatising' image which moves from Deleuze's time-image modernity (in the New Wave) towards a more essayist contemporary practice (in films such as *Film Socialism* (2010) *Goodbye to Language* (2014)

---

[12] In describing Bergson's notion of 'Being [as] alteration [or] duration', Deleuze describes such an intensive trajectory as one 'composite', multiphased image that must be 'dissociated' along its path: '*Between two things, between two products, there are only and there only could be differences of degree, of proportion [of intensities]*. What differs in [Bergson's] nature is never a thing, but a *tendency*. A difference of nature is never between two products or between two things, but *in one and the same thing* between two tendencies that traverse it, in one and the same product between two tendencies that encounter one another in it. Indeed, what is pure is never the thing; the thing is always a composite that must be dissociated; *only the tendency is pure, which is to say that the true thing or the substance is the tendency itself*' (2004a, 26; my emphasis).

and *The Image Book* (2018)). Echoing Badiou, this is what we may call 'the cinema's second' – or even third[13] – wave of 'modernity':

> Mention Godard first. He was also part of our historical frame of reference: the New Wave. The line of demarcation, the difference between the New Wave and what we are attempting to call cinema's second modernity [today], passes through him. (2013, 58)

Another filmmaker who intensifies Deleuze's time-image modernity is Lucrecia Martel – the mestizo director of the senses. With *Zama*, which is a highly dramatic film, there are plenty of affective moments that differentiate Deleuze's time-image into more disruptive viewing events. Add to Martel's contemplative style of filmmaking (as enabled by the long take) her manipulative use of sound arranged by musician Luciano Azzigotti, or her withdrawal from the sequentialised (chronological) tempo of the novel. There is also her off-screen work that so commonly pushes key audiovisual information outside of the cinematic frame, thus undermining the centrality of vision and action in order to generate a defamiliarising aesthetics resembling that of Zama's deliriums. Indeed, as many commentators have noted, there is a strong link between Zama's bewilderment and our own confusion as viewers: 'It takes more than one viewing to begin to piece together what's really happening in *Zama*', notes Romney in *Sight and Sound* (2018, 33); or as mentioned by Marchini in *Cineaste*: 'Inhabiting the tortured subjectivity of its protagonist, the film plunges the viewer into an affective maelstrom whose intensity doesn't relent for a moment of the almost two-hour running time' (2018b, 53). As a result, by dissipating the economy of narrative events, Martel favours a more contemplative film experience that can be defined above all by its sensory mode of address. This is, in the words of Rancière, an 'aesthetic regime' which confronts 'the old principle of form fashioning matter with identity' in order to introduce the 'sensible presence' of the phenomenological real (quoted in de Luca 2012, 200).

Deborah Martin has also stressed Martel's capacity to renew modern forms of film-thinking in what she sees as the experience of 'the uncanny'. In *The Cinema of Lucrecia Martel* (2016), she writes:

> [Martel's films] operate on the border of the known and the unknown, always gesturing to that which is just beyond our grasp, at the edges of the visible and of the thinkable. This is why the uncanny is such a prominent mode for Martel: the uncanny is

---

[13] 'Third modernity' as long as we take Deleuze's classical cinema to be the first modern period, as I have argued in Chapter 4, 'In Between Modernities and the Contemporaneous'.

an experience of doubt, of uncertainty, and Martel's films operate to communicate an essential lack of certainty, with all the anxiety and possibility that this entails (. . .) [Her films] exhibit a pervasive openness of frame and of meaning, an openness echoed by their representation of desire which proliferates promiscuously, eluding fixity. There is also a strong emphasis on the opening of perception: an idea which is diegetically staged, and which also results in cinematic experiments inviting a renewal of spectatorial perception (. . .) This openness and experimentation [is what] gives a radical political valence to Martel's work. (2016, 22)

This means that by placing images at the edge of the visible, by creating doubts about what we see, and by decelerating time to construct a filmic space for reflection, Martel's films place a strong emphasis on the opening of perception that shifts attention away from the classical dominance of vision towards the modern-sensorial. This is done by means of a body that, mainly out of its polyphonic functions, becomes our primary organ to apprehend what is experienced onscreen. As Martel suggests while referring to her aural approach to filmmaking:

In cinema, the most tactile thing one can use to transmit, the most intimate tool, is sound. Sound penetrates you, it is very corporeal (. . .) I work with the idea that sound can tell more than words. (Quoted in Martin 2016, 21)

Indeed, as it happens with *Zama*, Martel's acoustic prevalence not only expands to off-screen scenarios – that is, towards spaces where the viewer feels completely disorientated—but simultaneously deepens on-screen situations to create what we could call here a deep intensive-image, one which welcomes the viewer 'to [infinitely] discover what is in the image rather than coming to the image knowing what it is' (Marks 2000b, 178). This is exemplified, among other episodes in the film, when Zama visits the Governor (Daniel Veronese) and asks him to send to the King a letter of transfer on his behalf. In this meeting, we suddenly notice the embalmed ears of the supposedly deceased criminal Vicuña Porto (Matheus Nachtergaele), ears that the Governor hangs quite proudly around his neck. Here, we realise that behind the Governor's back there is a lackey who looks acutely, with his eyes wide open, at one of the ears resting on his chest. Unexpectedly, the conversation cuts off and the assistant's mumbling voice takes centre stage. Inwardly and mysteriously, he says: 'Vicuña Porto is dead . . . Do not touch [the ears].' He then, of course, touches the ears, but what really deepens and penetrates the image here is his sudden monologue which silences the previous interchange between Zama and the Governor and which so abruptly shifts our focus of attention: by zooming into the face of the subordinate, Martel conveys a deep visual richness that, quite unexpectedly, metamorphoses the whole dynamic of her *mise en scène*. This is a passage of high intensity that the filmmaker grounds in the potentiality of an image that is always more subterranean and excessive than its apparent material surface reveals it to be.

Besides her deep sonic labyrinth displayed in this episode, or in the other sequence described above when Indalecio's son tells Zama that his solitude is atrocious, there are many other instances where Martel's aural landscape densifies the image with subterranean intensities. Take, for example, the piercing whistling made by *the pájaro urutaú* and the *pájaro campana*, sounds that so often accompany the film's tropical settings, or the muttering noises of insects, like those of cicadas and flies, which travel from the (immaterial) off-screen space to the (material) on-screen body of Zama, as when they alight on his neck at the same time as he is attacked by mosquitoes on a hot tropical day. Such formation of meaning thorough images that are both sensually proximate and narratively disorienting, is one of the ways Martel contributes to this form of eventless cinema that Martin and Marks define, among other characteristics, by its 'sensual mode of address' (Marks 2000b, 194–242) – that is to say, an intensive-image capable of 'slowing [cinematic] time down' (Martin 2016, 7). How this is done in Martel's *Zama* will be the topic of my next and last section.

Third Drama: Intensification Passes Through the Body of Zama

Martel's film dramatises its own narrative development by the bodily decline of its protagonist. Recall the film's opening passage: Don Diego de Zama stands upright and confident at the riverbank waiting for a ship. A couple of shots later he spies on a group of naked women who are mud-bathing in the stream. Up to this point, Zama represents nothing so much as the classical voyeur as described by Laura Mulvey in her critique of (Hollywood) male-centred spectatorship, though the inconspicuous nature of his position of hidden observer will soon be exposed and derided by the active look of women: '¡Mirón!' [Nosy!], says one of the girls who caught him by surprise gazing behind the bushes. Once spotted, Zama runs backwards, nervously, until he is finally nabbed by Malemba (Mariana Nunes), the mulatta servant whose face he slaps.

This is the first of many failed encounters where Zama is put to shame by his own scopophilic actions, seduced and reduced to passivity by female agents who so easily captivate him, while simultaneously confusing him, or lying to him, as when he goes to the home of Rita (Paula Grinzpan) and finds out that there is a man on the second floor having sex with her. In this scene, Zama adopts once again the position of a male protector chasing the intruder with his sword and trying to calm Rita down with his heroic words: 'There's nothing to be afraid of . . .'; although Martel's film makes it very clear that Rita is not being raped as Zama thought: 'Are you hurt?' he then utters on-screen. Unlike the book, the film suggests that Rita is rather enjoying a night of sex with one of her lovers.

In this respect, Martel's film displays a feminist *contaminatio* of the novel which explicitly ridicules Zama's heroic virility, for the filmmaker reverses the dominant position of the traditional male voyeur into a passive observer – a seer – who is trapped by the secrets of Rita and womanhood. (The secret that is being preserved here is a form of hidden interiority that is driving Zama's mental confusion and, later on, his entire bodily collapse.) And it is under the affirmation of such a secret that the intensity of Martel's film gives itself to exterior as internal, that is to say, as 'the secret of secrecy' (Deleuze 2020b, 264) in which Zama's confusion (as well as that of viewers) begins to take shape. Luciana Piñares de Luenga (Lola Dueñas), the Spanish Lady married to his superior, the Minister of Real Hacienda, stands in this sense as the ultimate yet forbidden love relationship that both the literary and cinematic Zama desires; a woman that will flirt with him in the extreme but whose body he will never possess – despite her constant promises, notwithstanding her seducing him to the point of delirium.[14] Out of despair, when Zama gets into Luciana's house and spies on her, he realises that she has been sleeping with his subaltern, Ventura Prieto, thus not only cheating on her husband Honorio, and playing with his own expectations and desires, but also lowering his esteem.

In all of these cases, there are strained relationships with women that precipitate Zama's mental collapse. His psychological breakdown is not only due to his failed amorous encounters, or to his longing for his absent wife Marta, but also to the unfulfilled promise of a letter that would grant his reassignment to a more metropolitan post. Away from family and home, Zama is stuck in a claustrophobic yet open foreign space – a sort of Kafkaesque reverse of Gregor Samsa who is trapped in his own family house.[15]

Zama's waiting, in this way, is dramatised by his own bodily decline in both novel and film. It is a diminishing process that Di Benedetto and Martel know how to intensify: 'I do for you what no one did for me. I

---

[14] Luciana says to Zama: 'Every man is greedy for my body. Honorio, my own husband, lives in thrall to the flesh. I despise it and despise all men for their love of possession.'

[15] Zama could also be said to resemble Kafka's K, the protagonist of *The Castle* (1926/1999); someone who awaits with his life for a legal permit that he will never get. Like K, Zama agonises before getting what he wants.

say no to your hopes', says Zama at the end of the story to the criminal Vicuña Porto, who then proceeds to cut off his arms with a machete. Once enthusiastic, vigorous and rightful, our voyeur Zama ends up like a suffering fish resting on the ground. And this is precisely the dramatic arc put forward by Di Benedetto's story which later on Martel intensifies through Zama's body: '[Martel's] *Zama* is about a prolonged, agonized process of mundane waiting (. . .) a process that hollows out personal identity and dashes all lingering hope' (Martin 2018).

Put differently, what Zama's misfortunes bring to light here is that below the costumes of his rank there are always little conundrums, doubts, intensities that disrobe him completely, pushing him to the limit and to the unknown, as if there were internal gaps popping up through his body, gradually appearing on the surface of the image, moving from an internal confusion that loses itself to a subject that loses his body and sense of orientation in the film. In this capacity, Zama's interiority, which is the intensive-image as such, reveals itself in the indeterminacy of an exterior environment, in a perpetual waiting dashing all lingering hope, or in those female secrets visually materialised onscreen which diminish and demolish his standing body. And that is also the dramatic method conveyed in this chapter under Martel's adaptation qua contamination: a form of interiority that intensifies the presence of the absent in the novel; a de-visualising technique that affirms the silences and fractures of the writer's protagonist. Hence, the final moments of the film, when Martel inverts Di Benedetto's figure of the blonde (presumably European) kid for an image of the Indigenous, is clearly another means to problematise and politicise this indeterminacy of a mestizo character who can no longer see. Martel's Zama – a fractured 'I' – animates a new mode of thinking-feeling by virtue of the drama the book offers to her as a reader. In words of Didier Debaise:

> The question [of dramatisation in Deleuze] is to know how to intensify its importance. And if a method is needed, it is because the question of intensification, of the increase in importance of events, is not a natural attitude; it implies a change, an inversion in the habitual course of thought, a certain *askesis* of thought that allows it to be exercised in a new way. (2016, 10)

In the course of this chapter, *Zama*'s dramatisation, or what Deleuze calls 'the differen*c*iation of differentiation', has played out at three different levels – a moving image that, in each of its singular points, has revealed a new intensive drama. Firstly, following Rancière's paradoxes of the language of images, I explored how Martel's film was able to de-visualise Di Benedetto's text by pushing his elusive images towards higher levels of cinematic abstraction. This had to do, in general, with Martel's politics of adaptation, a mode of (mis)reading or transposition that she intuitively calls 'contamination' – an infection of the novel. At least three subtractive operations were more specific to her reimagining of the literary work. The first had to do with reversing the colonial past in which the novel was rooted. Here I argued that by deepening Zama's relationship to his locality in the Viceroyalty of the Río de la Plata, instead of reaffirming his own European heritage (as the book does at the end next to the image of the blonde kid in the creek), Martel complicated the question of Latin American identity by giving primacy to those voices of the subaltern. The second aspect dealt with transforming the book's first-person narrator into an almost speechless character throughout the film, so that by cutting out most of the storyline from his lips, Zama's interior monologues were transposed into more diffuse external dialogues, thus converting the centre of literary action in the book into more tactile episodes on-screen. Finally, the third dramatic subtraction referred to Martel's decision to erase the temporal brakes proposed by the novel so as to de-historicise its chronology, thus further complicating our sense of orientation in the film.

But the drama didn't stop there. Martel's *Zama* also dramatised Deleuze's cinemas more broadly. I claimed that by producing new relations around the principle of indeterminacy that so distinctly animates Deleuze's conception of the time-image, Martel's film was able to intensify his modern sequence in virtue of those unbearable affects that were forcing Zama (as well as the viewer) to think and feel anew. Her off-screen work and polyphonic form of cinema were some of the techniques in which the filmmaker conveyed an intensive form of audiovisuality that showed and told way more than what the surface of the screen could reveal, as if in the background of every image there were cracks, and already other images, expanding on the 'dramatic' arc of Deleuze's cinemas. The intensive-image, in this way, is expressing a differentiating continuity that not only marks the passage from Di Benedetto's book to Martel's film, but also one that liberates Deleuze's early 'drama' (e.g. in the classical movement-image) from its fixity or schematic coordinates, for this method which intensifies constantly must necessarily surpass the givens of resemblance by experimenting with those affects that are unknown to the viewer.

Lastly, in relation to the film itself, dramatisation was incarnated in the bodily decline of Zama; a character earlier idealised and self-assured, standing upright on the riverbank, but who ended up, not far from the same stream, lying like a restless cadaver on top of a canoe next to the Indigenous kid. Perhaps that boy was one of the children we saw at the beginning of the story, in the background of the image, or perhaps he was the son Zama had with the Indigenous woman in the film, so the boy could well be thought of as himself born anew as Indigenous (in the novel, on the contrary, Zama's son is 'frail and white', conceived by his Spanish servant, Emilia). Zama's existential crisis would probably then be resolved through such an inverted, black image of himself before becoming white and blonde as in the book. In this capacity, perhaps, Zama would no longer struggle to remain in the water, for the river would be part of his own fish-character and animality.

CHAPTER 7

What do Animals Teach Us About Intensity? On *Sweetgrass* and SEL's Bodily Praxis[1]

By 2001, before the Sensory Ethnography Lab (SEL) was established, director Lucien Castaing-Taylor and producer Ilisa Barbash began to explore Montana shepherding for what was going to be *Sweetgrass*; the first feature film produced by the Lab. With no interviews, a parametric narrative, and more animal noise than human, the film follows a handful of shepherds over a period of three months as they drive approximately 3,000 sheep through Montana's Absaroka-Beartooth mountains. Using long takes, close-ups and an inventive approach to sound, *Sweetgrass* draws on the filmmakers' ethnographic training to detail the way of life and process of work of pastoral life.

The film is structured into a year in the life of the sheep and the cowboys, beginning in winter and ending at the end of the summer pasturing, as John Ahern, one of the herders, explains. *Sweetgrass*, which emerges as a type of observational documentary drawing on the worlds of anthropology and film ethnography, opens an interesting direction in which to conceptualise animal ontology from the perspective of the intensive-image and its a-centric, post-human approach; it records the process of life between cowboy and sheep from an optical reality that, echoing Anat Pick, is not strictly centred 'on human form, perception and identity' (2007, 34). (Post human cinema presumes exactly a gaze which sees from an unconventional angle; that of a point of view from a non-human eye. It derives in a filmmaking style that attempts to decompose the notion of framing by presenting an acentred system of relations in which things become multiple referents, hence an intensive-image where things vary autonomously in relation to one another.) As stated on their website, and as seen

[1] A previous version of this chapter appeared in *Anthrovision Vaneasa online journal* 5 (1), 'The Colliding Worlds of Anthropology and Film-Ethnography: A Dynamic Continuum' (Escobar 2017a), and in the Literary Environments conference organised by Griffith University, Gold Coast Campus, under the title 'Animal Dwellings: The bodies of contemporary theory and SEL's documentary film Sweetgrass' (paper delivered 18 July 2017).

in other films related to the lab, such as *Leviathan* (V. Paravel and L. Castaing-Taylor, 2012); *Manakamana* (S. Spray and P. Velez, 2013); *The Iron Ministry* (J. P. Sniadecki, 2014);[2] *Ah humanity* (E. Karel; V. Paravel; L. Castaing-Taylor, 2015); and *Caniba* (V. Paravel and L. Castaing-Taylor, 2017), SEL harnesses perspectives:

> Drawn from the human sciences, the arts, and the humanities [aiming] to support innovative combinations of aesthetics and ethnography, with original nonfiction media practices that explore the bodily praxis and affective fabric of human existence. (Sensory Ethnography Lab)[3]

Undoubtedly, (audio) visual as much as written ethnography have had a particular interest in showing the societal patterns in which humans work and live. Animals, as an external element to understanding our own behaviour, have consistently been interlopers in such an anthropological enterprise. In Robert Flaherty's *Nanook of the North* (1922), as I have examined in the article 'The Colliding Worlds of Anthropology and Film Ethnography' (2017a), we see animals in focus alongside the dramatisation of Inuit life; or in Jean Rouch's *Les maîtres fous* (1953) while depicting the African Hauka cult, we watch horses possessed by spirits of colonial administrators to signify a human tradition that is only pertinent to the cult's members. It is an anthropocentric image that, beside negating any encounter with animal subjectivity, demonstrates our supposed entitlement to dominate and guard other animals as if they were second-class living species. This means that to critically take into account the topic of the animal, and the topic of their subjectivity through the body, it is necessary to think about 'the absolute other' in Derrida's terms (2002, 369) – the abject-other excluded from human consciousness and the realm of the symbolic.[4]

In keeping proximity with SEL's approach to visual culture through the senses and the body, this chapter focuses on the intensive proximity

---

[2] For further discussion, see the interview with J. P. Sniadecki on SEL's intensive approach to visual culture (Escobar 2017b).

[3] Lucien Castaing-Taylor established the lab in 2006 as a collaborative space between the departments of anthropology and visual studies at Harvard University to instigate a wide range of audiovisual productions, ranging from video installations to sync-sound films made by anthropologists-artists.

[4] As Derrida states in his lectures on *The Beast and the Sovereign* while referring to Lacan's 'imaginary' animal: 'This distinction [between human culture and animal nature] can appear to be subtle and fragile, beginning with the distinction between the symbolic and the imaginary that in the end sustains this whole anthropocentric reinstitution of the superiority of human order over the animal order, of the law over the living being, etc., where this subtle form of phallogocentrism seems to bear witness in its way to the panic that Freud talks about: wounded reaction not to the *first* trauma of humanity, the Copernican (the earth revolves around the sun), not to the *third* trauma, the Freudian (the decentering of consciousness in view of the unconscious), but to the *second* trauma, the Darwinian' (2009, 131).

established by the different characters in the film. I argue that *Sweetgrass* is able to underpin the traditional dichotomies of Western rationality by presenting us with an environment that is meaningful for both human animals and non-human animals alike. First, however, and in order to account for *Sweetgrass*'s mutually inclusive environment, I will draw on the status of the animal in contemporary cultural theory and social anthropology to sketch what Brian Massumi calls an 'intensive politics' of the animal – that is, 'a politics of animality and becoming' (2014, 38–54). It will be argued that by projecting an alternative in affect theory to the old Cartesian dualism between the 'soulless animal' and the 'quasi-divine man', recent debates in the humanities and the social sciences are rethinking the status of the animal to establish a more horizontal alliance among the living, what Deleuze calls an 'intensive proximity among species' (quoted in Pisters 2003, 156).

In Search of the Body: Philosophical and Artistic Strategies in Re-Thinking the Status of the Animal

In her article 'Nenette: Film theory, animals, and boredom' (2013), Barbara Creed asks whether or not it is possible to represent animal subjectivity and the animal's gaze in film (2013, 41). One way to address the inquiry, Creed observes, is through Margot Norris's *Beasts of the Modern Imagination: Darwin, Nietzsche, Kafka, Ernst, and Lawrence* (1985). In this work, Norris states that while the ideas of Darwin and Nietzsche have led to subversive interrogations of the anthropocentric premises of Western rationality, the works of Kafka, Ernst and Lawrence have developed a more affective discourse which allows the animal to speak again in the arts. By distinguishing the human as a 'being-in-language' from the animal as a 'being-in-its-body' (1985, 12; 2013, 43), Norris and Creed assert that these artists and philosophers have reversed the traditional Cartesian hierarchy separating the human from the rest of the living by placing the body, and all its power to affect and express, at centre stage again.

Similar remarks are made by Derrida in his seminars on *The Beast and the Sovereign* (2009) while criticising Lévinas's definition of the animal as lacking a proper 'face' (and what Lévinas calls the face, facial expression, is precisely what addresses the other in all its ethical potentiality). Not having a face, and thus a gaze, would then mean to refuse the other animal as bearer of sovereignty and meaning. Like Norris and Creed,[5] Derrida

---

[5] For further reading on Lévinas's denial of the animal face, see Creed's chapter on 'Levinas and Bobby' in *Stray: Human-Animal Ethics in the Anthropocene* (2017, 91–6).

also looks at Lawrence's work, specifically his poem 'Snake' (1923), in order to pose a poetic contestation to Lévinas's awkward remark when asked if the animal had a face: 'I don't know . . . Would you say that the snake has a face?' (Lévinas quoted in Derrida 2009, 237). Lawrence's snake, quite contrary to Lévinas's claim, is already a 'someone' endorsed with agency and subjectivity; his serpent is 'like a king in exile' whose face he addresses under the personal pronoun 'he': 'Someone was before me at my water-trough, and I, like a second comer, waiting . . .' (Lawrence 1923, 11). A closer inspection of this autonomy of the animal face will be referred to later in the chapter under *Sweetgrass*'s intensive close-up of a bellwether ewe that is similarly questioning Lévinas's anthropocentric face by means of a non-human gaze.

In line with these poetic interrogations of the traditional Cartesian project, I also claim that if the differences among creatures reside in corporeal categories – which further favours a de-hierarchisation of the role of human language in arbitrating meaning and reality – then it is 'bodily perspectivism' that *Sweetgrass* can reactivate in film. Relying on the documentary's proximity between cowboy, filmmaker and sheep, I will argue that its non-subject centred approach to visual culture calls for an intensive-image based on Nietzsche's 'perspectivism', described as an embodied point of view that is variable and multiple. As Nietzsche writes in *The Genealogy of Morals*:

> Let us be on guard against the dangerous old conceptual fiction that posited a 'pure, will-less, painless, timeless knowing subject'; let us guard against the snares of such contradictory concepts as 'pure reason', 'absolute spirituality', 'knowledge in itself': these always demand that we should think of an eye that is completely unthinkable, an eye turned in no particular direction, in which the active and interpreting forces, through which alone seeing becomes seeing *something*, are supposed to be lacking; these always demand of the eye an absurdity and a nonsense. There is *only* a perspective seeing, *only* a perspective knowing; and the *more* affects we allow to speak about one thing, the *more* eyes, different eyes, we can use to observe one thing, the more complete will our 'concept' of this thing, our 'objectivity' be. (Quoted in Hales 2019, 25)

So, what additional strategies could be adopted to unmark the dichotomies that have separated the human eye from other animal perspectives? Is it possible to de-anthropomorphise our own relationship to other beings? In 'Why Look at Animals?' (1984) John Berger discusses the gradual fading of non-human animals from urban metropolitan life in what he sees, quite paradoxically, as a form of disappearance that reappears in a visible form today: 'as pets, as stuffed toys, as subjects of live action and animated films' (1984, 26). For Berger, we render the animal inauthentic every time a film, a drawing or a meme of the animal becomes more important than the real living creature. (For Deleuze, this urban disappearance of the animal qua animal is also quite central. In *L'abécédaire* (Deleuze and Parnet 1988–9/2011) for example, he openly declares to detest dogs barking next to his door or pet lovers who talk to their dogs as if they were babies. Animal domestication represents, in his words, 'the shame of the animal kingdom' (2011, 5)[6] – and from this it follows that there cannot be animal-becoming under such a domesticated, urban setting.)

In response to Berger's essay, Pick's 'Why Not Look at Animals?' (2015) inverts the previous question of 'Why Look at Animals?' by observing the implicit connections in media culture between looking and extinction. She offers a response to Berger's disaffection with animal imagery and its subjectivity by stating that: '[Not looking] can give rise to an extinctionist impulse that desires the end of images, or even the end of the debased modern animal' (2015, 108). Her thesis concerns current audiovisual instances where our visibility of the non-human animal is inextricably linked to forms of surveillance and control. She refers, among other examples, to the policing nature of the wildlife film under its tracking technology which ironically provides us with an animal's view of the world:

> What the privileging of the first-person perspective occludes is how images are procured in the first place: the trapping and continuous tracking of animals, subject to the desires of humans – and to the durability of the device. (2015, 114)

This violence against, and separation from, the other animal is thus interrogated under the same anthropomorphic premises posed by Derrida, Creed and Norris. For Pick and Berger, correspondingly, the human-animal encounter is made good only in an environment where intimacy among creatures can exist in mutual inclusion, and this proximity becomes for them the best way to embrace a more authentic correspondence among

---

[6] In his collaborations with Félix Guattari, Deleuze also claims that the animal has acquired an inferior status in psychoanalysis. As described in *A Thousand Plateaus*, Lacan defines the animal by its lack of language, thus, cancelling their expressivity as subjects and signifiers. And it is also in Freud, according to Deleuze, where the animal is reduced to a mere symbolic value through his analysis of the Wolf Man's neurotic dreams, the Rat Man's obsessive thoughts, or Little Hans's phobic relation to horses. Even for Jung, who partially de-oedipalised psychoanalysis, the animal remains an occurrence in the world of dreams and fantasies. In Deleuze and Guattari's words: 'The least that can be said is that the psychoanalysts, even Jung, did not understand, or did not want to understand animal-becomings (. . .) They see animals as representatives of drives, or a representation of the parents. They do not see the reality of a becoming-animal, that is affect in itself, the drive in person, and represents nothing' (2005, 303).

the living. It is an ethico-aesthetic approach based on embodiment and the senses that also *Sweetgrass* displays next to its 'animal relationship with other animals' – a point that I will further investigate under the film's bodily praxis and its recognition that whatever we humans do is, of course, animalistic.

Other documentaries that provide an intensive-image from where to look at other species today include *Nénette* (N. Philibert, 2010); *Bestiaire* (D. Côté, 2012); *Becoming Animal* (E. Davie and P. Mettler, 2018); *Los reyes* (I. Osnovikoff and B. Perut, 2018); *Space Dogs* (E. Kremser and L. Peter, 2019); *Gunda* (V. Kossakovsky, 2020); *Cow* (A. Arnold, 2021); among many others. Additionally, and in terms of this book's intensive-image and its process of intensification that heightens in films from the classical to the modern and the contemporary periods, as explored in my critique of Deleuze's two ages of the image, *Sweetgrass* also relies on early ethnographic works that convey a similar interest in the expressive potential of animals. This is done by means of 'films in which not so much nothing as nothing very much happens' (Epstein quoted in Abel 1988, 66), as early filmmaker and film critic Jean Epstein defines cinema's *photogénie*. In this regard, Merian C. Cooper and Ernest B. Schoedsack's *Grass: A Nation's Battle for Life* (1925), from which *Sweetgrass* not only takes its title but also its style of filming and approach to the human-animal question, is a silent observational documentary that follows a large nomadic tribe and their livestock as they move across the Karun River and the Zagros Mountains in Persia (contemporary Iran). As a dramatised representation of the human-animal migration, Cooper and Schoedsack's work,[7] as many critics lamented at the time of its release, exhibited what the intensive-image expresses; namely boredom, disunity and incompleteness (Malek 2011, 315–16). It lacked the central perspective of the classical hero, or the family unit as in *Nanook of the North*, to tell the story. In fact, this 'boring picture', devoid of narrative cohesion, regarded by the filmmakers as a 'damned half picture' (Cooper 1947, 1) or 'a great lost opportunity [to develop] a good picture' (Schoedsack 1983, 41) has recently been praised by film scholars who rather celebrate the 'exquisite framing of long shots' (Smaill 2014, 73; Malek 2011, 318) and the long duration of its images to study these human-animal interactions in great detail as well as to immerse the viewer into a – by now gone – mutually inclusive environment. More than a sensory-motor picture, *Grass*'s intensive-image conveys compelling sensory qualities, as well as a Bazinian construction of time, that is at the core of

---

[7] The well-known directors would then go on to direct *King Kong* (1933).

Sweetgrass's aesthetics of *temps mort*, long shots and the liveliness of the animal world.[8]

Now, before discussing *Sweetgrass*'s sensorial approach and its embodied perceptual imagery, I would first like to explore another strategy coming from anthropology and the humanities, which tries to remove such a taxonomy separating the human from the rest of the animals. In his *Cannibal Metaphysics* (2009/2014), the anthropologist Eduardo Viveiros de Castro proposes an original (and at times also science fictional) account of Nietzsche's perspectivism. Throughout his ethnographic research with the Amerindian groups of the eastern Brazilian Amazon, he puts forward a pluralist ontology that seeks to discover what a point of view means for the bearer of the look. For the anthropologist, the world presented by the Amerindians is one inhabited by a wide range of subjective agents who live in intense proximity with one another: plants, animals, humans, objects, gods and the dead are all interconnected and equipped with the same general ensemble of perceptive disposition; what he describes in terms of 'multinaturalism' or 'bodily perspectivism' – namely, the capacity of all entities 'to occupy a point of view' (2014, 24).

In this sense, if all entities are said to hold a point of view, one wonders how is it that their different perspectives become equally valid in the Brazilian Amazon? And also, how is it that the Amerindians can know about the way other entities relate to the world? According to the anthropologist, the first question can be answered by the common ontological status of all species: if every entity can be thought of as 'agencied' or 'thinking', the author says, it is because they share the same condition of 'personhood'. According to Viveiros de Castro, every living entity is conceived as having, whatever its bodily form, the soul of a human character, so that all species are part of the same epistemological kingdom – that of the human agent where the look is said to be equally valid and true. This means, moreover, that while the Cartesian soul becomes the universal category for all Amerindian entities (because they all share this condition of personhood) the body, on its part, stands for the differential element of each particular species (so that this proximity among species can only pass through their 'being-in-the-body').

In his text 'Whose Cosmos, Which Cosmopolitics?' (2004) Bruno Latour also recalls the native's emphasis on the body as described by

---

[8] Another early film that manifests these early intensities of a slow, contemplative cinema is *Limite* (1931), by Brazilian director Mario Peixoto. The work constructs quite rhythmically a spatio-temporal dynamic that in many regards is reminiscent of Jean Epstein's *photogénie*, and of Sergei Eisenstein's characters as expressed by the film's recurrent image of its woman protagonist bound by handcuffs gazing into the camera.

Viveiros de Castro. Latour revisits the old disputatio in Valladolid that Spanish's colonisers held in order to decide whether or not Amerindians had a soul susceptible of being saved. The issue back then was to determine whether the Indigenous person had enough 'soul' or 'reason' to be taken as part of the human kingdom. But what is less known is that beside the Spaniards' controversy there was also a debate at the time held by the Amerindians in the Amazon. As stressed by Latour, the natives' problem was not so much to decide whether or not Spaniards had souls, but rather if they had bodies, because for them all entities had souls: '[But] what made them differ is that their bodies differed, it is bodies that gave souls their contradictory perspectives' (2004, 452). Terms reversed, Amerindian views of the world are indeed multiple, because their methods are determined not by metaphysical categories, but by corporeal experiments. The body becomes for them the structure of Nietzsche's perspectivism, and the more affects we allow to speak about one thing, then the more eyes we will have to observe that thing.

This leads to the second question: How is it that one can 'know' about the other? Here, Viveiros de Castro argues that to really understand how other entities behave and see the environment, the Amerindians – via shamanism – have to abduct foreign agencies and become their corporeality, what João Guimarães Rosa calls 'the who of things' (quoted in Viveiros de Castro 2014, 61). This means, as Ciro Guerra's film *Embrace of the Serpent* (2015) so clearly visualises, that if all entities have souls and their souls represent the universal attribute, then what makes their perspectives differ is 'the who' of their bodies, so that it is by becoming their corporality that the shaman can show how they perceive the environment.

But as we know from Deleuze and Guattari, the act of becoming has nothing to do with mimesis – that is, the imitation or reproduction of other bodies. (It is in *A Thousand Plateaus* (2005) where Deleuze and Guattari challenge Descartes's theory of the 'animal as machine' through their proposal of animal-becoming.) On the contrary, to become is understood as a process that inspires to find a 'zone of indifferentiation' between entities; a dissolution of identities that erases the boundaries between the one and the other; a zone of ontological parity in which affects come closer together. As they write in their chapter '1730: Becoming-Intense, Becoming-Animal, Becoming-Imperceptible . . .': 'To become is (. . .) to find the zone of indifferentiation where one can no longer be distinguished from an animal, an insect or a molecule' (2005, 277). I believe this argument best explains Viveiros de Castro's (seemingly anthropomorphic) notion of animal-becoming, because as far as all species share the same status of personhood and are equipped with unique perceptual dispositions, then one can no longer establish a demarcating line separating the human from the rest of the living: if the human is transformed into an animal, then it is also the animal who is transformed into a human. As Viveiros de Castro writes: 'What we take for blood jaguars see as beer; what humans perceive as a mud puddle becomes a grand ceremonial house when viewed by tapirs' (2014, 71).

Viveiros de Castro's work on Amerindian cosmology establishes a mutual inclusion among the living that also Massumi investigates under his 'animal politics' qua 'politics of becoming' (2014, 50). Drawing on the work of Bateson, Deleuze and Simondon, Massumi accounts for a human-animal inclusivity that places the body as the locus for thought, consciousness and emotion – all attributes on which the 'human soul' has claimed a long-standing monopoly. As he writes in *What Animals Teach Us about Politics* (2014):

> Animal politics is a *politics of becoming*, even – especially – of the human (. . .) It places the human on a continuum with the animal precisely in order to better respect the proliferation of differences: the movement of nature by which life always goes a-differing (. . .) Is it not the height of human arrogance to suppose that animals do *not* have thought, emotion, desire, creativity, or subjectivity? (2014, 50–1)

By treating the human as one among other animals, as represented very intensely in the films *Grass* and *Sweetgrass*, Massumi develops an integral politics of the body where the trap of projecting human characteristics on non-human animals is avoided by what he calls an 'animo-centric environment' (2014, 52). Here, the human enters into a broader animal realm where 'the priori dominance' in language is lost without losing the intensity of the animal body: 'It calls on the human to become animal, not on animals to renounce vital powers long wrongly assumed to be the sole province of humans' (2014, 52).

It is, once again, the metaphysical distinction between 'human culture' and 'animal nature' that is proclaimed to be useless next to Massumi's autonomy of the affective body. To the question *What [do] Animals Teach Us About Politics?*, the author proposes a non-cognitive approach to ethics and aesthetics that is indissociable from Deleuze and Guattari's 'intensive politics':

> Given the noncognitive nature of this ethico-aesthetic activity, the evaluation necessarily pertains to affect (. . .) Intensity is the supreme value of this manner of politics, for the simple reason that it is experienced as a value in itself, a-body with the pure mood-signs of ludic expressionesqueness. (2014, 41–2)

What animals teach us about politics is, in other words, a manner of expression based on the intensity pertaining to the realm of the body. It is a sensuous project that places the affective elements of each member at play in relation to one another and in connection to their varying perceptual dispositions. As it will be discussed in the next section, this 'intensive proximity' among species is precisely the type of corporeal practice populating *Sweetgrass*'s 'perspectivism'.

Sweetgrass and 'Becoming-Sheeple'

'The beginning is more than half the whole' (Aristotle quoted in Rancière 2016, 124). In *Sweetgrass*, this more than half the whole introduces us to the look of a sheep. After a prolonged moment of wind howling over a black screen, the film opens with a sixty second close-up of the face of a single bellwether ewe in a snowy landscape. The animal is first seen chewing by the camera in profile, then and still chewing, the ewe becomes aware of the camera and looks in its direction, and finally stops chewing and looks directly into the camera. For an extended moment, filmmaker and sheep are sharing the experience of observing each other. Filmed from a sheep-butt level, it is as if Castaing-Taylor is one of the sheep, or another animal belonging to the herd. It is also at this moment when we realise that the ewe is not only looking at the filmmaker but also at us, and probably at the entire Cartesian project discussed above. Right from its beginning, *Sweetgrass* sets its tone for the intensity of the film to come.

The bellwether staring into the camera reminds us of Berger's belief that: 'A power is ascribed to the animal, comparable with human power but never coinciding with it' (1984, 5). As Megan Ratner suggests in her article 'Once Grazing, Now Gone: Sweetgrass' (2010), the director Castaing-Taylor has largely focused on the subjective experience of the animal, 'of what it was like to inhabit their bodies, rather than to stare at them as objective bodies/animals' (2010, 24). Here, the close-up of the leading sheep looking back at the camera works as an interesting mechanism to place the animal and all its subjectivity at centre stage again in the arts. In fact, when in 1924 Béla Balázs emphasised the importance of the close-up, it was mainly to argue that by capturing the non-phonetic language of gestures this technique could depict, in great detail, all the expressivity of the human face in films:

> What is exciting is to discover a hidden quality, in the corner of the mouth, for example, and to see how from this germ the entire new human being grows and spreads over the entire face. (Balázs quoted in Elsaesser and Hagener 2010, 60)

Balázs's close-up, which according to Deleuze does not account for an enlargement of the cinematographic image but for an 'absolute change' in its spatio-temporal coordinates (2005, 96), as mentioned in his section on 'the affection-image' (2005, 89–104), represents in *Sweetgrass* a similar abstracting plane in that it portrays the pure isolated expression of a face. Here, *Sweetgrass*'s opening close-up, which according to Deleuze's Balázs should raise the face 'to the state of an Entity' (2005, 96) is no longer coincident with the expressivity of the human subject as described previously under Lévinas's anthropocentric face, but with the intensity of an animal gaze that questions the very idea of subjectivity as pertaining to the realm of humanity. In his later writings with Guattari, as noted by Orna Raviv, Deleuze's facial close-up is not centred on such a sovereign presence of the human entity, but coincident with those non-human, or post-human perspectives as explored in SEL's documentaries:

> ... while, for Lévinas, the face is a human modality, for Deleuze, the face should also be related to what is not human, thus allowing a space of posthuman ethics to emerge. Deleuze recognizes the cinematic screen as a plane where the human face loses its unique status and prestige. He and Félix Guattari's posthumanist philosophical view challenges the very idea of subjectivity (...) and they find the face, even in a landscape. (2019, 6)

In fact, there are few close-ups of the human face in *Sweetgrass*, which forces the viewer to follow the film's trajectory from a different viewing position. Here, the journey of Ahern is framed in closer proximity to his gathering with other animals than with the rest of the cowboys. He dwells like any other creature, usually singing to the sheep, talking to the horse and playing with the dog. He makes little eye contact when talking to other people, like his peer Pat Connolly for example. Yet, Ahern expresses a whole range of emotions (when he is happy, or worried or bored) while talking to his other animal companions. Also, the filmmaker, who has merged completely into the cowboy's itinerary, stands as another means by which to subjectify the animal – as well as to animalise the human. For Castaing-Taylor, who worked as a one-man crew shooting video and recording sound, the film involved forms of labour analogous to what the rest of the group were doing: carrying a heavy camera, climbing largely on foot into the upper reaches of the Absaroka-Beartooth range and, once there, keeping up with the cowboys' schedule. (And even when the filmmaker did not deny the presence of the camera in the film, he made an effort to mitigate its effects.) Hence, what is learnt from these examples is that the documentary welcomes a proximity among species where viewers and filmmaker can no longer be differentiated from the cowboy or the rest of the animals from the herd. It is an 'animo-centric environment' in which various entities come closer together through their 'being-in-the-body' or embodied points of view. As Lucien Castaing-Taylor puts it, the camera is employed as an 'almost prosthetic extension of [my] body rather than an instrument meant to shoot' (quoted in Ratner 2010, 23).

In addition to the use of the close-up and the filmmaker's bodily praxis, the film's long-take aesthetics is another mechanism that allows the viewer to absorb scenes in their totality at a slow pace. In 'Documentary Film and Animal Modernity in Raw Herring and Sweetgrass' (2014), Belinda Smaill explores the long-take in SEL's film as a particular technique to frame animal life and human labour in a relation of mutual inclusion. In her view, the long duration of the shot and its multiple angles from which to contemplate the environment provides a valuable time to study the animal body, an aspect which acknowledges 'the long-standing role of animals in the human world of agriculture' (2014, 76). Smaill argues that if the film dwells on the beauty of animal imagery, it does so through the long take where the viewer can appreciate their gestures in great detail. This can be exemplified, among other episodes of the film, when Ahern talks to his horse beside his tent: 'You got away from those sheep all night didn't you? Yeah, that's it. You got away from those damn sheep for a night. Probably a relief, isn't it?' Then, a dog walks into the shot and sits at the edge of the frame. After almost three minutes lingering on this frame only, the shot cuts to another image of the sheep. In this way, the film's aesthetics of *temps mort* and the tactility of its environment represents an intensive-image where the viewer, in a contemplative state of repose, can linger and examine calmly all the elements on-screen, rather than coming to the image already knowing what it means.

Hence, in *Sweetgrass*, the filmmaker is more concerned 'to get the feel for what the shepherds are doing than in clarifying the action for the viewer' (Ratner 2010, 23). In a way, by relying on the close-up and the long duration of the shooting, as well as by adopting non-verbal communication among the living, the film proposes an intensive approach to audiovisuality that intertwines human-animal relationships by their mutual actions rather than by the imposition of rational, 'symbolic' speech. Like in the cases of *The Wild Child* and *The Enigma of Kaspar Hauser*, as discussed in Chapter 3, this is an intensive-image which removes linguistic communication, or the subject as master signifier, in a form of bodily expression that often leaves the viewer in a state of wonder, with a somewhat unsettling feeling of not knowing what to look at or hear on-screen. (In this sense, the film's soundscape, designed by Ernst Karel, is another element that intensifies the viewer's acoustic experience of the space, usually juxtaposing images and sounds in a chaotic poetic way.) As stressed by Barbash and Castaing-Taylor:

> Everyday cognition consists rather of multi-stranded fragments of sensation, imagery, language, and memory, all jostled together messily. We sought to reflect this in the film's aesthetic and sound-image relationship. (Quoted in Ratner 2010, 25)

As mutual participants during the herd trail, animal-becoming is at the heart of the film's bodily perspectivism. Sheep, cowboys and filmmaker assemble here a type of multiplicity that makes their hierarchies disappear; a dissolution of identities that makes it impossible to say where the boundary between the human and the non-human is. Echoing Massumi, this is an intensive politics, or a politics of becoming, that expresses the vitality of the animal body: 'a pure and necessary expression of the inexpressible in becoming' (2014, 63). In fact, having educated himself on the history of the domestication of sheep, Castaing-Taylor coined the term 'sheeple', a quite original concept referring to these shepherd-sheep gatherings occurring in the Absaroka-Beartooth trail:

> Sheep and humans have existed uneasily with each other since we first domesticated them in Mesopotamia ten-thousand-odd years ago in the Neolithic Revolution; sheep were quite possibly the first domesticated livestock animal. They gave humanity our first staple proteins: milk and meat. Not to mention their skins, for shelter – and a couple of thousand years later, also their wool. They couldn't survive without us, because of the way we've bred them over the millennia. So, I don't think you can distinguish between 'people' and 'sheep'. It's more that we're so many variations of 'sheeple'. (Quoted in MacDonald 2013, 324)

Sweetgrass ends down town in Big Timber, once the summer pasturing is over. Ahern has a chat in the car with another ranchworker. Asked by his peer about the future, Ahern does not reply. The screen goes black and the film informs via text that the Absaroka trail is now being closed down. Away from the trail, the cowboy must now look for new employment; an isolated urban dweller who once entered into alliance with other species. Up in the mountains, however, cowboy and filmmaker demonstrated that such a politics of becoming can erase the boundaries between human 'culture' and animal 'nature'. What it takes to live in *Sweetgrass*'s animocentric environment is to recognise, first of all, that we are all *different* animals, and that our perceptions of the environment are the expression of our *differing* animality. This perspectivism of the image which undermines the masterful associations of the human gaze, between optical and sound events, is the last example of my exploration of an intensive-image in cinema to indicate a mode of audiovisuality based on the poetics and politics of the animal body; that of a point of view coming from an undomesticated, more experimental eye.

Conclusion: The Passion of Intensity

The intensive-image is a category that resists strict definitions. It is an image that merges feeling with form, depth with voluminous surfaces, or an eye that is *in front of* and already *in* the visual field it perceives. It is an embryonic-image that has a life of its own, a shape or structure that never stops changing, always differing in multiple varying ways; hence it is a moving – and sonic – image without beginning or end, on condition that it is intensity which lives in continuous flow, ranging vertically from one epoch to another and simultaneously passing between these epochs horizontally. Accordingly, this book has argued that the concept of the intensive-image challenges Deleuze's argument that the cinema should be separated into two periods, the pre-war classical of the movement-image and the post-war modern of the time-image, thereby emphasising what unifies rather than separates a variety of films ranging from the silent to the present era. I have developed the concept of the intensive-image, based primarily on Deleuze's writings on intensity which he defines as difference, sensation and flow, and which I have referred to as a displacing image, or a series of images, that interweave classical and modern films constantly.

This new category questions contemporary understandings of Deleuze's film-philosophy along with commonly accepted readings of his cinema books as divided by two opposite regimes of art: one is characterised by the classical movement-image, which Deleuze describes as a 'dogmatic image of thought', that is, as a system of resemblance in which images are connected with one another rationally; and the other a modern time-image characterised by its rupture with the previous system, by virtue of the fact that these images are devoid of links with one another by opening themselves up towards indeterminate, unresolved directions. Here, the concept of intensity has taken its cues from that 'linking absence' of Deleuze's modern regime, but instead of locating his direct time-image of thought in films emerging in post-war Europe, I have argued for the existence of a deterritorialising image that has read the modern-*new* as already embedded in the classical-*old*. This is the intensive-image complex that breaks off from the core of Deleuze's classical epoch supposedly guided by reason and central characters who bring the screen-world under their control.

Intensity is thus understood as the birthplace of two types of movement: one that pushes the cinema forward (in images that constantly differentiate in time) and another that moves the cinema backward (in the eternal recurrence of an origin). Hence, the first feature of the intensive-image is that it rediscovers what Deleuze calls the 'essence' or 'the soul of the cinema' – a sort of image-purification that only occurs with the advance of his time-image modernity – in pre-war, classical films, thenceforth accounting for an art that has always made manifest the fragmentary by producing open blocs of sensation that, for Deleuze, provide an emancipation from mimesis and its closed representational structures. Thus, by breaking free from such a chain of audiovisual relations, this book has proposed that cinema is an art intimately bound up with the question of time, the new and its becoming – a becoming, nonetheless, that produces the new by precisely conversing with the old, so that cinema's orientation towards a future is always and already present in the potentialities and divergences of its past. And from this follows the second characteristic of the intensive-image.

'Intensity – difference of intensity – is the sufficient reason of all phenomena, the condition of that which appears' (Deleuze 2014, 222). The crucial point of this statement is that intensity acquires the status of a thermodynamic principle which causes images to move, and which allows them to differentiate in time, under the cinema's process of variation. And yet, despite its continuous flow, the becoming of this image is always said to belong to the same source, which is that of sensation and its unmediated form of affection. On the one hand, this implies that in the background of every intensive-image, be it classical, modern or contemporary, there are differences that condition it so that even when intensity is explicated outside of itself (in the actual image we qualify) there are relations of force, or affective gestures at play, that remain invisible, unresolved, implicated in themselves. This reading of intensity qua potentiality of divergence has opened up a space to propose an implicative hypothesis that frees the flow of cinematic movement from its fixity in sensory-motor arrangements. Hence, by attesting that intensities are the sufficient ground for images to move and change, the second characteristic of this concept has permitted me to define the intensive-image in terms of films which cannot be reduced to an overall unit or perspective, thus leading to a non-totalisable multiplicity of points of view. The art of film, defined here as a heterogeneous field of relations, is what enables the potentiality of the intensive-image to always create new genesis and sensations.

In surveying the concept of the intensive-image as a cinematic formation hitherto neglected in Deleuze's writings on film and intensities, this book has sought to define its meanings and conventions through a close analysis of film texts, including the avant-garde, poetic, popular, ethnographic and experimental film traditions encompassing the classical, modern and contemporary periods. Accordingly, each of the preceding chapters has discussed relevant aspects of the intensive-image to demonstrate its originality, formal characteristics and relationship with the history of image-forms.

Chapter 1 examines Deleuze's film-philosophy and its reception: it aims to rethink his theorisation of the cinema as constituted by two opposite regimes of signs. By drawing on the concept of intensity in *Difference and Repetition*, this chapter reads Deleuze's conception of the moving image as one singular element that *moves* and transforms *in time*. This means that *Cinema 1: The Movement-Image* and *Cinema 2: The Time-Image*, rather than forming two separate categories belonging to different ages, are understood as a single intensifying tendency that experiments with the art of crossing a verge – that is to say, they form a passage of intensity that differentiates from the classical to the modern as well as current film periods. Hence, 'Towards the intensification of the cinema', the title of this chapter, introduces the first ontological disparity with Deleuze's system: that of the cinema being a morphogenetic process through which the intensive-image mutates into different states of itself. The chapter ends by looking at recent forms of slow and poetic films, which render visible not only the transformations taking place in the history of Deleuze's cinema(s) but transformation itself as the actual procedure of an image that has intensified, or become gaseous. Pedro Costa's *Colossal Youth* is the case study I employ in order to visualise this process of image-intensification under his poetry of displacements and exchanges that dissipates narrative meaning in favour of more contemplative and sensory experiences.

Chapter 2, 'Luis Buñuel's Nomadic Vision: Departures from an Originary World' returns to a film and filmmaker Deleuze had studied in *Cinema 1* in order to demonstrate that another reading, one in line with the theory of intensities, is possible and largely congruent with Deleuze's own writings. By reconsidering Deleuze's naturalist reading of the early Buñuel, this chapter challenges his notion of the 'impulse-image' – an image in which difference is subordinated to a larger circuit of perceptual and affective events, thus unable to acquire its full deterritorialising effect – and argues that the originary impulses of Buñuel's characters are not constitutive of a closed tightening cycle between *sur-real* source and *real* milieu, as argued by Deleuze, but rather can be attributed to the immanent circumstances in which his characters are immersed. Naturalism, in this sense, is not read as another liminal case of Deleuze's classical sensory-motor cohesion. On the contrary, it resonates as a modern heterogeneous system of relations in which the impulse, proper to the disproportionate bodies of Buñuel's early characters, expresses the poetic excess of what Pasolini calls a 'free-indirect-discourse' in cinema. This poetic surplus, I argue, subtends the formal features of Buñuel's intensive-image: a site of destruction and loss where viewers are irremediably threatened by an experience of formlessness – that is, the ocular associations arranged under Buñuel's de/forming poetry of horror as well as the poetic quality of his early films, defined by its affective or pre-verbal space in which rational dispositions towards meaning are thwarted. This thesis is explored in *Un chien andalou*, a classical film-text which arguably produces intensities that overturn or at least question Buñuel's 'closed cyclicality' as argued by Deleuze.

The following chapter offers a discussion on two New Wave films, François Truffaut's *The Wild Child* and Werner Herzog's *The Enigma of Kaspar Hauser*, to reflect about the cinematic child as a model for intensive thinking. Following Deleuze's reading of Hume, I explore the proposition that the screen characters Victor of Aveyron and Kaspar Hauser demonstrate a capacity to shatter the perceptual habits of adult subjectivity by enacting a mode of being that is not yet qualified by the ego's habitual associations but by the deterritorialising powers of the imagination. Here, I hypothesise that Victor and Kaspar, although akin to Deleuze's wanderers of his modern era, are nonetheless trapped in the teleological sequencing of his classical plot, so that the two films assume the form of an antinomy which interweaves the intense forces of the 'child-seer' (in the time-image) with the rational organisation of the movement-image schema. However, rather than locating the intensity of the child on the side of neorealism exclusively, as Deleuze does in *Cinema 2*, I suggest that these constructed experiences of childhood are echoed by another beginning: that of the cinema, for it is in borrowing some conventions from the silent film period that each filmmaker fuses the formal characteristics of the classical with an image of infancy that eludes any simple reduction to signification. Consequently, in collapsing this separation between classicism and modernism, the intensive-image offers a more cyclical understanding of the old in connection with the new, as it is in this coexistence of past and present, or beginning and end, that filmmaking revitalises itself – a matter of the very old that, as in the cases of *The Wild Child* and *The Enigma of Kaspar Hauser*, is producing something new.

Chapter 4, 'In Between Modernities and the Contemporaneous', returns to the epistemological aspects of Deleuze's film-philosophy, but now from the point of view of Deleuze's historicising thesis, widely criticised by writers from Jacques Rancière and Alain Badiou to David Bordwell. Here, I explore the proposition that Deleuze's two cinemas dwell in between modernities rather than in between a classical and a modern era of the image. This could mean that whereas *Cinema 1* is read as an enlightened, Kantian image of adequation (*adaequatio intellectus ad rem*) which breaks with the classical, Thomist reference to being (*verum est ens*), *Cinema 2* converts the previous promise of enlightened reason under a Nietzschean image of madness and nihilism. However, it is once again through Kant, or more precisely through Kant's notion of time as 'terror and transformation' that Deleuze's film-philosophical passage will occur. This is what I term the 'in-between modernities' of Deleuze's cinemas, described under the deterritorialising quality of the intensive-image which manifests the breakdowns of representation and action as accounted for by Kant's experience of modernity. In the second section of this chapter, which focuses on a certain notion of the contemporaneous, I thus expand and incorporate the fissures of Deleuze's time-image into the previous (Kantian) image of reasoning. Drawing on Bergson's 'gigantic memory' which makes his idea of virtuality a permanent intensifying structure, I explore the idea that Deleuze's cinemas, both virtual parts, are similarly caught up in a Bergsonian movement that differentiates over time and which reaffirms the cracks in temporality itself that Deleuze associates with his idea of contemporariness – that is, an empty form of the present that Nietzsche calls 'the untimely'.

Section Two of this book, 'The Politics and Poetics of the Intensive-Image in Contemporary Cinema', explores the implications of this thesis by working through different forms of the intensive-image in contemporary films. I analyse three recent works which provide eloquent illustrations of the aesthetics of intensity, as well as a method of analysis that is consistent with the difference-oriented philosophy this image intends to create.

This section opens with the study of Yorgos Lanthimos's *The Lobster*, a surrealist black comedy that expresses the indeterminate potential, and always dynamic nature, of the notion of intensity. Here, my analysis traces two maps by looking at the film's politics of resistance. The first map, which is delineated through extensive cartography, marks the physical spaces in which the action of the film takes place. This is a diagram that covers three geopolitical locations, all of which are said to be equally oppressive in practice although dissimilar in ideology. At the centre of the story, there is a city-state(ment) that commands the actions and movements of characters; at one axis, there is a hotel-space that extends the programmatic agenda of the *polis*; and at the other (opposite) axis, there is a forest-space that deviates from the rules of the urban edict. By mapping this system of relations, I seek to connect the normalising powers of *The Lobster*'s itinerary with the issue of surveillance as developed by both Michel Foucault's disciplinary society and Gilles Deleuze's subsequent paradigm of information. The second map, which I offer as an alternative route to the panoptical ensembles of Lanthimos and Foucault, is no longer conceived as a plane delineated in extension but rather as an invisible line surpassing the film's official norms. This is an intensive map which I draw via two forms of political resistance: resistance as an external act performed by characters who mock the conventions set up by dogmatic administrations; and resistance as an internal act enacted by a filmmaker who leaves the image open for virtual navigation. Intensity, in this way, is explored as a double resisting operation: one that defies *The Lobster*'s itinerary by embracing unknown destinations; and another that animates the image to remain hidden for the look of both characters and viewers.

Chapter 6 is a study of Lucrecia Martel's *Zama* and the politics of her script adaptation from Antonio Di Benedetto's book of the same name. Martel's film, I argue, is defined by a complex 'method of dramatisation' that is played out at three interconnected levels. It appears first in her adaption of Di Benedetto's novel. I argue that she pushes the writer's elusive images towards higher levels of cinematic abstraction. This is done by means of a process that de-visualises, or renders more ambiguous, the standing of the literary protagonist. Second, in relation to Deleuze's cinematic periods, I suggest that Martel's film practice reveals a disruptive and polyphonic form of aesthetics that enlarges Deleuze's time-image modernity towards more 'dramatic', indeterminate scenarios. Finally, Martel's method of dramatisation appears in relation to her tactile approach to the film itself. Here I suggest that the 'drama' is incarnated in the bodily decline of her protagonist, by maintaining that Zama's mental confusion, initially problematised in Di Benedetto's book, is further obscured on-screen under issues of both personal and cultural identity, as well as under a feminist contamination of the novel. This dramatising method is exemplary of the workings of the intensive-image in cinema; as the determinant in the process of intensification, this is an image that continually implies a change, or a detour from previous sequences, in order to increase their sensation, and to allow for the unresolved potential of the cinema to always be thought in a new way – 'it is intensity which dramatizes' (Deleuze 2014, 320) and it is dramatisation that intensifies the importance of this new image-category. In this capacity, Martel's politics of script adaptation favours a proliferating structure that renders more ambiguous the literary connections in the film. This is understood in terms of a baroque intensive-image that opens the story out in a non-totalisable arrangement of events, and which allows the filmmaker, in her words, to 'contaminate' the literary referent by blending the real and the imagined in a reservoir of virtual images which never really activate a stable form of identity.

Chapter 7, 'What do Animals Teach Us About Intensity?', analyses Sensory Ethnography Lab's first documentary film *Sweetgrass* in order to think about the animal as a figure of the political. I argue that SEL's film, which is a hybrid observational work moving between the worlds of ethnography and documentary cinema, affectively interrogates the traditional dichotomies of Cartesian philosophy by portraying an environment that is meaningful for both human animals and non-human animals alike. The film puts forward an experimental approach to visual culture which undermines the anthropocentric ways in which humans have seen the world and its alterity – it records animal life from a bodily praxis that is not centred on ocularcentrism. Here, and to account for the type of post-human or acentric cinema that SEL is promoting, I interrogate the status of the animal-other in contemporary cultural theory and social anthropology by sketching a non-subject-centred approach to the environment, with references to Massumi's 'animo-centrism' and Viveiros de Castro's 'perspectivism'. SEL's ethnographic documentary, as with the critical approach of affect theory presented in this chapter, conceptualises animal-ontology from the perspective of an intensive-image that records pastoral life from a foreigner angle – that of a point of view coming from another animal eye. Additionally, in consideration of the ways in which the intensive-image entwines the cinematic past and its present, *Sweetgrass* also relies on *Grass: A Nation's Battle for Life*, an early ethnographic work that manifests the intensities of a slow, contemplative cinematic tradition. More than a sensory-motor picture, I argue that *Grass*'s intensive-image conveys compelling sensory qualities, as well as a Bazinian construction of time, that is at the core of *Sweetgrass*'s aesthetics of *temps mort*, long shots and its renewed ability to introduce 'the recreation of the world in its own image' (Bazin 2005, 21).

* * *

In conclusion, if intensity proves to be a relevant concept to investigate the field of film theory and philosophy, it is not only because of the significance Deleuze attaches to this idea, but also because of the implications it holds for his film taxonomical construction – that is, as an image or a sequence of images that are pushing the *new* cinema backward (into the classical) and the *old* cinema forward (into the modern). His omission of the 'intensive-image' is, therefore, of particular importance for a film studies community that, as this book does, focuses on a cinema which develops in opposition to the action-sequence thrill achieved by the conventions of the Hollywood studio production – that is, a testimony to a more poetic and inactive film tradition that stretches from Buñuel's *Un chien andalou* or Dreyer's *The Passion of Joan of Arc* to Godard's recent video essays and Martel's *Zama*. This poetic lineage, designated by the concept of the intensive-image, has been explored in an alliance between philosophy and film, structurally linked to notions of flow, difference, embodiment and sensation. Here, in all of its thermodynamic character, intensity has been understood as an image that carries an important Deleuzian imprint – that of his philosophical concepts breaking up territories – and for this reason, I have also used the meanings and conventions of the intensive-image to problematise Deleuze's thesis and bridge his division between the two periods: classical and modern.

Postscript

From this point of view, intensity is always experienced as a force that arrives unexpectedly, from the outside, like an *event* that provokes the power or potential of images to displace the viewer, and the *cogito* that thinks. Intensity, in other words, represents a *passion* that happens to the subject, embracing them during the viewing experience. And so, once open to intensity, the viewing subject has no other choice but to submit to its effects.

Bibliography

Abel, Richard. 1988. *French Film Theory and Criticism, 1907–1939: Volume 1, 1907–1929*. Princeton: Princeton University Press.

Adorno, Theodor W. and Max Horkheimer. [1947] 2002. *Dialectic of Enlightenment: Philosophical Fragments*. Ed. Gunzelin Schmid Noerr. Trans. Edmund Jephcott. Stanford: Stanford University Press.

Agamben, Giorgio. [1990] 1993. *The Coming Community*. Trans. Michael Hardt. Minneapolis: Minnesota University Press.

— [1993] 2007. *Infancy and History: On the Destruction of Experience*. Trans. Liz Heron. London: Verso.

— [1994] 1999. *The Man without Content*. Trans. Georgia Albert. Stanford: Stanford University Press.

— [1995] 2000. *Means without Ends: Notes on Politics*. Trans. Cesare Casarino and Vincenzo Binetti. Minneapolis and London: University of Minnesota Press.

— [2006] 2009. *What is an Apparatus? and Other Essays*. Trans. David Kishik and Stefan Pedatella. Stanford: Stanford University Press.

— 2014. 'Resistance in Art'. Lecture, The European Graduate School, August. https://www.youtube.com/watch?v=one7mE-8y9c

Allen, Esther. 2016. 'Preface'. In *Zama*, Antonio Di Benedetto. Trans. Allen Esther. New York: *New York Review of Books*: vii–xx.

Ambrose, Darren. 2013. *Film, Nihilism and the Restoration of Belief*. London: Zero Books.

Andrew, Dudley. 2013. 'Every Teacher Needs a Truant: Bazin and *L'Enfant Sauvage*'. In *A Companion to François Truffaut*. Ed. Andrew Dudley and Anne Gillain. Chichester: Blackwell Publishing.

Andrew, Dudley and Anne Gillain (eds). 2013. *A Companion to François Truffaut*. Chichester: Blackwell Publishing.

Arendt, Hannah. [1958] 1998. *La condición humana*. Trans. Ramón Gil Novales. Barcelona: Paidós.

— 1970. 'Reflections Civil Disobedience'. In *The New Yorker*, 12 September. https://www.newyorker.com/magazine/1970/09/12/reflections-civil-disobedience

Aristotle. [340 BC] 1998. *Nicomachean Ethics: Books VIII and XIX*. Trans. Michael Pakaluk. Oxford: Clarendon Press.

Artaud, Antonin. [1926] 1965. *Artaud Anthology*. Trans. Jack Hirschman. San Francisco: City Lights Books.

Badiou, Alain. [1997] 2000. *Deleuze: The Clamour of Being*. Trans. Louise Burchill. Minneapolis: University of Minnesota Press.
— [2010] 2013. *Cinema*. Ed. Antoine de Baecque. Trans. Susan Spitzer. Cambridge: Polity Press.
— 2018. *L'immanence des vérités: L'Être et L'événement. 3*. Paris: Fayard.
Barlett, A. J., Justin Clemens and Jon Roffe. 2014. *Lacan Deleuze Badiou*. Edinburgh: Edinburgh University Press.
Barthes, Roland. [1964] 1972. 'The Metaphor of the Eye'. Trans. Richard Howard. In *Critical Essays*. Evanston: Northwestern University Press: 239–48.
Bataille, Georges. [1928] 2012. *Story of the Eye*. Trans. Joachim Neugroschal. London: Penguin Classics.
— 1985. *Visions of Excess: Selected Writings, 1927–1939*. Ed. Allan Stoekl. Trans. Allan Stoekl, Carl R. Lovitt and Donald M. Leslie Jr. Minneapolis: Minnesota University Press.
Baudry, Jean-Louise. [1975] 1986. 'The Apparatus: Metapsychological Approaches the Impression of Reality in Cinema'. In *Narrative, Apparatus, ideology*. Ed. Philip Rosen. New York: Columbia University Press: 299–318.
Baudry, Leo. 1976. *The World in a Frame: What We See in Films*. New York: Anchor Press.
Bazin, André. [1967] 2005. *What is Cinema? Volume 2*. Trans. Hugh Gray. Los Angeles: University of California Press.
Bégin, Richard. [2009] 2010. 'Raúl Ruiz o el Barroco en acción'. In *El cine de Raúl Ruiz: Fantasmas, simulacros y artificios*. Ed. Valeria de los Ríos and Iván Pinto. Santiago: Editores Uqbar: 181–201.
Bellour, Raymond. 2010. 'The Image of Thought: Art or Philosophy, or Beyond?' In *Afterimages of Gilles Deleuze's Film Philosophy*. Ed. David. N. Rodowick. Minneapolis: University of Minnesota Press: 3–14.
Benjamin, Walter. [1936] 2003. 'The Work of Art in the Age of Mechanical Reproducibility'. In *Selected Writings. Vol. 4: 1938–1940*. Trans. Harry Zohn. Cambridge, MA: Harvard University Press.
Berger, John. 1984. 'Why Look at Animals?' In *About Looking*. London: Writers and Readers Publishing: 3–28.
Bergson, Henri. [1896] 1990. *Matter and Memory*. Trans. Nancy Margaret Paul and W. Scott Palmer. New York: Zone Books.
— [1889] 2015. *Essai sur les données immédiates de la conscience (grands caracteres)* Paris: Ligaran.
— [1907] 1998. *Creative Evolution*. Trans. Arthur Mitchell. New York: Dover Publications.
Bertetto, Paolo. 2016. *Il cinema e l'estetica dell'intensità*. Sesto San Giovanni: Mimesis-Cinema.
— 2017. 'Concept, Sensation, Intensity: Deleuze's Theory of Art and Cinema'. In *Sociology and Anthropology* 5 (9): 729–97.
Bolaño, Roberto. [1997] 2011. 'Sensini'. In *Llamadas telefónicas*. Madrid: Anagrama: 7–13.

Bonitzer, Pascal. 1992. 'Hitchcockian Suspense'. In *Everything You Always Wanted to Know About Lacan: But Were Afraid to Ask Hitchcock*. Ed. Slavoj Žižek. London: Verso Books: 15–28.
Bordwell, David. 1985. *Narration in the Fiction Film*. Madison: University of Wisconsin.
— 1986. 'Classical Hollywood Cinema: Narrational Principles and Procedures'. In *Narrative, Apparatus, Ideology: A Film Theory Reader*. Ed. Philip Rosen. New York: Columbia University Press: 17–34.
— 2002. 'Intensified Continuity: Visual Style in Contemporary American Film'. In *Film Quarterly* 55 (5): 16–28.
Borges, Jorge Luis. [1941] 2005. 'La biblioteca de Babel'. In *Obras Completas I*. Buenos Aires: Emecé: 465–71.
— [1956] 1962. 'Death and the Compass'. In *Fictions*. Trans. Andrew Hurley. New York: Groove Press: 147–56.
— [1960] 1974. 'The Game of Chess'. In *Dreamtigers*. Trans. Mildred Boyer. Austin: University of Texas Press: 59.
— [1960] 2005. 'Del rigor de la ciencia'. In *Obras Completas I*. Buenos Aires: Emecé: 431–43.
Boundas, Constantin V. 2009. *Gilles Deleuze: The Intensive Reduction*. London: Continuum.
Bradshaw, Peter. 2015. 'The Lobster Review – dating satire loses flavour at the tail end'. In *The Guardian*. https://www.theguardian.com/film/2015/oct/15/the-lobster-review-
Braidotti, Rosi. 1994. *Nomadic Subjects: Embodiment and Sexual Difference in Contemporary Theory*. New York: Columbia University Press.
— 2013. *The Posthuman*. Oxford: Polity Press.
Bryant, Levi R. 2011. *The Democracy of Objects*. Ann Arbor, MI: Open Humanities Press.
Buchanan, Ian and Claire Colebrook (eds). 2000. *Deleuze and Feminist Theory*. Edinburgh: Edinburgh University Press.
Buchanan, Ian and Patricia MacCormack. 2008. *Deleuze and the Schizoanalysis of Cinema*. London: Bloomsbury Publishing.
Buci-Glucksmann, Christine. [1987] 2010. 'El ojo barroco de la cámara'. In *El cine de Raúl Ruiz: Fantasmas, simulacros y artificios*. Ed. Valeria de los Ríos and Iván Pinto. Santiago: Editores Uqbar: 143–72.
Butler, Judith. 1988. 'Performative Acts and Gender Constitution: An Essay in Phenomenology and Feminist Theory'. In *Theatre Journal* 40 (4): 519–31
— 1990. *Gender Trouble: Feminism and the Subversion of Identity*. New York: Routledge.
Calvino, Italo. [1972] 1997. *Invisible Cities*. Trans. William Weaber. London: Vintage Classics.
Canning, Peter. 2000. 'The Imagination of Immanence: An Ethics of Cinema'. In *The Brain is the Screen: Deleuze and the Philosophy of Cinema*. Ed. Gregory Flaxman. Minneapolis: University of Minnesota Press: 327–64.

Carpentier, Alejo. [1953] 1998. *Los pasos perdidos*. London: Penguin Books.
Chion, Michel. 1994. *The Voice in Cinema*. Trans. Claudia Gorbman. New York: Columbia University Press.
Ciment, Michel. 2003. 'The State of Cinema.' Address delivered at the 46th San Francisco International Film Festival in 2003. http://web.archive.org/web/20040325130014/http:/www.sfiff.org/fest03/special/state.html
Codell, Julie F. 2006. 'Playing Doctor: François Truffaut's *L'Enfant Sauvage* and the Auteur/Autobiographer as Impersonator'. *Biography* 29 (1): 101–22.
Colebrook, Claire. 2006. *Deleuze: A Guide for the Perplexed*. New York and London: Continuum.
— [2002] 2020. *Understanding Deleuze*. London: Routledge.
Colman, Felicity. 2005. 'Deleuze's Kiss: The Sensory Pause of Screen Affect'. In *The Warwick Journal of Philosophy*. (16): 101–13.
Comolli, Jean-Louise. 1980. 'Machines of the Visible'. In *The Cinematic Apparatus*. Ed. Teresa de Lauretis and Stephen Heath. London: Macmillan: 121–42.
Conley, Tom. 2007. *Cartographic Cinema*. Minneapolis: Minnesota University Press.
Cooper, Merian C. 1947. 'Grass Outline'. In *Coopers Papers BYU*, Folder 8.
Cooper, Sarah. 2013. 'Surreal Souls: Un chien andalou and Early French Film Theory'. In *A Companion to Luis Buñuel*. Ed. Rob Stone and Julián Daniel Gutiérrez-Albilla. London: Blackwell Publishing: 141–55.
— 2016. 'Narcissus and *The Lobster* (Yorgos Lanthimos, 2015)'. In *Studies in European Cinema*. 13 (2): 163–76.
Creed, Barbara. 1993. *The Monstrous Feminine: Film, Feminism, Psychoanalysis*. London: Routledge.
— 2007. 'The Untamed Eye and The Dark Side of Surrealism: Hitchcock, Lynch, and Cronenberg'. In *The Unsilvered Screen: Surrealism on Film*. Ed. Graeme Harper and Ron Stone. Wallflower Press: London: 115–33.
— 2013. 'Nenette: Film theory, animals, and boredom'. In *NECSUS: European Journal of Media Studies*. Spring (16): 35–50.
— 2017. *Stray: Human-Animal Ethics in the Anthropocene*. Sydney: Power Polemics.
Cronin, Paul (ed.). 2002. *Herzog on Herzog*. London: Faber & Faber.
Deamer, David. 2016. *Deleuze's Cinema Books: Three Introductions to the Taxonomy of Images*. Edinburgh: Edinburgh University Press.
Debaise, Didier. 2016. 'The Dramatic Power of Events: The Function of Method in Deleuze's Philosophy'. In *Deleuze and Guattari Studies* 10 (1): 5–18.
De Certeau, Michel. [1980] 1984. *The Practice of Everyday Life*. Trans. Steven Rendall. Berkeley: University of California Press.
— [1988] 1992. *The Writing of History*. Trans. Tom Conley. New York: Columbia University Press.
de la Durantaye, Leland. 2009. *Giorgio Agamben: A Critical Introduction*. Stanford: Stanford University Press.

DeLanda, Manuel. [2002] 2013. *Intensive Science and Virtual Philosophy*. London and New York: Bloomsbury Academic.
— 2010. *Deleuze: History and Science*. New York: Atropos Press.
Deleuze, Gilles. [1953] 1991. *Empiricism and Subjectivity. An Essay on Hume's Theory of Human Nature*. Trans. Constantin V. Boundas. New York: Columbia University Press.
— [1956] 2004a. 'Bergson, 1859–1941'. In *Desert Islands and Other Texts: 1953–1974*. Ed. David Lapoujade. Trans. Michael Taormina. London: Semiotext(e): 22–31.
— [1956] 2004b. 'Bergson's Conception of Difference'. In *Desert Islands and Other Texts: 1953–1974*. Ed David Lapoujade. Trans. Michael Taormina. London: Semiotext(e): 32–51.
— [1956] 2004c. 'Nietzsche's Burst of Laughter'. In *Desert Islands and Other Texts: 1953–1974*. Ed. David Lapoujade. Trans. Michael Taormina. London: Semiotext(e): 128–30.
— [1957] 2007. 'Course on Hume' (1957–1958). In *Two Regimes of Madness: Texts and Interviews 1975–1995*. Ed. David Lapoujade. Trans. Ames Hodges and Mike Taormina. London: Semiotext(e): 175–80.
— [1962] 2006. *Nietzsche and Philosophy*. Trans. Hugh Tomlinson. London: Bloomsbury Publishing.
— [1963] 2008. *Kant's Critical Philosophy: The Doctrine of the Faculties*. Trans. Hugh Tomlinson and Barbara Habberjam. London: Continuum.
— [1964] 2003. *Proust and Signs*. Trans. Richard Howard. Minneapolis: University of Minnesota Press.
— [1967] 2004. 'The Method of Dramatization'. In *Desert Islands and Other Texts 1953–1974*. Ed. David Lapoujade. Trans. Michael Taormina. London: Semiotext(e): 94–116.
— [1968] 2014. *Difference and Repetition*. Trans. Paul Patton. London and New York: Bloomsbury Academic.
— [1969] 2015. *Logic of Sense*. Trans. Constantin V. Boundas. London and New York: Bloomsbury Academic.
— [1973] 2020. 'Gilles Deleuze and Félix Guattari: Interview on Anti-Oedipus with Raymond Bellour'. In *Letters and Other Texts*. Ed. David Lapoujade. Trans. Ames Hodges. London: Semiotext(e): 195–239.
— [1976] 2007. 'Author's Note for the Italian Edition of Logic of Sense'. In *Two Regimes of Madness: Texts and Interviews 1975–1995*. Ed. David Lapoujade. Trans. Ames Hodges and Mike Taormina. London: Semiotext(e): 63–6.
— [1978] 2020a. 'Musical Time'. In *Letters and Other Texts*. Ed. David Lapoujade. Trans. Ames Hodges. London: Semiotext(e): 240–4.
— [1978] 2020b. 'Description of Woman'. In *Letters and Other Texts*. Ed. David Lapoujade. Trans. Ames Hodges. London: Semiotext(e): 253–65.
— [1980] 2007. 'Eight Years Later: 1980 Interview'. *In Letters and Other Texts*. Ed. David Lapoujade. Trans. Ames Hodges. London: Semiotext(e): 119–66.

— [1981] 2005. *Francis Bacon: The Logic of Sensation*. Trans. Daniel W. Smith. Minneapolis: University of Minnesota Press.
— [1982/1983] 2011. *Cinema 2: Los signos del movimiento y el tiempo*. Trans. Pablo Ires and Sebastián Puente. Buenos Aires: Editorial Cactus.
— [1983] 2005. *Cinema 1: The Movement-Image*. Trans. Hugh Tomlinson and Barbara Habberjam. London: Continuum.
— [1983] 2007. 'Cinema-I, Premiere. An Interview with Serge Daney'. In *Two Regimes of Madness: Texts and Interviews 1975–1995*. Ed. David Lapoujade. Trans. Ames Hodges and Mike Taormina. London: Semiotext(e): 210–12.
— [1984] 2007. 'Michel Foucault's Main Concepts'. In *Two Regimes of Madness: Texts and Interviews 1975–1995*. Ed. David Lapoujade. Trans. Ames Hodges and Mike Taormina. London: Semiotext(e): 246–65.
— [1985] 2013. *Cinema 2: The Time-Image*. Trans. Hugh Tomlinson and Robert Galeta. Minneapolis: University of Minnesota Press.
— [1987] 2007. 'What is the Creative Act'. In *Two Regimes of Madness: Texts and Interviews 1975–1995*. Ed. David Lapoujade. Trans. Ames Hodges and Mike Taormina. London: Semiotext(e): 317–29.
— [1988] 1992. *The Fold: Leibniz and the Baroque*. Trans. Tom Conley. Minneapolis: University of Minnesota Press.
— [1988] 2007. 'Preface to the American Edition of the Time-Image'. In *Two Regimes of Madness: Texts and Interviews 1975–1995*. Ed. David Lapoujade. Trans. Ames Hodges and Mike Taormina. London: Semiotext(e): 356–8.
— 1995a. *Negotiations: 1972–1990*. Trans. Martin Joughin. New York: Columbia University Press.
— 1995b. 'On The Time-Image'. In *Negotiations. 1972–1990*. Trans. Martin Joughin. New York: Columbia University Press: 57–61.
— [1995] 2007a. 'Immanence: a Life'. In *Two Regimes of Madness: Texts and Interviews 1975–1995*. Ed. David Lapoujade. Trans. Ames Hodges and Mike Taormina. London: Semiotext(e): 388–94.
— [1995] 2007b. 'Preface to the American Edition of the Movement-Image'. In *Two Regimes of Madness: Texts and Interviews 1975–1995*. Ed. David Lapoujade. Trans. Ames Hodges and Mike Taormina. London: Semiotext(e): 274–6.
Deleuze, Gilles and Félix Guattari. [1972] 2009. *Anti-Oedipus: Capitalism and Schizophrenia*. Trans. Robert Hurley, Mark Seem and Helen. R. Lane. London: Penguin Classics.
— [1988] 2005. *A Thousand Plateaus: Capitalism and Schizophrenia*. Trans. Brian Massumi. Minneapolis: University of Minnesota Press.
— [1991] 1996. *What is Philosophy?* Trans. Hugh Tomlinson and Graham Burchell. New York: Columbia University Press.
Deleuze, Gilles and Claire Parnet. [1988–9] 2002. *Dialogues II*. Trans. Hugh Tomlinson and Barbara Habberjam. New York: Columbia University Press.
— [1988–9] 2011. *Gilles Deleuze from A to Z*. Trans. Charles J. Stivale. London: Semiotext(e).

de los Ríos, Valeria. 2019. *Metamorfosis: Aproximaciones al cine y la poética de Raúl Ruiz*. Santiago: Ediciones Metales Pesados.

de Luca, Tiago. 2012. 'Realism of the Senses: A Tendency in Contemporary World Cinema'. In *Theorizing World Cinema*. Ed. Lucia Nagib, Rajinder Dudrah and Chris Perriam. London: I. B. Tauris: 183–204.

de Luca, Tiago and Jorge Nuno Barradas (eds). 2016. *Slow Cinema*. Edinburgh: Edinburgh University Press.

Deren, Maya. [1946] 2005a. 'An Anagram of Ideas on Art, Form and Film'. In *Essential Deren: Collected Writings on Film by Maya Deren*. Ed. Bruce R. McPherson. New York: Documentext: 35–109.

— [1946] 2005b. 'Cinema as an Art Form'. In *Essential Deren: Collected Writings on Film by Maya Deren*. Ed. Bruce R. McPherson. New York: Documentext: 19–34.

— [1951] 2005. 'New Directions in Film Art'. In *Essential Deren: Collected Writings on Film by Maya Deren*. Ed. Bruce R. McPherson. New York: Documentext: 207–19.

— [1951] 2016. 'About the Feminine'. In *Comparative Cinema* 4 (8): 9.

— [1953] 1963. Maya Deren in conversation with Willard Mass, 'Poetry and the Film: A Symposium'. In *Film Culture* 29: 55–63.

— [1959] 2005. 'Amateur versus Professional'. In *Essential Deren: Collected Writings on Film by Maya Deren*. Ed. Bruce R. McPherson. New York: Documentext: 17–18.

Derrida, Jacques. [1994] 2005. *The Politics of Friendship*. Trans. George Collins. London: Verso.

— 2002. 'The Animal That Therefore I Am'. Trans. David Wills. In *Critical Inquiry* 28 (2): 369–418.

— 2009. *The Beast and the Sovereign: Volume 1*. Trans. Geoffrey Bennington. Chicago: Chicago University Press.

Di Benedetto, Antonio. [1956] 2016. *Zama*. Trans. Esther Allen. New York: NYRB Classics.

— [1956] 2018. *Zama*. Ariana Hidalgo Editora: Buenos Aires.

Didi-Huberman, Georges. [2000] 2017. *The Surviving Image: Phantoms of Time and Time of Phantoms: Aby Warburg's History of Art*. Trans. Harvey Mendelsonh. Pennsylvania: The Pennsylvania State University Press.

— [2011] 2018. *Atlas, or the Anxious Gay Science*. Trans. Shane B. Lillis. Chicago: University of Chicago Press.

Dieleke, Edgardo and Fernández, Álvaro. 2018. 'Zama: heterocronía, voyeurismo y mundos posibles'. In *LaFuga* 21: 1–10.

Eco, Umberto and Jean-Claude Carrière. [2009] 2011. *This is Not the End of the Book*. Trans. Polly McLean. London: Harvill Secker.

Elsaesser, Thomas. [1986] 2014. 'An Anthropologist's Eye: Where the Green Ants Dream'. In *The Films of Werner Herzog: Between Mirage and History*. Ed. Timothy Corrigan. London and New York: Routledge Library Editions, v.8 Cinema: 133–56.

— 2019. *European Cinema and Continental Philosophy: Film as Thought Experiment*. New York: Bloomsbury Academic.

Elsaesser, Thomas and Malte Hagener. 2010. *Film Theory: An Introduction through the Senses*. New York: Routledge.

Escobar, Cristóbal. 2017a. 'The Colliding Worlds of Anthropology and Film Ethnography: A Dynamic Continuum'. In *Anthrovision Vaneasa online journal* 5 (1): http://journals.openedition.org/anthrovision/2491

— 2017b. 'En conversación con J.P Sniadecki, del Sensory Ethnography Lab'. Trans. Cristóbal Escobar. In *LaFuga* 20.

— 2017c. 'Hitchcock's Simulacra: Crystalizing the mental operations of Rear Window and Vertigo'. In *Yearbook of Moving Image Studies. Image Temporality: The Relation of Time, Space and Reception of Visual Media*. Ed. Lars C. Grabbe, Patrick Rupert-Kruse and Norbert M. Schmitz. Darmstadt: Büchner: 76–91.

— 2020. 'Correspondencias con Laura U. Marks'. Trans. Cristóbal Escobar. In *LaFuga* 24.

Fairfax, Daniel. 2016. 'Gilles et Jacques se disputen Béla: philosophies of cinematic modernism and the films of Béla Tarr'. In *Studies in European Cinema* 13 (1): 13–18.

Farber, Manny. [1969] 2009. 'Luis Buñuel'. In *Farber on Film: The Complete Writings of Manny Farber*. Ed. Robert Polito. New York: Penguin Random House: 662–7.

— [1971] 2009. 'Introduction to Negative Space'. In *Farber on Film: The Complete Writings of Manny Farber*. Ed. Robert Polito. New York: Penguin Random House: 691–7.

Feuerbach, Paul Johann Anselm. 1832. *Kaspar Hauser: The Foundling of Nuremberg*. Cambridge: Harvard College Library, Class of 1814: 12–13.

ffrench, Patrick. 1999. *The Cut: Reading Bataille's Histoire de l'oeil*. Oxford: Oxford University Press.

Flanagan, Matthew. 2012. *'Slow Cinema': Temporality and Style in Contemporary Art and Experimental Film*. University of Exeter. Unpublished PhD thesis.

Flaxman, Gregory. 2000. *The Brain is the Screen: Deleuze and the Philosophy of Cinema*. Minneapolis: University of Minnesota Press.

Fotiade, Ramona. 2013. 'Fixed-Explosive: Buñuel's Surrealist Time-Image'. In *A Companion to Luis Buñuel*. Ed. Rob Stone and Julián Gutiérrez-Albilla. London: Blackwell Publishing: 156–71.

Foucault, Michel. [1961] 1988. *Madness and Civilization: A History of Insanity in the Age of Reason*. Trans. Richard Howard. New York: Vintage Books.

— [1961] 2009. *History of Madness*. Trans. Jonathan Murphy and Jean Khalfa. London: Routledge.

— [1966] 1968. *Las palabras y las cosas*. Buenos Aires: Siglo XXI.

— 1975. *The Birth of the Clinic: An Archaeology of Medical Perception*. Trans. A. M. Sheridan Smith. New York: Vintage Books.

— 1977. *Discipline and Punish: The Birth of the Prison*. Trans. Alan Sheridan. New York: Random House.

— [1978] 1990. *The History of Sexuality: An Introduction*. Trans. Robert Hurley. London: Penguin Books.

— [1979] 2004. *The Birth of Biopolitics: Lectures at the College de France, 1978–1979*. Ed. Michael Senellart. Trans. Graham Burchell. New York: Picador.

Freud, Sigmund. [1913] 1965. *The Interpretation of Dreams*. Ed. and trans. James Strachey. New York: Avon.

— [1930] 2002. *Civilization and its Discontents*. Trans. David McLintock. London: Penguin Classics.

Fuentes, Carlos. 1973. 'The Discreet Charm of Luis Buñuel'. In *The New York Times Magazine*, March. https://www.criterion.com/current/posts/109-the-discreet-charm-of-the-bourgeosie

Gedmünden, Gerd. 1994. 'The Enigma of Hermeneutics: The Case of Kaspar Hauser'. In *Reading after Foucault: Institutions, Disciplines, and Technologies of the self in Germany, 1750–1830*. Ed. Robert S. Leventhal. Detroit: Wayne State University Press: 127–50.

Goddard, Michael. 2004 'Towards a Perverse Neo-Baroque Cinematic Aesthetic: Raúl Ruiz's Poetics of Cinema'. In *Senses of Cinema* 30 (February).

— 2013. *The Cinema of Raúl Ruiz: Impossible Cartographies*. New York: Columbia University Press.

Goethe, J. W. von. [1829] 1989. *Wilhelm Meister's Journeyman Years*. Frankfurt: Suhrkamp.

Grosz, Elizabeth. 2000. 'Deleuze's Bergson: Duration, the Virtual and a Politics of the Future'. In *Deleuze and Feminist Theory*. Ed. Ian Buchanan and Claire Colebrook. Edinburgh: Edinburgh University Press: 214–34.

— 2004. *The Nick of Time: Politics, Evolution, and the Untimely*. Sydney: Allen & Unwin.

— 2008. *Chaos, Territory, Art: Deleuze and the Framing of the Earth*. New York: Columbia University Press.

— 2012. 'Time is Out of Joint'. In *Time and History in Deleuze and Serres*. Ed. Bernd Herzogenrath. London and New York: Continuum.

— 2017. *The Incorporeal: Ontology, Ethics, and the Limits of Materialism*. New York: Columbia University Press

Gunning, Tom. 1990. 'The Cinema of Attractions: Early Film, Its Spectator and the Avant-Garde'. In *Early Cinema: Space, Frame, Narrative*. London: BFI Publishing: 381–8.

— 1995. 'Aesthetic of Astonishment'. In *Viewing Positions: Ways of Seeing Films*. Ed. Linda Williams. New Brunswick, NJ: Rutgers University Press: 114–33.

Hales, Steven. 2019. 'Nietzsche's Epistemic Perspectivism'. In *Knowledge from a Human Point of View*. Ed. Ana-Maria Cretu and Michela Massimi. Synthese Library (Studies in Epistemology, Logic, Methodology, and Philosophy of Science) 416: 19–35.

Harbord, Janet. 2016. *Ex-centric Cinema: Giorgio Agamben and Film Archaeology*. Bloomsbury Academic: New York.

Hughes, Joe. 2009. *Deleuze's Difference and Repetition: A Reader's Guide*. New York: Continuum.
Hume, David. [1739] 1888. *A Treatise of Human Nature*. Oxford: Clarendon Press.
Huyssen, Andreas. [1983] 1987. 'Foreword: The Return to Diogenes as Postmodern Intellectual', In *Critique of Cynical Reason*. P. Sloterdijk. Minneapolis and London: University of Minnesota Press: ix–xxv.
Ingold, Tim. 1992. 'Editorial'. In *Man*, New Series 27 (4): 693–6.
Insdorf, Annette. 1994. *François Truffaut*. New York: Cambridge University Press.
Isaacs, Bruce. 2005. 'Non-Linear Narrative'. In *New Punk Cinema*. Ed. Nicholas Rombes. Edinburgh: Edinburgh University Press: 126–38.
Itard, Jean Marc Gaspard. [1801] 1932. 'First developments of the Young Savage of Aveyron'. In *The Century psychology series: The wild boy of Aveyron*. Trans. George and Muriel Humphrey. New York: Century: 3–51.
Johnston, Trevor. 2015. 'Animal Instincts'. In *Sight and Sound* 25 (11): 81–3.
Kafka, Franz. [1915] 2016. *The Metamorphosis*. Trans. Susan Bernofsky. London: Penguin Classics.
— [1926] 1999. *The Castle*. Trans. Mark Harman. New York: Schocken Books.
Kant, Immanuel. [1781] 2008. *The Critique of Pure Reason*. Trans. Max Muller. London: Penguin Classics.
— [1790] 2005. *Crítica del juicio*. Buenos Aires: Losada.
— [1803] 2007. 'Lectures on Pedagogy'. In *Anthropology, History, and Education*. Ed. Günter Zoller and Robert B. Louden. Cambridge: Cambridge University Press: 434–85.
Kaplan, E. Ann and Ban Wang. 2008. *Trauma and Cinema: Cross-cultural Explorations*. Hong Kong: Hong Kong University Press.
Karalis, Vrasidas. 2012. *A History of Greek Cinema*. London: Continuum.
Kennedy, Barbara. M. 2000. *Deleuze and Cinema: The Aesthetics of Sensation*. Edinburgh: Edinburgh University Press.
Kerr, Walter. 1975. *The Silent Clowns*. New York: Knopf.
Klossowski, Pierre. [1969] 1997. *Nietzsche and the Vicious Circle*. Trans. Daniel W. Smith. Chicago: University of Chicago Press.
Langer, Susanne K. [1953] 1977. *Feeling and Form: A Theory of Art Developed from Philosophy in a New Key*. New Jersey: Prentice Hall.
Lant, Antonia. 1995. 'Haptical Cinema'. In *October* 74: 45–73.
Lapoujade, David. 2017. *Aberrant Movements: The Philosophy of Giles Deleuze*. New York: Semiotext(e).
Latour, Bruno. 2004 'Whose Cosmos, Which Cosmopolitics? Comments of the Peace Terms of Ulrich Beck'. In *Symposium: Talking Peace with Gods, Part 1, Common Knowledge*. Durham, NC: Duke University Press: 450–62.
— 2011. *We Have Never Been Modern*. Trans. Catherine Porter. Cambridge, MA: Harvard University Press.

Latsis, Dimitrios S. 2013. 'Genealogy of the Image in Histoire(s) du cinema: Godard, Warburg and the iconology of the interstice'. In *Third Text* 27 (6): 774–85.
Lawrence, D. H. 1923. 'Snake'. In *Birds, Beasts and Flowers*. London: Martin Secker: 113–17.
Leibniz, Gottfried. [1679] 1973. *Leibniz-Philosophical Writings*. Ed. G. H. R. Parkinson. Trans. Mary Morris. London: J. M. Dent & Sons.
Lenoir Rémi and Robbie Duschinsky. 2012. 'Foucault and the Family'. In *Foucault, the Family and Politics*. Ed. Robbie Duschinsky and Leon Antonio Rocha. Palgrave Macmillan Studies in Family and Intimate Life. London: Palgrave Macmillan: 19–38.
Linnaeus, Carl. 1735. *Systema Naturae*. Netherlands: B. de Graaf.
Losilla, Carlos. 2012. *La Invención de la modernidad, o cómo acabar de una vez por todas con las historia del cine*. Madrid: Editoriales Cátedra.
MacDonald, Scott. 2013. *American Ethnographic Film and Personal Documentary: The Cambridge Turn*. Oakland: University of California Press.
MacKenzie, Iain and Robert Porter. 2011. *Dramatizing the Political: Deleuze and Guattari*. London: Palgrave Macmillan.
Malek, Amy. 2011. 'If you're going to educate 'em, you've got to entertain 'em too: An Examination of Representation and Ethnography in *Grass* and *People of the Wind*'. In *Iranian Studies* 44 (3): 313–25.
Malson, Lucien. 1981. *Les enfants sauvages: mythe et réalité*. Paris: France Loisirs.
Marchini Camia, Giovanni. 2018a. 'It's Not Literary Adaptation . . . It's Literary Infection. An Interview with Lucrecia Martel'. In *Cineaste* (Summer): 45–6.
— 2018b. 'Review: Zama'. In *Cineaste* (October).
Marks, Laura U. 2000a. 'Signs of the Time: Deleuze, Peirce, and the Documentary Image'. In *The Brain is the Screen: Deleuze and the Philosophy of Cinema*. Ed. Gregory Flaxman. Minneapolis: University of Minnesota Press: 327–64.
— 2000b. *The Skin of the Film: Intercultural Cinema, Embodiment, and the Senses*. Durham, NC and London: Duke University Press.
— 2015. 'What a Body Can Do. Answers from Trablus, Cairo, Beirut and Algiers'. *Paragraph* 38 (1): 118–35.
Marrati, Paola. [2003] 2008. *Gilles Deleuze: Cinema and Philosophy*. Trans. Alisa Hartz. Baltimore: Johns Hopkins University Press.
Martel, Lucrecia. 2017. 'Llevar al Cine una Obra Maestra'. In *El País*, March. https://elpais.com/cultura/2017/03/31/babelia/1490954491_002830.html
Martin, Adrian. 2004. 'Displacements'. In *Raúl Ruiz: Images of Passage*. Ed. Helen Bandis, Adrian Martin and Grant McDonald. Rotterdam: Film Festival Rotterdam: 45–53.
— 2014. *Mise en Scène and Film Style: From Classical Hollywood to New Media*. Basingstoke: Palgrave Macmillan.
— 2018. 'Review: To the Victims of Expectation – Lucrecia Martel's "Zama"'. In *Mubi Notebook*. https://mubi.com/notebook/posts/review-to-the-victims-of-expectation-lucrecia-martel-s-zama

— [2018] 2020. *Mysteries of Cinema: Reflexions on Film Theory, History and Culture*. Perth: UWA Publishing.
Martin, Adrian and Cristina Álvarez López. 2021. 'Deadline: In a Lonely Place'. In *Cinea*. https://cinea.be/deadline-in-a-lonely-place/
Martin, Deborah. 2016. *The Cinema of Lucrecia Martel*. Manchester: Manchester University Press.
Martin-Jones, David. 2011. *Deleuze and World Cinemas*. London: Continuum.
Marx, Karl. [1867] 1993. *Capital Volume II*. Trans. Ben Fowkes. London: Penguin Classics.
Massumi, Brian. 2002. *Parables for the Virtual: Movement, Affect, Sensation*. Durham, NC: Duke University Press.
— 2014. *What Animals Teach Us About Politics*. Durham, NC: Duke University Press.
Metz, Christian. 1974. *Film Language: A Semiotics of Cinema*. Trans. Michael Taylor. New York: Oxford University Press.
Michaud, Philippe-Alain. [1998] 2007. *Aby Warburg and the Image in Motion*. Trans. Sophie Hawkes. New York: Zone Books.
Mulvey, Laura. 1975. 'Visual Pleasure and Narrative Cinema'. In *Screen* 16 (3): 6–18.
Nagib, Lúcia. 2015. 'The Politics of Slowness and the Traps of Modernity'. In *Slow Cinema*. Ed. Tiago de Luca and Jorge Nuno Barradas. Edinburgh: Edinburgh University Press: 25–46.
Nietzsche, Friedrich. [1873] 1997. *Untimely Meditations*. Ed. Daniel Breazeale. Trans. R. J. Hollingale. Cambridge: Cambridge University Press.
— [1882] 1974. *The Gay Science*. Trans. Walter Kaufmann. New York: Random House.
— [1887] 2003. *The Genealogy of Morals*. Trans. Walter Kaufmann. New York: Dover.
— [1901] 1968. *The Will to Power*. Trans. Walter Kaufmann. New York: Vintage.
Norris, Margot. 1985. *Beast of the Modern Imagination: Darwin, Nietzsche, Kafka, Ernst, and Lawrence*. Baltimore: Johns Hopkins University Press.
Pasolini, Pier Paolo. [1965] 2001. 'The Cinema of Poetry'. In *Post-war Cinema and Modernity: A Film Reader*. Ed. John Orr and Olga Taxidou. Trans. Marianne de Vettimo and Jacques Bontemps. New York: New York University Press: 37–53.
Paz, Octavio. [1950] 2000. *El laberinto de la soledad*. México City: Fondo de Cultura Económica.
Peirce, Charles Sanders. 1950. 'The Principle of Phenomenology'. In *The Philosophy of Peirce: Selected Writings*. Ed. Justus Buchler. New York: Harcourt: 74–97.
Perez, Gilberto. 1998. *The Material Ghost*. Baltimore: Johns Hopkins University Press.

— 2019. *The Eloquent Screen: A Rhetoric of Film*. Minneapolis: University of Minnesota Press.
Pick, Anat. 2007. 'Ecovisions: Seeing Animals in Recent Ethnographic Film'. In *Vertigo* 3 (4): 33–7.
— 2015. 'Why not look at animals?' In *NECSUS: European Journal of Media Studies*. Spring (19): 107–25.
Pisters, Patricia. 2003. *The Matrix of Visual Culture: Working with Deleuze in Film Theory*. Stanford: Stanford University Press.
Plato. [c. 375 BC] 2006. *The Republic*. Trans. Desmond Lee and H. D. P. Lee. London: Penguin Classics.
— [c. 369 BC] 1992. *Theaetetus*. Trans. M. J. Levett. Cambridge: Hackett Publishing Co.
Purse, Lisa. 2011. 'The Action Sequence'. In *Contemporary Action Cinema*. Edinburgh: Edinburgh University Press: 56–75.
Quaranta, Chiara. 2020. 'A Cinema of Boredom: Heidegger, Cinematic Time and Spectatorship'. In *Film-Philosophy* 1 (24): 1–21.
Rancière, Jacques. [2001] 2016. *Film Fables*. Trans. Emiliano Battista. London: Bloomsbury Academic.
— 2011. *Béla Tarr: Le temps après*. Paris: Capricci.
— [2011] 2014. *The Intervals of Cinema*. Trans. John Howe. London: Verso.
Rapan, Eleonora. 2018. 'Shepard Tones and Production of Meaning in Recent Films: Lucrecia Martel's Zama and Christopher Nolan's Dunkirk'. In *The New Soundtrack* 8 (2): 135–44.
Ratner, Megan. 2010. 'Once Grazing, Now Gone: *Sweetgrass*'. In *Film Quarterly* 63 (3): 23–7.
Raviv, Orna. 2019. *Ethics of Cinematic Experience: Screens of Alterity*. London: Routledge.
Rodowick, David. 1997. *Gilles Deleuze's Time Machine*. Durham, NC: Duke University Press.
— 2010. *Afterimages of Gilles Deleuze's Film Philosophy*. Minneapolis: University of Minnesota Press.
Rölli, Marc. 2009. 'Deleuze on Intensity Differentials and the Being of the Sensible'. In *Deleuze Studies* 3 (1): 26–53.
Romney, Jonathan. 2000. 'The Man Who Fell to Earth (Werner Herzog's The Enigma of Kaspar Hauser)'. In *Sight and Sound* 10: 24–6.
— 2018. 'Burden of Dreams'. In *Sight and Sound* (June): 32–4.
Ross, Harris. 1987. *Film as Literature. Literature as Film: An Introduction to and Bibliography of Film's relationship to Literature*. New York: Greenwood Press.
Rousseau, Jean-Jacques. 1755. *Discours sur l'origine et les fondements de l'inégalité parmi les hommes*. Amsterdam: Marc-Michel Rey.
Ruiz, Raúl. [1995] 2013. *Poéticas del cine*. Santiago: Universidad Diego Portales.
— 2017. *Diario: Notas, recuerdos y secuencias de cosas vistas*. Santiago: Universidad Diego Portales.

Russell, Dominique. 2003. 'Blinding Women: Buñuel, Feminism and the Representation of Rape'. In *Buñuel: El Imaginario Transcultural; L'Imaginaire Transcultural; The Transcultural Imaginary*. Ed. Gaston Lillo. Ottawa: University of Ottawa: 180–98.

Schefer, Jean Louis. [1980] 2016. *The Ordinary Man of Cinema*. Trans. Paul Grant. London: Semiotext(e).

Schoedsack, Ernest B. 1983. 'Grass: The Making of an Epic'. In *American Cinematographer* (February): 40–4.

Sennett, Richard. 2018. *Building and Dwelling: Ethics for the City*. New York: Farrar, Straus and Giroux.

Shakespeare, William. [1600] 2000. *The Merchant of Venice*. Ware: Wordsworth Editions.

Silverman, Kaja. 1981. 'Kaspar Hauser's "Terrible Fall" into Narrative'. In *New German Critique* 24–5: 73–93.

Simondon, Gilbert. [1964] 2009. 'The Position of the Problem of Ontogenesis'. Trans. Gregory Flanders. In *Parrhesia* 7 (4): 4–16.

Sloterdijk, Peter. [1998] 2011. *Spheres. Volume I: Microspherology*. Trans. Wieland Hoban. London: Semiotext(e).

Smaill, Belinda. 2014. 'Documentary Film and Animal Modernity in Raw Herring and Sweetgrass'. *In Australian Humanities Review* 57 (November): 61–80.

Sobchack, Vivian. 1980/1981. 'Synthetic Vision: The Dialectical Imperative of Buñuel's Las Hurdes'. In *Millennium Film Journal* (Fall): 140–50.

Stam, Robert. 2000. 'Beyond Fidelity: The Dialogics of Adaptation'. In *Film Adaptation*. Ed. James Naremore. New Brunswick, NJ: Rutgers University Press: 54–76.

Strickland, Peter. 2016. 'Yorgos Lanthimos by Peter Strickland'. In *Bomb Magazine* 135. https://bombmagazine.org/articles/yorgos-lanthimos/

Talu, Yonca. 2016. 'Review: The Lobster'. In *Film Comment*. https://www.filmcomment.com/article/review-the-lobster-yorgos-lanthimos/

Tarkovsky, Andrei. [1986] 1989. *Sculpting in Time: Reflections on the Cinema*. Trans. Kitty Hunter-Blair. Austin: University of Texas Press.

Taylor, Lucien. 1996. 'Iconophobia. How anthropology lost it at the movies'. In *Transition* 69 (1): 64–88.

Thomas, Allan James. 2019. *Deleuze, Cinema and the Thought of the World*. Edinburgh: Edinburgh University Press.

Totaro, Donato. 1999. 'Gilles Deleuze's Bergsonian Film Project: Part 2. Cinema 2: The Time-Image'. In *Off Screen* 3 (3). https://offscreen.com/view/bergson2

Varela, Francisco J., Eleanor Rosch and Evan Thompson. 1991. *The Embodied Mind: Cognitive Science and Human Experience*. Cambridge, MA: MIT Press.

Viegas, Susana. 2016. 'Gilles Deleuze and early cinema: The modernity of emancipated time'. In *Early Popular Visual Culture* 14 (3): 234–50.

Viveiros de Castro, Eduardo. [2009] 2014. *Cannibal Metaphysics*. Ed. and trans. Peter Skafish. Minneapolis: Univocal.

Weber, Max. [1922] 1963. *The Sociology of Religion*. Trans. Ephraim Fischoff. London: Beacon Press.

Wigley, Samuel. 2008. '*Colossal Youth* is a colossal confusion'. In *The Guardian*, 29 April. https://www.theguardian.com/film/filmblog/2008/apr/29/pedrocostasultraminimalcolo

Williams, Linda. 1981. *Figures of Desire: A Theory and Analysis of Surrealist Film*. Chicago: University of Illinois Press.

Zoro Sutton, Javier. 2017. '¿Qué es lo que me hace decir te amo? Sobre *The Lobster*'. In *LaFuga Revista de Cine* 20: 1–7.

Index

400 Blows, The, 64, 80–1

acentric cinema, 51, 183; *see also* post-human cinema
action-image, 28, 31–2, 90
adaptation, 74, 80, 85, 102, 145, 151
    contamination as adaptation, 141, 147, 160–1, 182
    politics of adaptation, 139, 147, 161, 182
affection-image, 8, 9n, 15, 19, 28, 31, 49, 173
affective discourse, 27, 165
affective mode of address, 2, 156
Agamben, Giorgio, 50n, 75, 79, 86–7, 109–10, 126, 126n, 127–8, 133–4, 154
Andrei Rublev, 102
animal-becoming, 167, 167n, 170, 175
Antonioni, Michelangelo, 20, 34, 42, 99n
Aquarela, 31
Aristotle, 50n, 76, 88, 102, 126n, 137
art cinema, 16, 51
avant-garde, 1–2, 7, 15, 15n, 23, 47, 59–60, 65, 67, 113, 144, 179

Badiou, Alain, 33, 110–12, 112n, 146, 156, 181
Balázs, Béla, 19, 172–3
baroque, 16–18, 17n, 151
Barthes, Roland, 65

Bataille, Georges, 64–5, 67
Bazin, André, 40, 66, 81, 83, 95, 96n, 101
becoming, 5, 6, 21–2, 28, 30, 60, 85–6, 89, 94, 105, 107–8, 170, 178
    becoming-man, 79, 84–6,
    becoming-molecular, 45
    becomingness, 141, 152
    becoming-woman, 125
    image of becoming, 92
    maritime-becoming, 118, 133, 135
    politics of becoming, 165, 171, 175
    see also image-in-becoming; intensity
Benning, James, 51, 95
Berger, John, 166–7, 172
Bergson, Henri, 3n, 5n, 14, 21, 28n, 29–30, 32, 35–6, 39–40, 42, 94, 96, 99, 110–11, 155, 155n, 181
    Creative Evolution, 21, 28n, 36, 94, 110
    Matter and Memory, 21n, 110–11
Bertetto, Paolo, 10, 30
Bordwell, David, 15, 94, 181
boredom, 51, 165, 168
    cinema of boredom, 2, 154
    see also slow cinema
Borges, Jorge Luis, 69, 88, 106, 143
Boundas, Constantin V., 11–12
Buñuel, Luis, 16, 19, 23, 36, 42–3, 52–71, 62n, 65n, 66n, 92, 94, 99n, 101, 105, 136n, 179–80, 184
Butler, Judith, 108, 123

Cahiers du cinéma, 101
Castaing-Taylor, Lucien, 163–4, 172–5
cinema of attractions, 53
cinema of slowness *see* slow cinema
cinematic boredom *see* boredom; *see also* slow cinema
cinematic classicism *see* classical cinema
cinematic modernism/cinematic modernity *see* modern cinema
cinematic poetry *see* poetic film
classical cinema, 2, 4, 7, 9n, 10–11, 14, 18–23, 11n, 28–36, 38–9, 42, 50, 55–6, 58–61, 63–4, 66–9, 73–4, 83, 89–90, 92, 96, 99–101, 104–6, 108, 110, 113, 152–4, 156n, 168, 177–80, 184
  classical Hollywood, 27
  see also movement-image
classical philosophy, 5n, 97
Colebrook, Claire, 4, 93
Colossal Youth, 44–50, 52, 55, 179
contemplative cinema, 2, 11n, 52, 154, 156, 168n, 179, 183; *see also* slow cinema
contemporary cinema, 4, 7, 15, 15n, 22–3, 29, 35, 51, 95, 113, 139, 152, 154–5, 168, 178–9, 181
contemporary painting, 50, 109
Cooper, Sarah, 69–70, 119, 123, 124
Costa, Pedro, 22–3, 35, 44–51, 109, 154–5, 179
Creed, Barbara, 74, 165, 165n, 167
crystal-image, 55
  crystalline, the, 17, 113
  crystalline narration, 90

DeLanda, Manuel, 13, 30, 119
Deleuze, Gilles
  Anti-Oedipus, 4
  A Thousand Plateaus, 86, 134n, 167n, 170
  Cinema 1: The Movement-Image, 3, 8, 9n, 18–20, 21n, 31, 35, 37n, 39, 49–50, 56, 59, 62, 90, 96, 101, 111, 179, 181
  Cinema 2: The Time-Image, 3, 10, 20, 35, 37n, 40, 43, 50, 55, 59n, 62, 90, 93, 95, 96n, 99, 101, 111, 179–81
  Difference and Repetition, 1, 4, 6–7, 38, 109n, 126n, 141n, 152, 153n, 179
  Empiricism and Subjectivity, 6–7, 76
  Francis Bacon: The Logic of Sensation, 37n
  Kafka: Toward a Minor Literature, 37n
  Nietzsche and Philosophy, 1, 152
  Proust and Signs, 37n
  The Fold, 37n
  Logic of Sense, 7, 107n
  'The Method of Dramatization', 154
  What is Philosophy?, 9, 11
  'What is the Creative Act?', 128
Deren, Maya, 14–16, 18–19, 23, 108, 144, 152
Derrida, Jacques, 103, 124–5, 137, 164, 164n, 165, 167
de-visualisation, 7, 50, 52, 142, 145, 147, 152, 154
Di Benedetto, Antonio, 139–52, 159–61, 182
difference in degree, 10, 155n
difference in nature/kind, 10, 22, 155n
differentiation, 5, 7, 11–12, 28, 141, 153, 160
  differenciation, 141, 153, 153n, 160
  zone of indifferentiation, 170
displacement, 9, 47–8, 59, 66, 70, 94, 119, 133n, 155, 179
dogmatic image of thought, 28, 30, 38–9, 58, 64, 97, 177
Dovzhenko, Alexandre, 19–20, 20
dramatisation, 139, 141, 143, 147, 152–4, 160–1, 164, 182
Dreyer, Carl Theodor, 19, 108, 184

duration, 18, 20, 28–30, 32, 39–41, 46, 52, 94, 99, 112n
durée see duration

Eisenstein, Sergei, 93, 169
Enigma of Kaspar Hauser, The, 23, 72–6, 79–80, 87–91, 174, 180
extensity, 4–5, 10, 13, 39, 153
    extension, 4–5, 14, 21, 153, 182
    extensive difference, 5
    extensive movement, 10, 21, 36

film-poetry, 15–16, 23; *see also* poetic cinema
Flaxman, Gregory, 22, 30, 40
Flow/*rheûma*, 14, 21, 28, 30, 177–8, 184; *see also* intensity
Foucault, Michel, 96, 103–6, 108, 117, 120–5, 128–30, 182
free-indirect-discourse, 7, 16, 18, 45, 47, 55, 67, 69, 180; *see also* Pasolini, Pier Paolo
French New Wave *see nouvelle vague*
Freud, Sigmund, 47–8, 69, 100, 104, 109–10, 133, 164n, 167n
Fuentes, Carlos, 54, 61–2, 65

gaseous, 29, 44–51, 152
    becoming-gaseous, 31, 179
    gaseous-image, 35, 51, 142
    gaseous intensity, 48–9
    gaseous perception, 29n, 30, 154
Germany, Year Zero, 41–4, 63
Godard, Jean-Luc, 4, 105, 109, 109n, 111–12, 155–6, 184
Grass: A Nation's Battle for Life, 168–9, 183
Grosz, Elizabeth, 12–13, 49, 58
Guattari, Félix, 4, 7, 9, 12, 27, 37, 44, 46, 51, 60, 80, 85, 129, 134, 134n, 167n, 170–1, 173

Heidegger, Martin, 46, 51, 109
Herzog, Werner, 23, 73–80, 87–91, 99n, 139, 180
Heterogeneity/heterogenous, 60, 68
Hitchcock, Alfred, 37, 37n, 127
homogeneity/homogenous, 5, 30, 32, 154
Hume, David, 5n, 6, 76–9, 86, 180

ideality/idea, 141n, 153–4
idealism, 97
image-in-becoming, 8, 11, 15, 35; *see also* intensive-image; becoming
immanence, 56, 98
    cinema of immanence, 58
    see also plane of immanence
impulse-image, 8, 19, 55–6, 58, 64, 179
individuation, 5
intensity, 1–15, 19–23, 27–30, 35, 44, 46, 48–50, 58, 60, 66–7, 71, 74, 78, 80, 83–4, 86, 88, 91–5, 99, 107–8, 109n, 110, 113, 119, 126–7, 132, 134, 137, 140–2, 145, 152–4, 156, 158–9, 163, 171–3, 177–84
    aesthetics of intensity, 181
    cinematic intensity, 80, 105
    intensive, the, 5, 11, 12–13
    poetic intensity, 147
    power of intensity, 12, 20, 74, 153
    see also intensive-image; thermodynamic intensity
intensive-image, 1–2, 6–10, 12–14, 16, 18–19, 22–3, 29–30, 35, 44, 46–7, 49–51, 55–6, 58–60, 65, 67–8, 83, 90–5, 99, 101, 105–10, 112–13, 118–19, 127–8, 132, 140–1, 146–7, 152–4, 160–1, 163, 168, 177–84
    image of intensity, 34, 111
Italian neorealism, 3, 28, 64, 180

Kafka, Franz, 37n, 57, 143, 149, 159n, 165
Kant, Immanuel, 4–5, 38–9, 42, 75–8, 82, 84, 95–101, 103n, 181

Keaton, Buster, 22, 33–4, 36, 101
Klossowski, Pierre, 5n, 18

Lacan, Jacques, 105, 109–10, 164n, 167n
Latour, Bruno, 98, 169–70
liquid, 28–31, 35, 40–1, 48, 139–40
   liquid-image, 43
   liquid perception, 14, 41
Lobster, The, 2, 23, 61, 103, 117–38, 154, 181–2
Los olvidados, 23, 43, 54, 62–4, 66n, 99n

Mann, Anthony, 23, 33–6
Marks, Laura U., 8n, 50, 158
Massumi, Brian, 11–12, 165, 171, 175, 183
Martel, Lucrecia, 23, 35, 51, 61, 95, 139–61, 182–4
Martin, Adrian, 9, 19, 33, 151, 158
mental-image, 37, 55
mise en scène, 82, 145, 151, 158
Mizoguchi, Kenji, 19, 95
Modern artists, 103
modern cinema, 2, 4, 7–8, 10–11, 14, 18, 21–3, 29–30, 32–3, 35, 40–2, 50–1, 54–5, 57–64, 66, 73, 83, 88–95, 98–101, 104–5, 108, 111–13, 133, 139–40, 142–3, 152–6, 156n, 168, 177–84; *see also* time-image
modernity, 95–105, 103n, 111, 121, 129, 181
   modern State, 122, 124
modern metaphysics, 5, 96–7
modern painting, 49
montage, 32, 40, 95
   archaeological montage, 109, 112, 155
   Hollywood montage, 27
   genealogical montage, 112
   German school of montage, 20
   Soviet school of montage, 3, 93
morality, 42–4

movement-image, 1–2, 8, 9n, 18–20, 21n, 28, 30–40, 43–2, 45, 50, 54–5, 58–9, 63–5, 68, 70, 80–4, 93, 96–100, 105, 177, 180
multiplicity/multiple, 4, 10, 13–14, 39, 54, 71, 76, 110, 175
   multiplicity of images, 16, 18
Murnau, Friedrich Wilhelm, 20, 93, 112n
Mulvey, Laura, 142, 158

naturalism/natural philosophy, 55–6, 58–60, 62, 66, 66n, 92, 180
New German Cinema, 74; *see also* New Wave cinema
New Wave cinema, 3, 64, 73–4, 89, 111, 155–6, 180; *see also nouvelle vague*
Nietzsche, Friedrich, 1, 5n, 6, 14, 18, 38–9, 86–7, 89, 99, 103, 105, 107, 109, 152, 165, 166, 169–70, 181
Nihilism, 87, 103, 181
   nihilist position, 99, 103
North American New Wave, 41; *see also* New Wave cinema
nouvelle vague, 54, 74, 111, 155–6; *see also* New Wave cinema

off-screen space/off-screen, 7, 20n, 29, 48, 140, 151, 156–8, 161
on-screen, 20, 47, 89, 127, 145, 154, 157–9, 161, 174
organic narration, 2, 15n, 17n, 28, 104
originary world, 55–7, 179
   origin, 90–1
Ozu, Yasujiro, 22, 22n, 95

parametric narrative, 30, 163
Pasolini, Pier Paolo, 16, 18, 45, 47–8, 55, 67–9, 147, 180
   cinema of poetry, 16, 47, 68
Passion of Joan of Arc, The, 19, 108, 184
Peirce, Charles Sanders, 3n, 49–50, 50n

Peixoto, Mario, 22, 108, 169n
perception-image, 19, 28, 45, 49
Perez, Gilberto, 19–20, 33–4, 55, 105, 140, 155
Pisters, Patricia, 84–5
plane of immanence, 11, 57–8
  immanent plane, 3n, 58n
Plato, 28, 38–9, 97, 124
  Platonism, 38, 43, 56
poetic film, 1–2, 8, 14–20, 23, 47, 55, 66–8, 95, 179, 184
  poetic language of film, 14, 68, 70, 108, 144
  see also film-poetry
poetics, 34
  poetic consciousness, 46, 67
  poetic excess, 8, 68, 71, 180
  poetic intensification/intensity, 146–7
post-human cinema, 2, 163, 173, 183

Rancière, Jacques, 11n, 22, 33–4, 48–9, 145–7, 152, 154, 156, 160, 181
Ray, Nicholas, 33–4, 36
Rossellini, Roberto, 37, 42–3, 63, 99n
Ruiz, Raúl, 9, 16–18, 21, 51, 144, 147

Schefer, Jean Louis, 66–7, 101
Sensory Ethnography Lab, 23, 163–4, 183
sensory mode of address see affective mode of address
sensory-motor schema, 15, 20, 22n, 32, 43, 59, 90, 96, 111, 155, 179
  sensory-motor closure/cohesion, 22, 37, 62–3, 92
  sensory-motor formula, 35–6, 42, 66, 108, 183
slow cinema, 2, 11n, 22, 51–2, 154, 158, 169n, 179, 183
Straub, Jean-Marie and Danièle Huillet, 34, 93
stray characters, 58, 64
  stray, the, 74

surrealism, 16, 55–6, 68
Sweetgrass, 23, 163–9, 171–6, 183

Tarkovsky, Andrei, 67, 102, 144
Tarr, Béla, 11n6, 51, 95
temps mort, 154, 169, 174, 183
That Obscure Object of Desire, 53, 57, 61–2
thermodynamics, 9, 13, 30
  thermodynamic intensity, 6, 14, 92, 184
  see also intensity
threshold, 75, 119, 131
  between *Cinema 1* and *Cinema 2*, 37, 83
time-image, 1–3, 8, 11n, 16, 19, 21n, 22, 28–9, 31–2, 34–5, 37, 39–44, 50, 54, 56–9, 62–4, 66, 83, 90, 93–4, 98–100, 103–6, 142, 154–6, 161, 177–82
Truffaut, François, 23, 64, 73–86, 89–91, 180
Tsai, Ming-liang, 95

Un chien andalou, 16, 23, 43, 53–5, 61–2, 64–70, 136n, 180, 184
untimely, 1, 105–8, 110, 181

Viegas, Susana, 33, 63, 93
virtual/virtuality, 11–12, 37, 57, 98, 111, 128, 128n, 142, 181
  virtual ideas, 12
  virtual images, 151, 183
  virtual movement, 62–3, 66
Viveiros de Castro, Eduardo, 169–71, 183

Warburg, Aby, 61–4, 105–6, 108, 112–13
Wild Child, The, 23, 72–5, 79–86, 89–91, 174, 180
will-to-power, 6, 14

Zama, 23, 51, 61, 139–62, 182, 184

EU representative:
Easy Access System Europe
Mustamäe tee 50, 10621 Tallinn, Estonia
Gpsr.requests@easproject.com

www.ingramcontent.com/pod-product-compliance
Lightning Source LLC
Chambersburg PA
CBHW051124160426
43195CB00014B/2336